I AM COMPASSIONATE CREATIVITY *

111 Stories from Preschool to Providence

By Kāli Quinn

*For Felton —   March 2022
with all the love in
the world for your
            health +
Edited by Gil Poulin   happiness +
continued authenticity.
So grateful to know you. always,
                              Kāli.*

With prominent exception of my grandparents, my parents, and my brother, there are no other proper names used within this text. Although these stories include other people, they are my stories. They are told from my perspective and remembrances.

I am Compassionate Creativity: 111 Stories from Preschool to Providence

Published by Compassionate Creativity

www.compassionatecreativity.com

First Edition.

ISBN: 0997393335
ISBN-13: 978-0997393330 (Compassionate Creativity)

Cover design by Robin McGuirl

Cover Photo by Dawn Quinn & Jeff Smithson

Author Photo by John Shaw

Edited by Gil Poulin

FOR

Dawn & Evan
Jule & Thom

TABLE OF CONTENTS

1. Remembering where you came from: land and people.

2. Searching for & returning to your eternal questions.

3. Knowing that your every action has a lasting effect.

4. Reviewing your relationship with technology.

5. Holding the flashlight on things that no one else is.

6. Finding freedom through music.

7. Knowing what calms you and finding out what calms those closest to you.

8. Asking elders what life was like for them and listening for as long as they will share.

9. Discovering what helps you to express yourself.

10. Realizing the difference between quality and quantity, especially when it comes to love.

11. Empathizing through a lens of multiple causality.

12. Seeking out the middle road.

13. Turning everyday experience into an adventure.

14. Taking care of your precious gifts.

15. Revisiting, with great care, the moments that shifted your life.

16. Letting your grief mysteriously give way to gifts.

SECOND MOVEMENT: ON TO THE WEST 115

FOURTH MOVEMENT: MOMENTOUS LISTENING *192*

SEVENTH MOVEMENT: ANOTHER KIND OF PROVIDENCE   *327*

Because when I look, really look, there is a glistening to things. What glistens? Things? Me seeing things? Just me?

- THOMAS P. QUINN, 1999

AN INTRODUCTION

 A memoir.
A field guide.
A curriculum.
A center.

Since I was a kid, I have always loved to make stuff and bring people together. I loved sports and science and math and trees and books and music and every new thing I learned about. Instead of choosing one of these things, theater seemed like the best way for me to continue to love and explore everything, to be curious and play. In college, I learned everything I could about theater. In graduate school I learned how to make my own plays. And then, for the first time in my life, I stepped out of school and began to negotiate my way through the world as a theater maker.

Throughout my twenties – juggling several projects, creating a company, figuring out how to make money, and beginning to teach – what I loved began to disintegrate. I continued to encourage my students and audiences to be present, but I became less and less present with myself. Instead of slowing down, I sped up. I filled each waking second with another great project, and if I encountered bumps along the way, I worked harder, in more places, and for longer hours. From the outside, these headlines and resume bullet points looked great, but on the inside, I was flailing, unsure of how and if I could keep going.

"What is your question?" asked one my students. "What are

you asking of the world?"

I had been so focused on what the world had been asking of me that I had never thought about this way. I defined myself as a teacher and a performer, but *what was at the core of my work?*

I took out my journals and notebooks from throughout the years to see what patterns I could find. *What repeated? What seemed to matter most?* Flipping through, I came across a page entitled *Advice to a Young Artist Like Myself.* I could hardly remember writing it, but it was exactly what I was looking for. These were my values and yes, they all circled around how to be compassionate and creative at the same time.

I returned to the same student and shared these values and my question: *How do we cultivate Compassionate Creativity for ourselves and our communities?*

"This is awesome. Let's share this with the world."

Thus, the *Compassionate Creativity Project* was born:

Every day for the last 111 days of 2014, we emailed these values and a connected story to 111 people around the world. Within the first few weeks, this project became way more powerful and effective than I had ever anticipated, and it affected me more than I ever imagined it would. The balance between having a place to share my own reflections, and being able to hear how others connected to them, brought me to the heart of each day. Some of the people I knew, and others I met for the first time through their responses:

"Oh this is my life right now too!"

"I needed to hear that and pass it along today."

"I love thinking about all of these things and practicing them. "

"Well, that just pulled some moisture out of the old peepers."

"I like that you have asked this question, because it is something that has bothered me for years."

"This is beyond exactly what I needed to read today. I am deep into scary, transitional times in every area of my life. Thank you. It feels like something I was just supposed to do, be part of these 111 days."

Every morning I woke up excited to see who had reflected and what stories of their own they had shared in our online group. Seeing people who didn't know one another connect and support one another through shared values and stories was infinitely inspiring.

Compassionate Creativity wasn't just a project. The expression, consistency, and community reminded me of who I am and who I was from the beginning: I am Compassionate Creativity. During the most challenging times in my life, I was most challenged to be Compassionate Creativity, but these were also the times I needed to find this combination the most.

So what is compassion? What is creativity? And what does it mean to put these two together? Asking these questions has been a life-long process for me, and through this book I share with you discoveries from my first thirty-five years.

Every story shares how I navigated through a moment of uncertainty by remembering who I was, what I loved, and how to collage the pieces together. Each story starts with the value I learned during that process, and each story concludes with questions for you to reflect on.

In this way, this book is a memoir. It is a field guide. It is a curriculum. And, it becomes a Center for Compassionate Creativity.

Taking time away from teaching and performing to reflect on and write out these stories has been an incredibly healing process for me, and I hope that my journey can bring you joy through your own connections and interpretations. Let these stories become medicine, fuel, fire, and companions. Let them remind you of your best abilities, dreams, and intentions. Let them encourage you to consistently value your life as your art and your art as your life, sharing the story of who you are with those around you... Not just living, but finding your own best practice of being alive.

Out of my own losses and lessons, I now give to you the love, beauty, honesty, and open arms of Compassionate Creativity.

Peace and play your way from here,

Kāli Quinn

Kāli Quinn

kali@compassionatecreativity.com

AN INVITATION

 Everyone is an artist.
Everyone is an actor/activist.
Everyone a teacher.
An expert.

If you are a doctor, you might understand that I had my appendix out when I was five and my tonsils out a year later. You might ask me how I broke my wrist and how old my dad was when he died of a heart attack.

If you are a computer, while helping me retrieve my forgotten password, you might learn that I was born in Mercy Hospital in Buffalo, New York or that my first grade teacher was Mrs. Carberry. You'd see that the first concert I went to was Verdi and that my dog's name was Beckett.

If you are a cop, you might ask why I have a New York State plate but a Rhode Island driver's license. You would see that I am thirty-four years old.

If you are an accountant, you might try to understand how I worked in seven states last year or why I had spent so much money creating theater when the numbers didn't seem to equate to an income.

If you are on the committee at that university where I recently submitted a job application, you might see that I identify as a white female.

If you are a student, you might ask me what class I teach and when and where it will be meeting.

If you are a customs officer, you might ask why I was in Guatemala and if I was really was a clown.

If you are a human being, whatever your post or position, age or creed, I invite you to come sit by the fire, listen, warm your hands, and sing...

PRELUDE: A SONG OF CHILDHOOD

Connect to Compassionate Creativity by...

1. Remembering where you came from: land and people.

South Buffalo, New York. April 1981.

There are so many places and people we have all come from. Moments of welcome. Of feasts and farewells. I didn't start in this lifetime. I come from many people. Some of whom I know. Others who I don't and never will, but their blood runs in mine. Their memories and ideas and choices. Their discoveries and hardships, their ways and who they loved and where they lived – formed me and inform me, usually without me having any knowing as such.

We each arrive to a place, a passport, a culture, a language, and a set of circumstances that were whirling before our birth and now welcome us into the mix. The two people that came together to make us were once children themselves. Maybe they planned on or didn't plan on being parents. Either way, here they are looking down at parts of themselves, reworked into a new being. A new life. An extension of their own.

To think that my life started so, so long ago as part of so many people all over the world coming together into my two parents astounds me: the exponential quality both understood and totally unfathomable, the amount of gratitude and praise and grief and care and responsibility... it takes my problems and wishes and doubts and relationships into part of a long stride while also having such an impact in every direction on those yet to come.

My grandmother, with her husband, created four children. Those four children, along with their partners, created eighteen grandchildren. By the time my grandmother passed away, those children grew up, found love, and created eleven more people. Now there are at least double that plus great, great. Great. That's a lot of people! Without my grandmother and grandfather being together, to date, fifty-something people would have never existed.

My mom and dad and both of their parents were all from Buffalo. Snow and football and all. My parents met in a bar in South Buffalo called O'Malley's, where my dad worked. They had their first date on the fourth of July at a picnic near Buffalo and became husband and wife a few years later and settled down in Buffalo.

I arrived three weeks later than I was expected to: a new native of Buffalo.

Like my mom's name, Dawn, I was named for new beginnings. A name that also means barn dances. Spelled like the Hindu goddess but with a line over the A to make it sound long. *Kāli.*

My tree stretches with great grandparent seeds from Ireland and Ukraine and Germany, and at times if I listen carefully, I can feel the food and music and countrysides of those places running through my veins too, but closer to the surface is my Buffalo: streets and eats and all four seasons. I learned from early on that Buffalo isn't a place that one leaves or can leave behind. Buffalo is a way of life: roots and baggage, weight and wings, an anchor, a heartbeat.

I grew up hearing sentiments that echoed, "Blood is thicker than water" and "All is fair in love and war." I don't believe in these sayings. I quickly learned about those who worked hard to raise me no matter what and that there is hunger for justice deeply embedded within each of us. I want to live by the truth, choosing how to speak my identity and lineage and testify how it's not war but love that provides:

I am Kāli Quinn
Daughter of Thom and Dawn
Raised alongside Evan
By a dog named Beckett
With Ukrainian Eggs from the Broadway Market
And Irish Dancing of Southern Buffalo
Introduced by second-generation American grandparents
Of the Old First Ward
A Papa on one side who dyed his beard green on St. Patrick's Day

A Grandma on the other who made pierogi and potato pancakes
And fed by countless teachers and seeds of creativity.

Held in the palm of the great Lake Erie
A place originally inhabited by the Attawandaron
And then blessed by the Seneca
Keepers of the Western Door
And one of the five tribes of the Iroquois People
Called River of Horses by the French
And occupied by the British at Fort Niagara
Years later the conclusion of the Erie Canal
And terminus of the Underground Railroad
City of Lackawanna Steel
And Good Neighbors shoveling snow.

Raised on values of love, curiosity, compassion and connection
I am Kāli Quinn
Child of the Universe
Roaming the earth
Since Earthday 1981.

⌘

Where and whom do you come from? Write the poetry of you in any way you'd like. For inspiration, do some research about the place you grew up or your current residence. Leave space for what you don't know.

Gloriously announce yourself through these words out loud to yourself (or feel free to share with someone else).

2. Searching for & returning to your eternal questions.

Hamburg, New York. The 1980's.

My name is Kāli Quinn. I am six. My teaher is Mrs. Carberry. My favorite animals are dafens and wolfs. My favorit color is people.

I flip through a folder that had been given to me when I finished high school. It includes writing that I had done from first grade through twelfth, ages five through eighteen. The pages move from big messy penciled letters with misspelled words amidst dotted lines to penned cursive stories to fully typed essays. There are three pieces of writing per year. Each one gives me a quick glimpse into what I cared about and how exactly I articulated it at the time:

Age 5: *When I grow up I will be a vetnareaen. Do you know why? Because I like aminals. I want to be a gimist. Too. I want to be a artist too. I want to be a teacher.*

Age 7: I did plays for babysitters and wrote songs for my cats. I wrote stories about dragons going to doctors because no one believed in them and a lost baby fox that was cared for by a young boy.

Age 8: I compared waiting for test results to *waiting for the dentist when you know you have a cavity.*

Age 9: *We worked out in gym, made beautiful art in art, sang up a storm in music, and went places in books in library. One of my favorite memories I have about fifth grade is our senior volunteer. We made beanbags, leaf name tags, potato heads, coasters, and many more decorations.*

Age 10: *If I had one gift to give, I would give it to the world.*
    It wouldn't be big. It would be small.
    It would be a gift to all.
    To some it wouldn't be much.
    It's something you can't hold or touch.

    It starts with everyone being nice to everyone.
    And ends with love in a ton.
    It doesn't cost anything.
    And to some it might sting.

    This gift would end all wars
    But it can't be bought in just any old store.
    Bought with love, care and light,
    My gift would be peace and to all a good night.

Age 11: In a paper about Ukraine and where my family had come from, I concluded how *the place where people live affects who they are.*

Ages 12-17: *Now I'm pleased to introduce you to a survivor who struggled to grasp her life during a time of revolution in France.* I wrote stories and book reports that all focused on the arc of someone moving from extreme hardship and isolation to amazing accomplishments.

Age 18: Before graduating, I wrote an essay about the

universal language of music... *Music is a syntactic system in itself without words. It can travel across nations, faiths, and decades. As an integral part of each human being's life, music nourishes by teaching, inspires through faith, and motivates as a community tool.*

And I sit back in wonder and amazement. Oh right... I have always been this me. I have always loved animals, especially dolphins and wolves. My favorite color is purple (or people!). I've always been fascinated by hearing other people's stories, especially about where they are from. I have always loved spending time in the presence of older folks. I have always believed in the transcendent power of connecting art and music.

In all I do, I continue to spiral round the same questions. These questions are the essence of who I am, what I care about, and what I strive for. With compassion and creativity as my guides, these are the questions I will continue to ask for the rest of my life:

How do we balance love, work, and play throughout our lifetimes?
How do we move on and what and who do we take with us?
How do we make peace with whatever happens along the way?

These questions are eternal. In searching for answers to them, I only continue to find more questions, more interests, more intrigue. These aren't questions that have answers. If I become afraid that these questions don't have answers or if I try too hard to make sense of these questions or figure them out, I will shut down, but if instead, I find a way to return to these questions with a sense of play and openness, they fuel my creativity. Making stuff allows me to compassionately explore these questions with my hands, heart, and mind. I then collage together my discoveries in the form of plays and poems and music and share these with others. In this exchange, I create a container for the questions to live and reverberate without needing answers. I elicit the audience's responses, interpretations, and connections, ready to listen to their perspective and encourage them to play along.

⌘

What are the questions you find yourself returning to throughout space and time?

What have you found to guide you through your eternal questions?

How do these questions and qualities connect to your current interests, projects, and relationships?

3. Knowing that your every action has a lasting effect.

Hamburg, New York. 1989.

I first learned about death when I found out that my middle name, Michelle, was a tribute to one of my dad's best friends who passed away days before I was born.

I first learned about family when my brother came into the world.

I first learned about companionship when my family adopted a dog named Beckett.

I first learned to re-use things when my grandmother saved egg cartons to store things and made cardboard sheaths to hold her steak knives.

I first learned that some people have more than others when my mom won a bike in a contest and, knowing that we didn't need one, she rigged a raffle at school so that a boy who was poor and made fun of could win it. And when my dad offered a man off the street a job for the night.

I first learned about friendship when my first grade teacher and I wrote letters for years after I left her class.

I first learned to see love in everything when my mom found rocks that were shaped like hearts and gave them to everyone as presents.

I first learned about passion when a teacher asked me what I was excited to learn about.

I first learned about compassion when my mom volunteered for an organization that helped families who were dealing with cancer.

I first learned about justice when I heard the story of my dad firing someone at his work on the spot because they called their co-worker a "faggot."

I first learned to turn things into other things when my dad drew random shapes on a piece of paper and then had me and my brother create our own picture out of what we saw.

I first learned that it's possible to create your own way through the world when my mom ran her own business, *Wallpapering and Painting Done by Dawn*, for fourteen years.

I first learned about play when my extended family would gather round the table and play cards together for hours.

I first learned to communicate openly when my parents encouraged me to talk about everything.

I first learned about the greater world when my mom took my brother and me on a trip to California to visit my uncle.

I first learned about the universe when my dad encouraged us to make up stories about where the stars came from.

I first learned about commitment when my mom showed up to every one of my plays and concerts and sporting events and made me lunch and dinner every day.

I first learned about my connection to the land when my parents purchased a small cottage on Lake Erie, and my brother and I would be on the sand and in the water all day long...

⌘

When did you first learn about these things?

How do they still have an impression on you today?

Notice how you teach someone something today just by being you.

4. Reviewing your relationship with technology.

Hamburg, New York. September 1988.

I have always had an aversion to screens and been in love with antiques. I love older things and older people and older ways. I long to know where things come from. I remember at a young age driving with my mom and telling her that I was "made for another time."

Stopping at the intersection she rolled her eyes: "Oh really? Have you heard your father talking about this?"

But I hadn't. Really. I was just me. I was inherently obsessed with *Little House on the Prairie* and could imagine living on a distant farm. The wind in my long, braided hair. The fields at my feet. Instead, I listened to crickets ringing along the summer breeze through a suburban window. Five houses away there was another one that looked exactly the same as mine (on the outside anyhow).

The first day of fourth grade I received an assignment to make an inventory of all the electronic things we could. I took this very seriously, as I did most assignments, especially when they had the unending potential of such a list.

By the time I arrived home from school I had already

numbered fifteen electronic devices into my black and white marbled notebook. Things I had noticed at school and on my way home: phones, overhead projectors, lights, and traffic signals. Getting off the bus, I had a mission, and I loved having a mission.

I marched through the front door searching for everything that was plugged in. The kitchen, of course, was full of new items for my list: refrigerator, toaster, microwave, and blender... my list was growing onto the next page! Were my classmates at home having as much fun as I was? Wow!

At dinner, my family became involved. We brainstormed more and more electronics together. My mom added the iron and washer and dryer as she had been using those all day for her linen business. My dad added a dishwasher and automatic doors, a coffee machine and a cash register – all that he had used while working in the cafeteria that day. My little brother added the light above the table. I had already had lights, but actually, yeah, that light was a chandelier. Maybe that got its own listing? Maybe every kind of light did? Yes! More and more pages filled in as we brought our plates to the sink.

While my family settled in for some nightly television watching before bedtime, I sat on the steps leading down to our living room, pencil and paper still in hand, hunting for new items... TV! How could I forget? Of course! The television!

And my list paused there for a while as I watched my family watching TV. They were so focused. It was like the TV was on, and they were turned off. I did some experiments to see if I could get their attention: silly moves, sounds and even leaving for ten minutes. Much to my surprise no one noticed. They were still glued to their TV program. Strange, I remember thinking.

The next day I handed in the pages of my homework assignment and was onto a new mission of my own: to see what my life would be like without any TV. Goodbye to *Little House on the Prairie* and Saturday morning cartoons! I was going to find other, more productive things to do with that time, to see what I had been missing while I was staring at those screens and how I wanted to choose to spend my time.

⌘

Describe your relationship with technology.

How does this relationship help/hinder your time, your space, your work, and the way you communicate with others?

What is your healthiest balance with technology?

5. Holding the flashlight on things that no one else is.

Hamburg, New York. April 1989.

I had my first birthday sleepover party when I turned eight. A few girls from school came over and we rocked out late-eighties-jean-jacket style. After cake and ice cream my mom granted us permission to take a walk around the block all by ourselves. If I fast-forward quickly through all of my elementary school years, my mind always wants to pause even for a moment with what happened next at the far end of the block. As we strutted our awesomeness around the curve, we saw an older kid on the side of the road pouring something down the drain. This caught the eye of one of my friends. "Hey, you can't do that," she said, as she looked closer. "That's oil. You can't just put that down that drain."

"Who did this group of newly turned eight-year-olds think they were anyway?" he must have been thinking as he rolled his eyes in our direction before continuing on with whatever it was that he was doing.

I remember part of me feeling so embarrassed. Did my friend think that she could just go around telling people in my neighborhood what to do? She was making all of us look so un-cool. At the same time, there was another part of me that knew she was right to speak up to this older kid. I knew that actions needed to be brought to light. I remember my choice to ignore that second part of me and take the side of the first, acting as if my friend's words had never existed. And as the boy pouring the suspicious liquid down the drain became invisible to me too, the other girls and I walked away round the bend. We left the girl who had spoken up behind.

As I continue to fast-forward through middle school and high school, I see more of these moments flash before me – moments where I knew that there was an injustice playing out right before my eyes and ears and that I paused not knowing quite what to do. What I had thought my reaction would be and what I actually chose to do in the moment were usually different things. What did I believe in enough to take a stand for? To fight for? To risk standing out and being laughed at or even being hurt? When did my head, heart, and gut align with a voice of my own that shouted *No, stop* or powerfully said *Yes, I support you... I support this cause*? What did I care about so much that I would defend it with all my life?

⌘

How do you define justice?

What do you believe in enough to take a stand for?

How do you bring light to this?

6. Finding freedom through music.

Hamburg, New York. 1990.

When I was nine, I got a new neighbor. An older woman - whom I identified as "old" because of the curve in her back, her white curly hair, and her kind smile. She had recently moved in with her son. He was nice too and seemed probably a little older than my parents' age at the time.

This new neighbor woman always waved while sitting on the lawn and always sweetly said hello to me (a gesture in which all the neighbors did not partake). I would wave back and smile as I continued to throw hoops or ride my bike: "Hello."

I wondered where she had come from and why she needed to live with her son. My grandmother lived in the same house for fifty-something years. A few miles from her, my other grandparents also lived on their own. I had understood that kids moved out, but now I was confused. Did parents eventually move in with their kids too?

Little by little I came to understand that this woman had to be locked inside when her son wasn't there because she "didn't have her wits about her." What were wits? Change in her pockets? Keys? Did I have some? Did I need them? Would I be given some wits at a certain age?

No. Soon after, I learned that not having her "wits" meant that she had something "wrong" with her. Something that occasionally made her go out on a walk without clothes on, something that made her repeat herself a lot, a reason I needed to reintroduce myself to her each time I met her. This intrigued me, and I didn't want her to be alone nor did I want to be alone after school, so I started going over to visit. To "babysit."

I would cross over to her driveway, walk up the steps, and unlock the door with my special key. Even though she always welcomed me first, sometimes I would need to explain to her who I was before sitting down with her. Then we would eat crackers and talk and talk and talk.

I would ask her questions about her life because I realized that she had lived a lot more of it than I had. And that she had been alive a long time ago, which I hadn't. I wanted to learn about a part of history that I was learning about at school from someone who really lived it. Someone who could tell me all about what it had been like for them. Sometimes I heard the same stories over and over again, but I didn't mind because I loved them, and there was always some detail that was absolutely new.

The coolest learned fact about my neighbor friend was that for most of her life she had been an organ player at a roller rink. I found this absolutely astounding. I loved music and roller-skating but only knew organs to be played at a church. I imagined her younger and playing the organ for hours on end as people skated out their prayers into the night.

The most amazing part of our afternoons was when she made her way over to the little organ that her son had brought from her old house. As if her bedtime ritual, with all her bodily wits about her, she pulled out the bench and sat down in the exact same indented place along the white vinyl. Then, as if returning home again after a trip, she gently rested her fingers along the white keys, and turned her head over her left shoulder toward me: "What will it be today? What would you like to hear?" She always looked so much younger in this moment.

"*Somewhere Over the Rainbow*, please." (My personal favorite at the time.)

And then like magic, even though she hadn't remembered what was happening from one moment to the next for the last two hours of our visit, she effortlessly performed the whole song. As if the same age through our enjoyment, we sang all the lyrics together. Some words were new to me but her heart knew every verse to every song. Swaying from side to side, she could play any song I asked for. The dulcet sounds would fill the house as I danced about our living room skating rink. I wondered if others might be able to hear us outside. Or maybe the whole house vibrated between the tones of her songs and the glorious happiness that streamed from her face looking up toward the light.

A perfect medicine, I thought... for what years later I understood to be Alzheimer's disease.

⌘

What music helps you to move more freely?

How does moving freely on the outside affect your movement on the inside?

7. Knowing what calms you and finding out what calms those closest to you.

Denver to Buffalo via Chicago. July 1991.

In 1991 two young girls sat side by side toward the back of a plane. One was me and the other was my older cousin. We were on our way back from visiting our uncle outside of Denver. My mom and brother had flown out with us on the way there, but on the way home it was just the two of us and this was our first time flying without our parents.

The night before, we had a fight. I can't recall the details of the argument. (Isn't that the way so many fights look in retrospect, childhood ones or otherwise? It's easy to remember the brawl without being able to ever recall what it was about. Maybe because it's usually motivated by a thousand causes all leading to a backing up in the pipeline of the relationship.) So let's sum up this fight as the intersection of having spent too much time together, being nervous about taking a flight alone, and simply not wanting to leave the newly discovered Rockies. All of these conflicts escalated into thrown fists and an early bedtime, leaving two grudge-holding cousins ready to be back in Buffalo in their own, separate homes.

A little ways into our flight, we started to experience

turbulence. Come to think of it, maybe that's when I learned that word. "Just like a bus on a bumpy road," I remember equating it to. Normal. But these bumps in the air only seemed to be getting worse and the other passengers, of all ages, were starting to look around. My cousin seemed unaffected. Ignoring me and bumps, she remained steadily focused on some magazine that she had found, left in one of the seat pockets.

But my heartbeat was beginning to speed up with each bump and only beat harder when the stewardess abruptly ceased doing her nails and started pacing up and down the aisle. As soon as I met eyes with her, she attempted to hide her obvious panic with an insane-looking smile. This wasn't good. This wasn't normal. Something was wrong. The plane started to thrash more and more, and I became sure that this was it. "Listen to me!" I said, breaking our silence, "I think we're gonna die…"

A sarcastic, almost reprimanding voice came out from behind the magazine followed by an exaggerated roll of her pre-teenage eyes, "No Kāli, we're not going to die."

I was horrified. This was the way that I was going to go? Really?

The turbulence intensified, and then I noticed the captain coming back to talk to one of the stewardesses. Something about "a water leak in the wing," I thought I heard. My stomach started flipping. "Shh…" she said to him, "There are children sitting right there. You don't want to scare them."

At that moment, my cousin realized the severity of our

plight. She dropped the magazine to the ground and grabbed my shoulder with a look of terror in her eyes, "Kāli, you're right... We are going to die."

And if we were, I was out to give her a dose of her own medicine. I answered back in the same sarcastic rhythm she had given me, "No, Leigh. We're not going to die."

About thirty blurry minutes later, we were safe on the ground in Chicago. I remember the other passengers applauded the landing while I grabbed my bag on a mission to hightail it out of there and call my mother. I found the first pay phone I could and explained to her that there was no way we were getting on another plane and demand that they would have to come pick us up as soon as possible.

"Well, what did she say?" my cousin inquired anxiously.

"I got the answering machines and left a message."

We lumbered toward our next gate was already boarding for Buffalo. Attempting to convince myself that flying two hours would be better than waiting ten hours for my mom and the ten-hour drive back, we shakily followed in line onto the new plane and found our seats. But I couldn't calm down.

My fears and indecision were interrupted by a gravelly but sweet voice coming up the aisle. "Hello, Girls," smiled the older woman taking the last seat in our row. "Don't worry," she continued as she settled in, "We are all going to be just fine. After all, we have angels watching out for us."

I wasn't certain whether either me or my cousin believed in angels, but this older woman had a certain shimmer about her that was convincing enough. With white hair backlit by the sunset, she sat at the window asking us where we were from and where we were going. My fears subsided as we answered her questions and asked her the same, and without realizing it, we were up in the air. Smiling and laughing, our continued conversation became the wings that I needed to fly back to Buffalo.

⌘

What calms you?

How can you create reminders of these throughout your day?

What are things that calm someone you love? How can you give one of these as a gift today?

8. Asking elders what life was like for them and listening for as long as they will share.

South Buffalo, New York. 1993.

A seventh grade version of myself once reflected:

You could say that life is like a book – some things fiction and some things fact. There are many pages we turn, many chapters we close, and many characters that we encounter through the plot. They become part of us in a way that binds our book for readers to come. Once upon a time, you come in contact with one person who helps you overcome conflicts and they have a great effect on the theme of your story. This character could be anyone really, but for me it has become my grandmother, Gramma Jule.

My Grandma Jule is my dad's mom. Her parents came from Ukraine, and she grew up in the Old First Ward as Julianna, the middle child of three. In her mid-twenties, my grandma married an Irish policeman. Together they had four children. She never learned to drive, but she proudly took the bus into downtown Buffalo every evening to clean the offices of city hall. Her husband passed away when their oldest child was nineteen and my dad, the youngest, was eleven.

"I will call you Jule like he did," my dad promised her then and remained close by.

Seventy-three long years of work, love, and dedication as a mother, grandmother, and great grandmother was what made her a candidate for my short story about someone I admire. I chose her because of the strength that she has had throughout her life.

I met my grandma just weeks before her sixtieth birthday when I came into the world three weeks after my due date. For the first year of my life, my mom and dad and I lived in the South Buffalo apartment above my grandma, in the same house my dad grew up in. When I was hardly two and my parents moved a couple miles away into their own house, my grandma was beside herself. She put her angst into pulling up the rugs in her house and proceeded to repaint the walls all by herself, vowing not to talk to my parents until they brought me back. Needless to say, she eventually calmed down and we visited often, but for her and me, often wasn't often enough.

We never wanted to be far from one another. I can't pinpoint why. There aren't reasons for things like this. My grandma had fifteen other grandchildren, all of whom she felt affection for, but I was different. I was "her pride and joy," my mom would say, trying to explain it. And it was true: I was her pride and joy and she was mine. We saw one another as nothing short of perfect, long-nose profiles and brown eyes alike, with pictures upon pictures to prove it.

My grandmother definitely knows how difficult it can be to grow up. She knows that closing chapters, over-coming conflicts, and all of the other things in between those pages aren't always so easy. She learned early on that life did not come with a handbook to guide her through. But with age, came knowledge through experience that is passed as advice to others.

When I was in fifth grade and my parents separated, my dad moved back into that original South Buffalo apartment that I was born into. He once again lived above his mom and from then on I spent every weekend with my grandmother. The beds were always made and her fridge was always full and ready. We played cards. We watched *Golden Girls* and every Sunday we waited for Buffalo Bills traffic to subside before we rubbed noses goodbye and parted ways. As my dad drove us back to the suburbs, I counted... Just five days of school before she and I would be together again.

⌘

What is your relationship like with elders? What draws you toward them or away from them?

Who is an elder that you can spend some time compassionately listening to today?

How might this conversation shift your perspective?

9. Discovering what helps you to express yourself.

Hamburg, New York. 1990-1998.

"Play me another one," my grandma asked after clapping and clapping. "Please?"

In fourth grade when my public school (amazingly) offered everyone the option of playing an instrument, I chose to play the flute, but when they told me to blow in the hole and I couldn't get any sound out right away, they said that my teeth were wrong asked me to choose again. The next instrument that came to mind was the violin. The girl who lived behind me had played the violin since she was three, and on summer days I would listen to her practicing for hours while I played on my swing set. "I'll try violin, please."

That moment began a lifelong relationship. I immediately ran home and our family became the proud renter of a violin that traveled next to me on the bus to and from school every day for the next five years.

My first lessons took place in a small closet off of our school's gymnasium. Five kids piled in elbow-to-elbow as learning how to play the violin. "You see this note?" said our teacher pointing to a black line with a circle between five horizontal lines. "It corresponds to a place on your instrument." We all looked at the teacher wide-eyed as he helped us figure out how to hold our instrument to our chin and put the right finger on the right string to find the note. Holding it there, our other hand picked up our bow and slid it along the strings at just the right angle and speed to hear the note on the page. Note by note we went through the same process over and over again little by little piecing together a phrase of music. Phew! This was gym class! This was math! This was history!

At nights, when my family watched TV, I would go up to my room and saw away. I was never forced to practice. I wanted to. This was learning a universal language that the whole world knew and my violin was my new best friend. A novel way to spend time, pass time, and feel time. Whether in 4/4 or 6/8 my fingers moved along the strings, perfecting song after song. When we went to my grandma's on the weekend, I would play for hours.

By sixth grade, instead of boy bands and *Beverly Hills 90210*, I preferred Verdi's Requiem and Sunday afternoon pre-concert talks at Kleinhan's Music Hall. "Do you know CPR?" my dad would joke, referring to the grey-haired bobbing heads falling in and out of sleep down our aisle even before the concert started. I elbowed him. They could sleep if that's what they wanted to, but I was transfixed. I loved to listen to the sound of the orchestra tuning as I waited for the handsome Chilean conductor to enter from stage right.

The piece opened with the cello section explaining death. Such somber sounds were nothing like I had ever experienced, and almost immediately, I pictured in my mind the sadness that was portrayed. It wasn't speaking in words, yet what an impact it had.

The chorus began to sing softly. They seem to plead for perpetual light to shine upon the dead. I was hardly thirteen years old, so the death that they mourned over was far from my conception, yet I felt it along with them. As they sang for what they had lost, I began to find the music that I thought I had always known.

Afterward we would go to a piano bar, and then drive home around Delaware Lake listening to 94.5, the classical music station, playing "Guess that Tune."

When I was in ninth grade, I bought my first violin by pooling together the money from my First Communion and a few years of babysitting. The next year, I started violin lessons with someone in the Buffalo Philharmonic, and demonstrating more and more commitment, my mom and dad helped me to upgrade to another violin.

"I want to play *Vivaldi's Four Seasons… Spring!*" I announced when I arrived in high school.

"That's pretty advanced. It's what the seniors are playing, and you are only a freshman."

I ordered the music and couldn't believe how hard it was. Note by note, I figured out where to place my fingers. I found the patterns. I played them slowly and sped them up little by little. I listened to the recordings over and over. I slept with the music under my pillow and the violin case open next to my bed.

This could not be taught in any classroom or explained in any other language, only by the music itself. These weren't just notes on a page. They were the expression of emotions that I never knew existed.

⌘

How do you express yourself with words? Without words?

How does expressing yourself shift your perspective?

10. Realizing the difference between quality and quantity, especially when it comes to love.

Hamburg, New York. 1995.

When I was fourteen I received a felt-tip penned letter on yellow legal pad paper, given to me by way of my dad's hand. He asked me to receive it as my first love letter. I smiled and scowled: I had been furiously angry with him for weeks because he chose to spend time with my brother instead of me.

For the past three years, my dad was the coach of my Odyssey of the Mind team. O.M. was a creative competition where six of my friends and I met every week for hours on end from November through March to build a play that was based on one of the given themes. We figured out a story and the props and the scenery. We made cardboard pterodactyls and ten-foot pop-up books. We acted and danced. The only rule was that all the decisions had to be figured out within the team. No one else could help but my dad was in the room always ready to give us a thumbs-up or take us to buy supplies for the next best idea.

"It's becoming petty," I remember my dad saying after year three, "Now that you are all getting older it's becoming about who likes who and which team wins. That's not as fun. You aren't doing it for the love of it anymore."

Sure, I cried and cried when we lost and my first boyfriend was on the team, but I still loved the creative part with all of my might.

"And now, it is time for me to coach your brother."

It wasn't going to be the same without him. This was our time together. Conflicted and jealous of my brother, I opened the letter up slowly and started to read it in my own time:

"Dear Kāli,
Please accept this as your first love letter…"

In a slanted cursive he went on to share with me what he called the "Mathematics of Love." With equations drawn between paragraphs he articulated to me how love was not a quantitative thing, that love wasn't something that could be measured or compared, but rather how love was an endlessly qualitative gift that one had to give. He laid out his decision to spend time with my brother and how it didn't demean his love for me. He explained that he still wanted to support me and go to concerts and hear all about my ideas. This was not an end. He was simply asking for my permission that our love take on a different form.

Part of me was ready to tear up the note or throw it out, but instead, I read his words over and over, wanting to understand what he was saying, how much he cared.

Still angry, I gave my permission, realizing for the first time how I could feel many different ways at the same time.

This letter became an X-axis to draw strength upon, to look at and touch, defining and redefining our relationship as the days and now years have passed. Tangible proof of love.

⌘

How do you show someone that you love them?

How do you trust when someone loves you?

11. Empathizing through a lens of multiple causality.

Hamburg, New York. 1996.

When I was fifteen, I took out some yellow legal paper and wrote my dad a new love letter: "When you don't take care of yourself, it hurts me. I don't want to be around you if you are going to continue to drink and smoke cigarettes. Please stop."

I had been raised in school on the notions of a "zero-tolerance orthodoxy" program that included a police officer coming into our seventh grade class, burning oregano, and telling us that if we ever smelled that to make sure we walked the other way. Drugs were bad. Alcohol was bad. And hence, as the equation continued, people who drank were bad too. But my dad was good. But he was bad. But he was good. But he was bad. But he was my dad. But I didn't want my dad to do these things. I didn't want this dad to be my dad, but I did.

Defeated, I got no response to my letter and our relationship fell silent for months. I didn't go to visit him on the weekends or call him for advice; he didn't come to my concerts or call me. I really thought that if I took myself out of his life, if he cared about me enough, he wouldn't be able to live without me and he would choose to shape up and everything would be better. If only equations of love were this easy to solve: supply and demand, like check and balance.

What I haven't told you yet is that my dad had a rare autoimmune disease called *Polymyositis*. I am reminded that it's rare because it has one of those automatic red wavy lines under it as I type this story. Isn't recognized here as a word.

Disease = Dis-ease = Without ease

Diseases are usually referred to by the name of the person who first recognized it or by the scientific rhetoric medical students learn to memorize.

Polymyositis, like the names of most diseases you hear for the first time, no matter your age, sound like some sort of foreign gibberish, gobbledygook. But when you go to the doctor not feeling good, and knowing that something isn't quite right and looking for answers, you are told that you have [this disease], the word sits with you. *Poly-myo-sitis*. When it sticks around and you fill it out on enough forms and you try to explain it to friends and co-workers, [this disease] becomes a common household word that rolls off your tongue. But it's not just a word. It's an interruption. A cause. A travesty. Something you have to deal with. A word with associations so deep and sensations so grand. A word that offers an answer and takes on resentment as the newest part of your identity: I have [this disease]. [This disease] runs in my family. [This disease] is one thing in a book, but it's a thousand new ways of living for me. It's what people see when I have a hard time walking up the stairs or I have no hair or when my arm doesn't look like everyone else's. [This disease] is part of me but not all of me. It's now become part of *who I am.*

Poly = many
Myo = of the muscles
Sitis = inflamed

Polymyositis is a chronic disease that comes and goes. It is quite difficult to diagnose and there is no pinpointed cause. And there is no cure, only some treatments including low doses of chemotherapy. It's not fatal exactly, just debilitating. Very debilitating. So much so that my dad couldn't lift my brother when he was born. The disease went into remission for several years, but resurfaced when my dad was in his forties. Although young, he could not walk upstairs without a lot of help from a sturdy railing. When he crossed his legs (which he loved to do), he would pick one leg up in his hands and move it to rest on top of the other before sitting back in his rocker and lighting a cigarette. This was a new identity for all of us.

This same person had also strongly identified as an athlete throughout his life. I have all the pictures and articles in a nearby shoebox to prove it. When he was growing up he played baseball and loved shooting hoops. He was tall: six foot, four inches. "The same height as Abraham Lincoln," I enjoyed boasting to my second grade classmates.

And today, when a sixty-something-year-old guy on a bar stool in South Buffalo finds out that I'm his daughter, they immediately remember my dad's pitching and hitting a baseball unlike anyone they'd ever seen. "That Quinnie was good," they repeat over and over and over.

"I know he was," I think as I remember playing catch with

him or as I walk by some kids playing catch and, without a thought or calculation, I pick up their missed ball and throw it directly to one of their gloves.

There is no doubt that I am a "Quinnie" too. And I'm proud of it, except for the drinking and smoking cigarettes part. But again, love is not that simple. We don't choose our genes or the diseases that may come into the mix. We are our family from the start and whatever circumstance arises becomes part of an ever-expanding, more complex equation that we can't figure out on our own. How could we ever be aware of all the elements at play? We don't know what baggage our parents are dealing with. We only know that we want them around forever.

⌘

What are things that you label as "bad" or "wrong?"

How can your Compassionate Creativity help you to see the multiple causes, known and unknown, for these things?

12. Seeking out the middle road.

Hamburg, New York. 1997.

On my sixteenth birthday, my dad sent me sixteen red roses. I wanted them, but I didn't want them. They were beautiful and hurtful. I remembered the letter, my ultimatum: "When you don't take care of yourself, it hurts me. I don't want to be around you if you are going to continue to drink and smoke cigarettes. Please stop." I stood my ground and waited for him to change.

"You are crazy," some of my friends said. Not because of how I was handling the relationship but because I was missing out on getting a car – the old clunker my dad had promised to give to me when I turned sixteen when he bought a newer one. Sure, having a license but not being able to drive was wearing on my teenage self, but I was stubborn and persistent too. I was certain, if I held my ground long enough, my dad would come around to seeing things my way. Then I would get the car. Then all would be well and perfect. The equation would be complete.

Needless to say, the summer passed with no talking, no driving and no fun. Two people. Same noses. Same yellow paper. Many equations. A confusing love.

That September, Beckett (the big, white fluffy dog named by

my dad that we had adopted when I was three) fell ill. My mom and my brother and I didn't know what to do. My mom called my dad, and he immediately came to be with us.

Beckett along our laps, we all sat together on the couch. The same couch where my parents had told us they were splitting up. The same coffee table. The same players. A different time. A different Beckett.

"I think you are going to have to take him in," a neighbor advised us as she stood looking at the scene of arms and tears and fur and love before her. Eventually we agreed and waited for the moment that we could all gain the courage to stand up and do it.

My dad drove. It had been years since we were all in the same car. I held Beckett in the backseat. "The moment that Beckett dies is the moment that you are going to grow up," I recalled my dad saying as he noticed Beckett aging. But I never believed that the moment would come. Perhaps love can only see and believe in more life until the moment comes when we love so much that we are gratefully able to say goodbye.

I looked into Beckett's eyes as he drifted off. He was the companion that had slept in my bed for the last thirteen years. He was the unconditional love that continued as my parents split up. Beckett had been our constant and once again, he brought us together here in his final moment, setting the table for reconciliation.

The next day, readying to bury Beckett in our backyard, my dad handed me the keys to his car. "This is your car now. Go get your grandma. She wants to be here too."

I unlocked the door, changed the seat, tipped the mirrors, and started up the engine. I was driving for the first time by myself. I looked out at Lake Erie. I wept for everything I had never let myself feel. For my family. For all its glories and fiascos. For my independence. And there went my childhood flying away on the wind.

My grandma stood waiting in her doorway as I arrived, while back at my house my mother continued to dig the six-foot hole she had started at sunrise.

Later that afternoon, a swing set rusting nearby, we all gathered round the wooden frame of our old sandbox. There, lowering Beckett into the ground we grieved: For ourselves. For one another. For all the decisions we had made and would make. For all the directions we had gone. For the things that we had never planned for and how we all did our best. For Beckett.

For more life.

Good and bad. Right and wrong. Letters and words and roses. Athletes and diseases and whiskey and genes upon genes. Old and new equations side by side by side.

My grandma was my grandma. My dad was my dad. My mom was my mom. My brother was my brother. They always had been. They always would be. This was my family. I couldn't change that or them. Only myself.

Causes and cures mysterious and many, dreams and wishes in hand, that afternoon my dad and I began to rekindle our relationship with all its imperfections.

⌘

What is something or someone that you have been trying to change? What do you need to change for yourself in order to compassionately continue to be in that relationship?

13. Turning everyday experience into an adventure.

Hamburg, New York. 1996-1999.

In high school, I was proudly one of the "Music Dorks." Music Dorks loved playing music and lived in the Music Department. We met there in the morning, came back for lunch, and took as many music lessons as we possibly could in between. Eventually we abandoned lockers out in the hallway and usurped one of the practice rooms as our home away from home. There we hung posters, did homework, played music, and made plans for the weekend.

We had great grades and never thought of getting drunk or doing drugs. We were too busy being silly, friendly, quirky, and we were always ready to play - music or otherwise. To turn a person's birthday into a huge expedition. To surprise our teachers with a life-size cardboard cutout of Darth Vader in their office. To order Chinese food and fill a living room with laughter all night. While stopped at intersections, we turned our socks into puppets out the sunroof of our beat-up car. We went late to school so that we could watch the moon set over the lake first. We had photos developed at midnight after daylong photo shoots through Buffalo streets. We ran to one another across the mile of a new Wal-Mart as if being reunited after years. We got lost on rural roads and counted cows or picked strawberries. When the odometer hit 99,999.9

miles, we pushed the car the last tenth of a mile to hit the 100,000 mark. On our way home from a late-night concert, we pulled over in a parking lot and had a dance party around the car. Before dropping the next person off, we drove the last three blocks in reverse. Anything to change it up. Anything to turn an everyday experience into an adventure.

Two months before graduating high school, my friends blindfolded me, shoved me into the car and pumped music through the radio as they drove me to a secret location. Several minutes and miles later I stood in the middle of a crowded Chuckie Cheese. Among the kids playing skeet ball and bopping gophers on the head in exchange for some silly prizes were some of my other friends, along with my mom, my dad, and my brother. We all played into the night. Eating our pizza, all the birthday boys and girls were announced and asked to come forward. With college decisions reeling in my mind and birthday love in my heart, I proudly took the stage. Feet taller than my present company, cardboard crown perfectly intact, they turned four and five and six as I turned eighteen.

⌘

How can you turn an activity you are doing today into an adventure? How does this shift of perspective shift your relationship to the activity and people involved?

How could you reconnect with your sense of adventure by reconnecting with an old friend today?

14. Taking care of your precious gifts.

Hamburg, New York. 1999.

Most of the Music Dorks knew what they wanted to go to college for: to teach music. But I wasn't sure what I wanted to do. I loved everything, and I had never thought about doing any of it as a profession. How could I choose? The personality tests that the guidance counselors gave us said I should be a teacher or a counselor, but what would I teach? Who would I counsel? I understood that college was upheld as the best thing ever, and I never questioned that for a second.

My mom drove me to my first college visit at a school well known for its music program. We went to meet with the chair of the department. I sat on the edge of my seat as he began to review my portfolio. "I'm sorry to say that you are not going to get in with this SAT score."

"Oh, that was just my first try. I'll take it again."

"Statistics say that no one goes up more than fifty points or so. You're not going to get in."

I swallowed, raised my eyebrows, thanked him and high-tailed it out of there with my mom following closely behind. This decision would all come down to a four-digit number of a test on English and Math skills? He didn't even look at me or ask me about why I loved music. Tears began to run down my cheeks and mix with rain as we made our way across the quad.

"Wait!" the man called after us, "I read more about you and hope you will apply. I see that you are good musician too."

I nodded and smiled, ran to the car, and asked my mom if we could stop at the University of Rochester. I had visited a friend there and felt great. The campus was beautifully set next to a river and the people I met were kind. I didn't know what I would go there for, but I knew I felt welcome and at ease.

Alongside the Music Dorks, I started to audition on violin for schools, but something didn't feel right. I didn't like the people I met at the auditions. They weren't the Music Dorks I knew. These people felt so serious and competitive. I had this nagging feeling that if I studied violin I would grow to hate it, and I didn't want to hate what I loved so much. I didn't want to force myself to practice for five hours a day alone in a practice room in order to fight my way to the highest stand in the orchestra. I wanted to play music to play music, not because it was my job. *Just because this was something I did well, didn't mean that I had to continue doing it, right?*

Amidst writing applications, my dad had some business in New York City and I went along to check out NYU. "Why wouldn't you study theater?" he asked in the car ride down. I had never even considered doing theater before.

I took the tour of the school while my dad was at work. It

ended outside of the theater building. Older kids walking in and out. They all seemed to have a purpose and know exactly where they were going. *Could I be here? Could I be one of them? Could I be an actor?*

That night we went out to dinner and a Broadway show. When we found out that our waitress was an actress, I asked her when she knew that was what she wanted to do with her life.

"When I saw *Annie* when I was six," she answered as she shrugged her shoulders and walked away.

My dad and I smiled at each other knowing it had been the same for me when I was three. When I had a red *Annie* dress and sang and danced every day. Suddenly the dots began to connect. I saw my life connected through theater. Of course… When I made my brother perform *Christmas Carol* with me every holiday. When I made masks out of paper bags. When I took acting lessons at Studio Arena. When I said "Freddy, faithful Freddy," in the school play in second grade. When I played the Artful Dodger two years in a row. When I made a new play for Odyssey of the Mind every fall. When I read *Love Letters* out loud with everyone I knew. When I chose to do theater over soccer in high school. When I looked at the auditions every Sunday for the last ten years in the *Buffalo News*.

But it was too late to audition for theater and doing theater as a job still felt unattainable. It was one thing to play the violin in an orchestra. It was another thing to get up in front of an audience and play a character. *Was it possible that my biggest fear was my biggest dream?*

Acceptance letters started coming back in the mail. I was accepted into Nazareth for music performance, Ithaca for music education, NYU for social work (an intriguing last minute choice when I needed to check one of the boxes), and Rochester for Liberal Arts.

I celebrated and toiled and debated and talked it over with everyone I knew day in and day out. This was the hardest decision of my life and it had come along so quickly. Wasn't I just in fifth grade? *How was I supposed to know? What was I supposed to do? Who was I supposed to be? Why was this moment that was supposed to be so exciting so troublesome?*

It didn't even cross my mind that I could take time off or do something else. It was a given that I would be part of my school statistics of "those who went on to college." Going to college had been upheld as the best thing ever, but no one was putting pressure on me except myself.

The Music Dorks accepted the offers from their music schools, went, graduated, went to graduate school, and sixteen years later, they are still teaching music. I'm sure it didn't happen all in one sentence like that, but from where I was, it sure felt like it. It felt like from the time they were teenagers, they knew something that I didn't and still don't.

"This isn't the end of your life, it's just the beginning," my mom advised. "You can make a choice and then make another one."

I didn't know it yet, but over the next four years, I would end up at each of these schools in one way or another, but first would go to Rochester. They had a good music school that I could take lessons at, and it wasn't too far from home.

I liked the campus and the river nearby. I didn't know what I would study, but I decided to say yes and bring my violin along.

⌘

What are your gifts?

What is the relationship between your gifts and the choices you have made throughout your life?

How could you reactivate one of your gifts today?

15. Revisiting, with great care, the moments that shifted your life.

Around Buffalo, New York. May 1999.

I didn't feel good so I went home from school early. My mom found me in my bed crying and crying. "What's wrong?" she asked. "I've never seen you like this before."

"I don't know, but I'm afraid. I feel like something bad is going to happen."

The next day I skipped the first part of school to take my grandmother food shopping. I was sure that there was something wrong with her, but she seemed completely fine. When we got back to her house, my dad was there. He had come home early from work because he hadn't been feeling well. It wasn't that out of the ordinary for him to be feeling sick but it was unusual that he would take time away from work. I went upstairs to see him. I lay on the couch with him and we talked. I don't remember what about.

"I love you," I said in Ukrainian (like my grandmother had recently taught me) as I kissed him goodbye. When I got to the back door, I stopped. I felt an overwhelming urge to add something else before stepping out. "A lot!" I yelled as I exited down the staircase. Hearing him laugh, I felt completely reassured that everything was great, so I went into school.

I don't know how to tell you this next part. I never know how to introduce it as part of a conversation or add it into a story without being worried about the person I'm talking with. I know that someone won't know what to say or feel bad for me or ask for details that I don't know how to share. I don't want to catch you off guard but I want to put it to you straight because I'm trying my best to tell you this story because, although I wish it wasn't, it's one of the stories that make up my life...

That next day, my dad died. My *dad*. The person who everyone said I looked like. The person who made half of me. The person who wrote me my first love letter. The person who drank and smoked and had a rare muscle disease that wasn't supposed to be fatal. The person I called when didn't know what to do. *My* dad.

Everyone would end up wishing that they were somewhere else that day but how could we have known?

My brother was with my dad, my mom was at a picnic, and I was finishing an essay for college writing placement. I kept calling him for help, but he didn't want to talk so I finished the writing on my own, dropped it in the mail, and drove out to the cottage. When I got there, my dad's car was in the driveway but my dad and my brother were nowhere to be found. I called their names but there was no answer. I heard the answering machine beeping and pressed play. It was my Aunt who was on her way to Buffalo from Maryland asking me to come to Lakeshore Hospital as soon as I could. How was she there already? Where was my brother? Where was my dad?

In that moment, I knew. I knew. This was the bad thing that was going to happen.

This was the longest ten minutes of my life. I drove. I knew. I prayed it wasn't true. I knew. I drove as quickly as I could. I knew.

As I got there, the doctor came out and announced that my dad had died. That he had experienced a heart attack and that there was nothing more that they could do. I remember the hands of my Aunt and Uncle and cousins going to their faces. I remember the tears and the word "no" repeating over and over again. I remember my brother sitting shaking his head. I remember standing there knowing that my whole life had been somehow leading up to this moment.

I remember stepping outside and the grass looking green. I remember my mom coming. I remember driving to my grandmother's. I remember hugging her. I don't remember much more of the days after that.

If I had grown up in the time of Homer's *Iliad,* I would have helped to put my dad's body on a homemade raft of sticks and lit the pyre as we watched the beautiful flames float out into the river away from us and into the night.

If I had grown up in Australia with an aboriginal lineage, I would have stopped saying my dad's name out loud. It would be disrespectful since he had now passed on to other worlds. That could have been the way I explained to you that he was dead. "We don't say his name anymore," I would say to you as we walked on along the outback with the sun on our backs.

If I had grown up Jewish, I would have sat at home for seven days after his funeral with a candle lit, continuing to mourn while people brought food. A year later we would have placed his gravestone and every time we visited we would put a rock on it.

I didn't grow up with any of these customs, but rather days later I sat in a Catholic mass where my family wasn't allowed to give a eulogy because we had decided to cremate my dad. We all came together and wholeheartedly believed that was what he would have wanted. We remembered him saying so.

It is, of course, easier to romanticize other cultures and feel oppressed by the way I grew up. I know that. But I also remember feeling the constriction of feelings. I remember one person singing at an organ. I remember my brother throwing a crucifix in the parking lot and saying this wasn't what my dad would have wanted. I remember thinking I might be dragged out for chuckling as the five priests on the altar, all from different schools throughout my dad's life, looked like a slow-motion version of The Supremes gesturing as they mouthed their words together. I thought my dad would find it funny too, and I laughed and laughed.

As my laughter subsided, I wondered if my childhood fascination with grief had somehow always been preparing me for this moment. I don't know that it's "normal" that a fourteen-year-old elects to write book reports on Faulkner's *As I Lay Dying* or Hemingway's *A Farewell to Arms* let alone *Hiroshima* for summer reading, but that was me. Intrigued by what people do and how they go on after such circumstances.

As a kid, if the uncle or aunt or grandma of one of my friends passed away, I felt compelled to go to the wake. To "pay my respects." I wasn't afraid but rather fascinated by the dead person lying there, a person whom I never met before and understood fully that I never would. While I was supposed to be up praying, I knelt on the bench just looking at them. Feeling that the body I was kneeling in front of was no longer that person, I would kiss my hand and then bring it to their head for a moment. My mom caught sight of this action once, and in the car ride home begged to know why.

"I don't know. I always do," I said, which only made her eyes widen further.

"You do?" And after a nod and an elongated silence driving over the skyway thinking I might have done something wrong, my mom turned to me at the first stoplight. "Well… what did it feel like?" she said.

And my fourth-grade self began to realize that death wasn't something everyone was fascinated by but rather something that the majority of people were all too afraid to talk about. It was not a subject that we were to ask questions about or that we even had the words for. No, death and grief was something that was kept hidden in the dark corners of the hearts and minds of all of us.

In high school, my best friend's parents ran a bereavement group. For several years, their phone number was given to the parents going through one of the worst things that any human could ever experience, the loss of a child. I remember looking at the two of them in awe as I learned this while sharing spaghetti at their dining room table. They always told stories about their son in a way that felt like I had met him. "Remember that time that he put the turtles in the kiddy pool?" I'd ask years later, and we'd all remember. These friends comforted me that summer. They always remember to call me on the anniversary of the day my dad died. They aren't too afraid to ask me how I am doing while also being open to the fact that I might want to talk about something else too.

Several days after my dad died I remember sitting in a tollbooth line thinking there was no way I could go on without him. I wanted to pull over and call it good, sure that my own life was over. But days before hadn't I been a wide-eyed, enthusiastic eighteen-year-old getting ready to go to college? It took some convincing, but I could faintly see the me that was standing on the other side of the vast chasm of that past week. That self was calling to me, but I was afraid she had died with him. In the far reaches to make myself feel better, to keep driving even one more exit, I remember thinking how I had enough stories about my dad that even if I told one a day for the rest of my life, I would never run out.

Some of these stories have been included in these pages so far, but from this point on, in all the stories my dad will no longer be living. He is dead. But I would quickly learn that a relationship doesn't end when someone dies. It's the responsibility of the living to take care of it and of themselves.

⌘

Remember a time that shifted the course of your life. How have you related differently to that moment over time?

Take a moment to remember who you were before that moment.

74

16. Letting your grief mysteriously give way to gifts.

Delaware Park, Buffalo, New York. 1999.

That summer, someone mysteriously invited me to be a part of a Shakespeare in Delaware Park. *Henry IV, Part 2* would play eight times a week for seven weeks starting in a couple weeks. I remember at the time everyone kept asking me if that was something I really wanted to commit to.

"Fifty-six shows? You will surely hate theater after that," some remarked.

"That's just too much right now," others recommended.

But, sitting at this crossroads, I was ready to find out…

The play was outside on a multileveled wooden stage, the backdrop being Delaware Lake, part of one of the famous parks Olmstead designed in the city of Buffalo. Behind the stage sat a trailer with costumes and some little dressing rooms with big mirrors. I wore a period corset and a heavy layered earth-toned skirt that was laundered every night and then appeared magically on my hanger the next day right above my assigned leather shoes.

I had performed in several plays in high school but this was my first interaction with a professional play (I even got paid!) and it ran like clockwork. Like a great soccer game, teammates came and went every which way. Handing off the baton, changing clothes, taking breaks, everyone sweated profusely and drank lots and lots of water before taking a bow and calling it a night. The next day we came back and did it all over again. Always the same template, but always a new day: different audiences and different rhythms. There was always a new smell in the air or new patterns along the sky. And no matter how I was feeling or what was going on, I was never late. This was the best place to be.

While awaiting their cue, all the actors sat overlooking the lake. Minus the plaid vinyl lawn chairs and fluorescent plastic sunglasses, this was a complete Elizabethan scene. Some actors read books while others napped or conversed. In the meantime, the play was being piped back to us through speakers so that we all knew what scene was going on and how the audience seemed to be responding. When it was our turn to grab the baton, the stage-manager came round and gave us a heads up to ready ourselves for our entrance. Everyone did this in their own way: some people stretched their jaws and made funny noises, others ran quickly in place, others took deep breaths with their eyes closed, a few sat quietly until the last possible moment when they suddenly burst onto stage and somehow beamed up to meet their highest level of energy.

Me, I made sure to be at my entrance early just in case something happened and I had to go on sooner. I made sure my violin was in tune and readied for my first note. I checked that my skirt was in place and that my nose wasn't running. Thank God that I didn't have to say anything! My part was small. I was to play my violin in two scenes: first during Act One in the tavern and then again in Act Two at the bedside of the king's death:

"Let there be no noise made, my gentle friends;
Unless some dull and favourable hand
Will whisper music to my weary spirit."

I entered just then, and as dusk bequeathed the sky, I played a simple, haunting melody… one that my fingers might even remember now if I let them. I repeated the drifting tune until the scene came to its end. The mosquitoes frolicked about. The audience enjoyed the last bits of their picnics. Their kids sat upon their laps – wanting to see the last bit of action before their eyelids began to droop. I had been one of those kids one day not so long ago.

I remember this summer perfectly and at the same time, not really at all. A huge brush stroke that held my experience of great grief in a moment of so many transitions. A place between endings and beginnings, these 56 shows gave me a ritual. A daily practice when I needed it most. A home. I had somewhere to be, something to be part of, and amidst all I was eternally reminded of what I loved, what I valued most, and who I was.

And thus, on a wing and a verse, began an odyssey into adulthood.

⌘

When did you experience a moment of great beauty within a moment of great grief? How did this gift help guide you?

FIRST MOVEMENT: INTO COLLEGE

Connect with your Compassionate Creativity by...

17. Connecting to people who have a common passion.

Rochester, New York. 1999.

Freshman year of college was my first time living away from Buffalo, and for all of the sixty-some miles, it was a big step, where I met people from all over the world.

A voice with a sweet southern accent stood out among the din of the Freshman welcome fair. "Might you be interested in auditioning for some theater this semester?"

"Yes! I didn't know there was a theater department here!"

"It is a program within the English Department. You could even major in English with a concentration in theater."

This man was speaking my language! Before I knew it I was in the theater office signing up for classes and auditions and taking a tour of the Drama House across the street.

"There are a few spots open, but freshmen aren't supposed to be able to live here," explained the Artistic Director, who was from South Africa, "Although, if you really are interested, I might be able to find a way…"

"Let's be roommates!" proposed the girl standing next to me taking the tour. She was from England and studying abroad for the year.

Together we dragged our stuff from our originally assigned rooms and roommates into the Drama House. This three-story building was one of the seven similar buildings on the Fraternity Quad, but it wasn't a fraternity. This was "special interest housing." Seventeen other intriguingly assorted undergraduate renegades who were interested in theater arts became our housemates. Seventeen other young people excitedly on their own for the first time in their lives.

"Good morning, World!" shouted my roommate out the window every morning.

I learned more from her and the other people in this house than I did from any other class that entire first year. They had grown up in completely different ways, in completely different places. They used different words than me and believed completely different things than I did. I was intrigued by their customs and study habits and worldly ways. At night when everyone was studying, I would go around to every room and steal people's clothes, collaging together quite the outfit and making people laugh on the next round of visits.

My first week living there, I auditioned for the play at the theater across the street. That semester I performed in two Restoration Comedies back to back. In the first show, *The Man of Mode*, I played a tomboyish servant to a woman played by a Japanese professor. In the second show, *The Libertine*, I played Elizabeth Barry, a young actress. The man who played my lover was from Iceland. That spring I played Briseis in a six-hour, thirty-odd person version of *The Iliad*. Guest designers came from Greece and Russia.

Little did I know it then, but by choosing to study theater in college, instead of getting lost in the seas of two-hundred people lecture halls during the day and fraternity parties at night, my days and nights would be spent in the world of the theater. Production after production, I would collaborate with classmates from across the globe. I would gracefully be handed from character to character to learn about the dustbowl and Troy and the American slave trade by living within these places and times. And by being in relation to all these people, real and imagined, I would learn more about myself.

⌘

How has your passion connected you to new people or places?

How have they taught you more about yourself?

18. Discerning when you are running away versus when you are moving toward.

New York City. 2000.

Learning how much I wanted to do theater, I decided to audition for New York University. At the time I remember telling a teacher friend that the most nature I ever wanted was to take a walk in Central Park. I hadn't grown up camping or hiking or skiing or farming. Beyond sitting on a pile of rocks at Lake Erie, I didn't know what my relationship to the land was like. I'd rather be in the flood of people moving on the concrete sidewalks of a bustling city: buildings my trees, bright lights my sun, subway lines my roots.

I got in! I got in! New York City, here I come!

After getting lost and ending up in front of Yankee Stadium where we all sat in awe for a few moments before asking for directions, my courageous mom and ecstatic brother drove into Manhattan and dropped me and my stuff off at my West Village dorm. I stood on the corner waving and sobbing as they started their seven-hour drive back to Buffalo. I was not at the University of Rochester any longer. The big city was my campus. Just as I had dreamed, I was now in the epicenter of theater. I lived and went to school on the same island as Broadway. What more could I ever want?

"What did you do this weekend?" friends back at Rochester asked jealously, "Did you see a show?"

The answer was usually no. When you visit New York City, you go to Times Square. When you live there, you avoid it like the plague and spend that time doing your laundry.

When I auditioned for NYU, I was moving toward something, but by the time I actually matriculated, I was definitely running away from a ton. For some, New York might be the perfect city to run away to, but for me it became utterly overwhelming. I was so unsure of myself that I felt tossed in the wind and unable to stop amidst the seas of people. Everyone seemed so sure of where they were going. But between honking cars and homeless families begging for money outside of my dorm, I would stand paralyzed not knowing which way to go or how to possibly take it all in, let alone get to school. I was over-stimulated to say the least.

I was scared. I laid in bed and cried a lot and couldn't understand what was wrong with me. I could tell that my roommate wondered too, but didn't ask, and she just stopped associating with me altogether. She was there with a purpose and wasn't going to let anything or anyone distract her.

But me, I didn't know who I was, and I didn't want to risk losing myself more. I wanted to find myself and here didn't feel like the place I was going to do it. If I stayed, I felt like I was going to become someone that I didn't want to be. A person whom I knew I wouldn't like very much.

On the inside, I missed my dad but didn't want to admit it. *He died more than a year ago. Shouldn't I be over it or have moved on by now?* I sure wanted to move on, so why couldn't I? I wanted to do everything that he wanted me to do. To do the things that people kept telling me they were proud of me doing, but I became only more tired and anxious.

My emotional extremes were juxtaposed with acting classes of physical endurance and intense self-exploration. This was a perfect antidote on one level, but I also started to see the dam I had built up over the past year. If it broke, I wasn't sure what would happen or who would help me handle the mess.

In classes, I was surrounded by theater people. The same sixteen theater people day after day. They talked and talked about theater. All their goals focused around theater. Their life was theater. So was mine, I had thought. But where were all the political science majors and the people studying biology? Where was the Japanese professor who did the plays for fun? I loved making theater with these people in Rochester. But that was different. That was behind me. I had chosen this new path. I had been accepted at the prestigious Tisch School of the Arts.

Here I am in New York City, I began to write as I sat in a little Italian restaurant near my dorm attempting to figure this all out... but that's as far as I could get. Realizing that this was the first time I had ever eaten out alone, I shut the journal. I looked around at the empty seats and at the paintings on the wall. I listened to the chefs speaking boisterously in Italian, wishing I could understand what they were saying.

I finished my food and opened the journal back up. There, I

reread what was inscribed to me before I left for college. "You dad loved so much to write and express himself, and it brought him great comfort," his friend wrote. "I hope this book will provide you with the same solace and outlet. You have so many wonderful adventures ahead of you. Be a sponge and take it all in. Then squeeze back out what you want to here."

I turned to the next page:

Here I am in New York City.

I put the pen to the page and began to squeeze:

I am right where I always thought I would want to be and now I'm not so sure at all. This city just seems sad. Everything about it. It isn't a good place to be if you are sad too because it only makes it feel worse. Maybe if I could still be wowed by it. There is so much to do, but I can't bring myself to do it. Maybe there is a hump to get over or something, but I can't. Because I don't want to, I guess. So my opportunity of a lifetime ended up being not so good. The opportunity is now saying, "Go home."

The next day I went with some classmates to the Central Park Zoo. We were assigned to observe the animals, to see which one we were most taken by, and to then study that animal's movements. For over an hour I watched a seal in his tank as he moved through the water with such grace and ferocity. At one point he even came up to the edge and looked right in my eyes. He stayed long enough for me to see a yearning in him. One that I saw reflected in myself.

From there we went to the library to research our animal. Facts and totems toward creating a character. I learned how a seal is a reminder of balance, of channeling creativity and imagination. A reminder that dreams are significant, but that one first has to listen to their body's natural rhythms.

I walked back to my dorm through the darkening city. Leaves were changing, and I was ready to go home to take some time to grieve.

⌘

How do you discern when you are running away from something versus going toward something?

How does each directionality affect your actions?

What is a current relationship or situation that you could reframe from running away to moving toward?

19. Going on silent walks.

Ithaca, New York. 2001.

The next semester, I returned to school in Rochester, vowing that I would spend my summers immersed in intensive theater training. The first summer, I participated in a program in Ithaca, New York where I was one of twenty-four twenty-somethings from all over the country living side-by-side and rehearsing day and night. By day three we were all close, very close. By the end of the summer, we were inseparable.

My days of summer tans were replaced by hours upon hours in a black box rehearsing. Over the course of the eight weeks, I played the part of a ten-year-old boy named Itys, a Cuban refugee named Talita, a palm-reading gypsy named Paloma, and one of the Mechanicals in *A Midsummer Night's Dream*.

One day our group of twenty-four was challenged to be quiet all day. If needed, we could speak in classes, rehearsals, and shows, but otherwise there was to be no other words or sounds coming out of our mouths. No conversation. No phone calls. No hello to passing someone on the street. Nothing. Just silence.

For most of us, this was new territory. We were young

theater people who were used to being dramatic, expressive, and boisterous all day long, but we also up to experiment. Trusting our teacher, ready and willing, this day became a lifetime of exploration. We sat along the edges of the hallway awaiting the start of class in silence. We walked to the dining center and ate in silence. This was hard for us, but it was enlightening.

Without all the extraneous sound and interaction, we all felt more connected than we had before, and we played differently. Without words, we listened to the rhythm of our walks and stepped along with each other. All day I was aware of what I wanted to say when and why, realizing that without speaking, I was okay. I became aware that I liked to talk a lot about a lot and that sometimes I didn't need to. When I didn't talk or comment on something, I took the time to look at it and breathe it in. A long-term friendship between myself and two other actors was solidified when the three of us sat together quietly writing at the end of the day. I went to sleep that night calmer, with less of a need to do anything.

Weeks later, at the start of a new semester in Rochester, along with the rest of the world, I experienced September 11, 2001. Part of me wanted to be there. To run there. One year ago I walked those exact streets with my friends from NYU, the towers were in full view down Sixth Avenue, blocks from our dorm. So many of my new friends from Ithaca were there, our teacher. *Why were all these people there and I was not? Were they okay?*

There were no words for what anyone anywhere on the planet was feeling that day. The world was in full

87

suspension, all of us together. Incomprehensible and yet true. In shock, not knowing what do but knowing that I needed to be away from the images replaying on the TV, a friend and I quietly walked down to the Genesee River and sat under our favorite tree. I knew it was okay to be silent. In fact, in that moment it was possibly the best thing that we could have done. We silenced our voices, our thoughts, our movements. We felt our backs along the ground. As the whole world changed, we watched the birds flying overhead and the water moving along in front of us.

⌘

Take a silent walk today by yourself or with someone else (even 5 minutes around your house will do!). What was this experience like for you?

20. Seeing everyone as parts of yourself.

Rochester, New York. 2002.

During my junior year, I was cast as the character of Alice in a new play by Patrick Marber called *Closer* that was making its way around regional theaters and college campuses after a good run in London. *Alice* was described as a sort of waif, a word that I didn't know until that moment. She never had much of a family or held onto many friendships. She made her way through life by constantly remaking herself. She started over by cutting her hair and changing her image. Oh, and she was a stripper.

At first glance, beyond being about the same age, there was not much I had in common with *Alice.* I had grown up in the same place for eighteen years, surrounded constantly by family on both sides and hanging out with the same friends who moved through the same grades knowing me as the same Kāli. I was president of the class for four years and part of every club and committee I could fit into my after-school schedule. I carried a Franklin Day Planner, and I had never had sex, let alone thought of touching drugs or alcohol.

Alice believed that you chose to love someone and that at some point something would just turn off. There would be a moment that you would stop loving that person and she would name it out loud right there and then: "I don't love you anymore." And completely unemotionally she would leave – "that's that" – and move on to her next life without ever looking back. Being *Alice* would teach me a lot about a lot.

First things first, I would need to cut my hair into a sort of bob with bangs, an awkward style that I hadn't sported since the second grade. I would also need to learn how to smoke or at least pull off being a smoker, a habit that I had always judged harshly in others.

The three other students in the play were good friends. Their hair would remain as it was, and they would all give me tips on how to smoke:

Anna would be played by a bold girl from Texas who studied political science. She was readily able to talk straight up with me about sex and drugs, with intriguing stories from both the national history with such subjects and her own experiences. *Anna.*

The guy who was assigned the role of *Dan* was from Pennsylvania. We had kept watch over each other since a rough freshman year that included our share of late night grocery outings and hospital visits. *Dan.*

The last of the quartet was a character named *Larry*, played by a boy who had moved to the United States from Russia when he was ten. Earlier that same semester he decided to devote himself to being fully Orthodox. In Judaism this meant that he would observe the Sabbath and that working from sundown Friday to sundown Saturday would not be permitted. So we all agreed that the one night off from rehearsal would be Friday. On Saturdays we carried his script across the street to rehearsal for him and his Rabbi somehow found a way of looking at that rehearsal as more of play than work. *Larry.*

This ragtag group was cast together exploring the quadrilateral love and lust of *Larry, Dan, Anna* and *Alice.*

"You know," piped up *Anna* one night as we walked home from rehearsal, "When you dance, I can tell that you've never had sex." I turned red as she paused in her step and put her hand on my shoulder. It's true that I was uncomfortable dancing during the strip number and between that and holding cigarettes, I wasn't sure I would be able to pull this off. I just couldn't understand how to be *Alice.*

Anna invited the others into a sort of huddle. "I think we all need to do some first-hand research," she continued, with a coy twinkle in her eyes and an unusual idea up her sleeve.

That weekend, after an eight-hour rehearsal, *Anna* and her friend drove us all out to a little town thirty minutes south of school. ID shaking in hand, I readied myself for what I was about to witness. When we pulled up to the small dark building it looked like an abandoned diner or an out-of-season ice cream stand. We double-checked the address on our directions, and sure enough a light flickered, illuminating that same number. This was it.

Silent, we opened the doors of the car looking cool, as if it was totally normal for our crew to do this kind of thing together on a Saturday night. Sure, why not? Moving through a smoky haze we were greeted by a kind of hostess not much older than us, along with the eyes of a handful of older men, some bearded, some with hats, who sat at their own tables in front of a small, raised stage. I wasn't ready for this. I had never even seen another naked woman before, let alone explored my own parts in-depth. "Table for four, please," I said with an abrupt confidence, not realizing that my friends had already moved into some of the chairs in the front row. The rest of the night is still a blur of wide eyes and laughter, research and dancing, thongs and tassels, and the possible perils and plights of nudity, sexuality and a shared humanity in process.

Quietly mystified, with fewer answers and a sea of questions streaming from every part of our bodies, we drove home. In our classes our learning so far had been mostly engaged in memorizing facts that we would circle on the next exam or gathering precise quotes to be used in end-of-semester papers, but outside of those classes, in the theater, we were engulfed in a world so big and beyond our comprehension. This passionate scavenger-hunt kind of education was becoming out of our control and into our souls.

"Listen closely," anguished our director in his British accent at the penultimate dress rehearsal, "Anna is the only character I truly understand or empathize with at all. Really... I don't know what the rest of you are doing but you'd better figure it out before tomorrow night."

The only one he understood was *Anna*? What about my character? What about *Alice*? I felt horrified. That was our only note after doing the entire show? All my weeks of work and research hadn't amounted to anything? I had been dancing better and smoking like the best of them.

The next day, I skipped all of my classes. I reread the script front to back. I walked near the river and down to my favorite tree. I thought about *Alice*. I spoke her words out loud, but I wrestled with her choices, her way of being. I felt scared, bewildered, confused. At 6pm I showed up to the last dress rehearsal, and without any new plan of attack, I got into costume and make-up. I glared at my short hair cut in the mirror. I stood looking at myself looking like *Alice*, but what more could I do?

Places were called, and I nervously waited backstage for my entrance. In the blackout, I moved to sit smoking and waiting on a bench, my rucksack of belongings at my side, just as I had done for the last fifty times, but something was different. Shifting in my seat, I felt tentative, not knowing how the next moment would unfold. This uneasiness continued for the entirety of Act One.

At intermission, the stage manager fired toward me before giving her five-minute warning: "That was amazing!" she said, engulfing me in her arms, "Wow, whatever you are doing... keep it up. It's magical."

But what was I doing? I had felt totally unsure of myself in every scene.

Act Two went by in a similar fashion. My confusion and bewilderment continued on through *Alice's* every word and action. I danced the strip number. I kissed *Larry* long and hard. I cartwheeled in soaking wet, wearing *Dan's* button-down shirt. I felt him spit on me after I slapped him in the face before telling him that I didn't love him anymore. I used the same words as the night before, but I didn't know what I was doing or why. I bowed, changed clothes, and was more

93

exhausted than I'd ever been after a performance.

"Wonderful work!" bellowed the director as he came in to give his notes, "Do you know what you did?"

I looked at him with a look that felt more like one of *Alice's,* "I have no idea."

"Perfect. Keep that up!"

Keep that up? I had always analyzed and understood every word and performed my best study of the character. What this play and director and character were demanding was another thing. I was presenting my ideas about *Alice,* not being *Alice.* I calculated my moves as I went. *Alice* wouldn't do that. And if I continued to analyze *Alice* like this, the audience would too. If I wanted the audience to empathize with *Alice,* I had to empathize with her myself. *Alice* was teaching me how, in order to create, I had to give over to the beauty of not knowing, having faith that it would somehow all accumulate to something. I had to see *Alice* not outside of myself, but rather as part of me. I needed to look out at the world through her eyes, from her perspective.

Another night down, my three other compadres looked at me and smiled. "I'm ready," I said, not knowing if that were true, but knowing that we would all be closer tomorrow.

⌘

Who is someone you see as being the opposite of you?

How can you find some new ways that you share similarities with them? How might this affect your relationship?

21. Checking your assumptions at the door.

Buffalo, New York. 2001.

I had been away at college having revelations in all directions, continually falling into pieces one week and then putting myself back together the next, reinventing myself anew in this new place, this new home. I was a totally different person… or rather I was becoming much more of the me that had always been in there somewhere but I hadn't yet found the courage to bring out until now. I liked this new me much better than the old one, but when I returned to Buffalo for a visit, it felt impossible to be this new person. Everyone expected me to be the me that they had known, and I couldn't help but fall into my old ways of being. This was endlessly frustrating. I didn't want to be that other person anymore. I wanted to be the new me everywhere, but I wasn't quite sure how to integrate it all.

The fight that raged inside me erupted into a heated dispute with my brother. It would, of course, be easier to battle with him or anyone else than with myself:

"Yeah, well… You're never going to be passionate about anything!" I said in the middle of that particular dinner. As soon as the words came out, I would have done anything to put them back in. Jaws dropped, the table fell silent, and my brother immediately slammed his glass down and stormed out the front door.

"I didn't mean it," I said to my mom and my grandma as I shrugged my shoulders and rolled my eyes. They shook their heads, lost in the sea of their own tongue-tied regrets and began to clean up. I knew that I had crossed a line and I would never be able to go back.

Although I didn't know what to say next, I took a breath and headed out to the porch to find my brother. Arms crossed, he turned his head, looked me straight in the eyes and said one of the most heart-wrenchingly honest things I have ever heard: "You don't know me."

Our eyes locked in the suspension of this possible truth.

This, the two-year-old brother that fell in the sump-pump when I was supposed to be watching him.

This, the brother I played dress-up with.

This, the brother named Evan who my dad liked to call Raoul.

This, the brother who stayed in the lake all day, face down, looking for treasures.

This, the brother who fought with me over who got to sit in the front seat every Sunday night.

This, the brother that was with my dad when he died.

This, the brother who years later would come to live with me in Brooklyn, who would come to visit me for a weekend in Vermont, help me move, and end up staying for months.

This, the brother who always remembered all the words to every song on the radio and now returns his own lyrics to me five minutes after I text him a new melody.

This, the brother who can now grow a beard, is over six feet tall, and has proposed to his girlfriend.

"You don't know me."

He was right. Even though he was my brother and I had known him for his entire, I didn't walk every step of his day with him. I didn't live with his thoughts, in his body. Even though we had experienced many of the same events as children, we were affected differently. We reacted differently. We remembered them differently. Somewhere along the way, I had started to make some major judgments about who he was, the choices he made, and what he needed most. And for the last three years, while I was away at college, I had no idea what was happening at home, just as he had no idea what had been happening to me. Without ever acknowledging it, we had begun to live completely separate lives in separate places. We glorified one another's experiences thinking that the other must have it better, ignoring the possibility that the other was also struggling. I wished I was there. He wished that he wasn't. But what could we do? Time had led us this far and we were so much more the same than we were different.

"You don't know me."

This, my brother. My only sibling. The baby I held in my arms when I was three. The only family I will have once my mom is gone. The only one who will remember how the lights in the dining room would dim at dinner. How the car said, "The door is ajar." How my mom laughed and how my dad raised one eyebrow when he wanted to appear more serious.

"You don't know me."

This, the brother whose shoulders I stood on out on the lake while waving to our parents to take pictures.

The only one who can remind me who I was all those years before leaving home.

Made from the same two people, we were both full of such passion.

"I'm sorry. I don't know you and I do know you," it took me years more to be able to finally say out loud. "I am proud to be your sister and I will be forever grateful to call you my brother."

⌘

What is an assumption that you are holding right now?

How is that assumption related to your own needs and fears?

22. Recognizing diversity and feeling interconnected at the same time.

Santiago, Chile via Philadelphia, Miami, and Panama City. 2002.

My mom helped me to cobble together her and my dad's frequent-flyer miles so that I could travel for free to Santiago, Chile where my college boyfriend was studying abroad. This was my first time out of North America, and it would take over twenty-four hours to get there.

"Remember, there is no way I am coming to Panama City to pick you up," joked my mother, remembering a scared call from Chicago long ago. She kissed me and waved me along onto my gate. "You've got to keep going and then in a week, come all the way back." She didn't even know where I was going. She'd never crossed the equator. She must have been so scared to let me go, but amazingly enough there she stood figuring out how to let me go all the same. She looked so strong and certain that I would be okay, that this was the best choice that we had ever made. "Go…"

As the plane took off, I drifted back to high school:

"I'm going to meet everyone in the entire world," I announced, gleaming amidst the crowded high school hallways.

My English teacher overheard and chimed in with his infamous monotone lilt: "Really, Miss Quinn?" He loved to call everyone by his or her last name. "You want to meet everyone in the world? How exactly are you going to do that? You want to meet everyone? Even the very bad people?"

"Yes," I said timidly while gaining confidence, not wanting to leave anyone out whether they were bad or good or tall or short or rich or poor or whatever. I looked around at the crowed hallway of football players and Music Kids and teachers of all shapes and sizes and ages. "Yes," I restated my claim, "I want to meet everyone."

This old memory, mixed with the new one of my mom waving, helped me board new planes in Philadelphia, Miami, and Panama City.

I passed so many people along the way. So many people on their way to so many places. Some sad. Some joyous. Some distraught. Some business people. Some mothers. Some both. Others students like me. All colors. All ages. Hats and turbans and buns and leg-braces. Blue eyes and brown eyes and green ones. Backs bent and straight. Tall and short. Some prayed. Some asked for money. Some gave money. Some observed. Some walked quickly. Others sauntered slowly. Some spoke. Some yelled. Some remained quiet. Thinking, dreaming, listening.

Coming out of the Chilean airport, people with all of these qualities and more fled by. I became an innocent child walking hand-in-hand with my boyfriend into the city. The streets of Santiago bustled noisily with things for sale. Colors and patterns, and lace and laundry streamed out of high windows. When we arrived at our nearby hostel, adrenaline having run out after twenty hours of travel, I quickly fell asleep. The montage of images from this new hemisphere continued on repeat until my nap was abruptly interrupted by the entire building starting to shake. The bed jolted along the floor.

"Oh, yeah," my boyfriend dropped in casually as he saw my eyes open in amazement and terror. "I forgot to tell you, there are little earthquakes like this here all the time."

"What?!" In a panic I jumped out of bed and ran to the window looking down on the streets of the city. Although the ground was rumbling, everyone was going about their business. "Holy shit." I remarked, jaw dropped. "There are so many people down there." There were people walking and riding in every direction. People everywhere. People that had always been here while I had been somewhere else. The world was so much bigger and greater and more humbling than I ever imagined it could be.

"Let's get out there and see what's going on!" I rattled off, extremely intimidated and excited all at the same time. I didn't even speak Spanish, but nonetheless, my quest to meet everyone in the world was still a worthy one in motion.

⌘

How can your Compassionate Creativity help you to notice how you are similar to people who might seem very different from you?

23. Befriending your neighbors.

Rochester, New York. 2002.

The first time I lived alone was when I watched a professor's house for the summer. During the day I worked at a nearby performing arts camp, and in the evenings I returned home to his plants and a cat named Porch and began to find my own rhythm: making dinner, reading a little, and talking on the phone a lot before falling asleep.

A couple of weeks into my stay in the middle of the night I awoke to a funny high-pitched sound, a squeak that I could only attribute to the cat playing with one of her jingly toys. After pulling the pillow over my head several times, I made my way to the living room to see what all the fuss was about. Both the cat and the toy were motionless, but the noise continued at my feet. I looked down slowly to see a writhing bat.

I quickly ran back into the bedroom and slammed the door. Not knowing what to do, I took the blanket off the bed and shoved it into small the space at the bottom of the bedroom door, but that didn't seem like enough protection. I pulled the dresser in front of the door and stood with my back against it. Starting to pant, I learned that apparently, I was afraid of bats.

Wait! I left the professor's cat out there with the bat! What was happening out there? The bat? The cat? I needed to do something now.

I climbed out the bedroom window onto the railing and down the porch and tiptoed across the street barefoot to arrive at the neighbor's door.

Knock. Knock. Knock.

No answer. Of course not. It was three in the morning.

Knock. Knock. Kn —

"Oh, hi. My name is Kāli. I live across the street. We met a couple days ago when you were moving in.... Umm..." I contorted my body, readying to deliver my quandary. "I have a bat in my house and I need your help."

He paused and rubbed his eyes, "Hold on. I'll be right back."

I stood there amidst the crickets until he returned equipped with a broom and a garbage bag: "Let's go."

We trudged across the street up to the porch on our joint mission. To his surprise I stopped short. "I don't have a key," I explained, "I crawled out my bedroom window to get out so that I didn't have to see the bat again. It's in the living room."

Before I knew it, I was standing on his shoulders to hoist myself through the window. Moving the dresser, I made a dash out through the bat territory to open the front door and let him in.

"You stay here," he whispered and then he was off.

"Be careful!" I called after him.

What felt like an eternity passed before he reappeared.

"Let's just say, the cat got the bat... The cat's fine. The bat's not."

"What?"

"The bat's in the bag. You can go back in now. It's safe." But I couldn't move an inch. "Go ahead... I'll come with you," he insisted.

Closing the front door and leaving the tied garbage bag and broom behind us, we stood in the doorway of the now bat-less living room.

"Are you okay?" he murmured.

"Yeah, I'm fine."

"Are you sure?"

"No." (I later learned that this man had a great philosophy that one should always ask every important question twice, knowing that the respondent might impulsively hide the truth on their first answer.)

"Well then, I'll stay here until you are."

Looking around the space I imagined the warfare between the bat and the cat. The same cat that now stood at our feet smiling in victory and basking in what was probably the most exciting night of her life.

"Are you okay now?" the neighbor chimed in after a minute or two.

"Yeah. I'm okay… I'll be all good here by myself."

"You sure?"

"Yep. I am. Let's get some rest."

"Goodnight," he waved with the broom and the bat bag in hand.

"I can't thank you enough," I yelled after him.

"No problem. That's what neighbors are for, right?"

"Yeah. Welcome to the neighborhood."

⌘

Who is a neighbor who was a great help to you or vice versa?

How could you reconnect with them or pass along the power of that relationship to a new neighbor/friend today?

24. Finding your center and moving from there.

Rochester to North Carolina. 2002.

My friends and I piled in the car and drove ten hours straight to somewhere in North Carolina with the goal to each be cast in a professional summer production. They call this kind of audition a cattle call because we were only three of the hundreds upon hundreds of college students driving into this rodeo called show business.

My hair was done, my shirt was tucked in, and I pinned on my number: 42. Headshot and resume in hand, I was herded into the auditorium with my group of fifty. Sitting through the other 41 competitors before it was my turn was daunting, illuminating, and terrifying. This wasn't an audition at the University of Rochester Theater Program. There were so many others here and they all had the same goal as me. These were the products of every college theater program across the States.

When it was my turn, let's just say I went for it. Trying desperately to compensate for all of the energy that I perceived my competitors had lacked. I became so invested in performing my monologue to its fullest that when the timekeeper cut me off, I couldn't even hear her. I was... on a roll. I was... living the dream. I was... on top of the world. I was… not going to be called back for a single part.

We turned right around and drove home. Somewhere between the Mason Dixon Line and the University of Rochester, these words made their way to the page:

They say don't beat yourself up
It's just one of many
Rejections come in bundles
Constructive as the criticism may be
It takes something along with it each time
Two positive thoughts for every negative
One out of a hundred this time
The chances are good
A lot of pretty faces
Milling around
See the sparkle
Ignite powerful memories
Know that I am real
Stand up straight
Sense my fear
Smile politely from ear to ear
Project but don't talk that way
Walk the walk
Talk the talk
Cliché taboo faux pas
Maybe if I was a man
Not the right size
Totally the wrong height
Just wait it out
They tell me
The next one could be the one
Break into that business of show

The extra eye shadow from this morning
Worn off by tears
Of questioning
Whether I am good enough
When I know that I am.

I knew that I wanted to pursue theater after college, but where and how could I do that while continuing to be myself?

⌘

When do you feel pressured to be someone other than yourself?

How do you react to criticism?

How do you return your center? What helps you to believe in yourself?

25. Giving random people random gifts.

Rochester to Lackawanna, New York. 2003.

When I was in high school I took the New York State Thruway every Wednesday for violin lessons. When I entered onto the highway in Blasdell I always saw the same woman working at the tollbooth. She had the most beautiful, beaming smile and would always welcome me with her glistening tone: "Hi there, Baby! Nice to see you again! How are you doing?" Now sure, she might have said these words to hundreds of people that passed through her gates every day, but honestly, when she handed me my ticket, I felt incredibly special. It would make my whole week. I would look forward to seeing her, sometimes more than the violin lessons themselves.

During my second year of college, when I took a semester off, I did a lot of art projects. Some friends called it my "hodge-podge sabbatical" because I would take random bits of magazines that I associated with certain people and collage them into presents: vases, bookmarks, cardboard shelves, and all sorts of random things. I remember making the tollbooth lady a special magnet collaged together with images of happiness and giving. I figured I could enter onto the Thruway during her usual Wednesday shift, give her this little gift, go one exit, and return home. But when I arrived there she wasn't there. I described her to the man now sitting in her booth who said that he wasn't sure where she was and that she had possibly been transferred. I gave him the magnet and he promised that he would do his best to get it to her wherever she was.

The next semester I returned to school. Years going back and forth on that same Thruway to and from Rochester, I always looked for that beaming smile on the way, but no matter the day of the week or the time of the day, she was nowhere to be found.

Finally graduating with all of my belongings packed into my car (including my endlessly meowing cat named Dell), I left Rochester, my new home and new friends of the last four years, to return to the old home, the place where I had grown up.

Almost back in Buffalo and still teary-eyed, I searched for exact change for the upcoming toll.

"Hi there, Baby! So nice to see you again! How have you been doing?"

That voice! That smile! My dream came true! It was really her!

Reunited, I leapt from my window and she from hers embracing in the space between. In this brief interaction, she explained how the gift had a special place on her fridge and that she had often wondered where I might be and if she would ever be able to thank me for all I had given to her. I echoed back how I had often wondered about her and that reuniting with her now meant the world to me.

"Congratulations on your graduation," she said as I drove away, "And welcome home."

⌘

Who is someone that you pass everyday but don't really know?

How could you give them a simple gift today to let them know that you see them, that they make a difference to your day?

What are the reasons this might be challenging for you to do?

26. Turning oddities into commonalities.

2003. South Buffalo, New York.

That summer between college and graduate school I lived in the apartment above my grandmother. I was the first person in the four years since my dad had passed away that she let stay.

One night as I was racing around the kitchen, trying to get our food on the table, she stopped me in my tracks: "You are not going out in that shirt."

My grandmother had never told me what to do or not to do. She had always been more of a friend than a parental figure… a benefit of the skip of a generation, I supposed.

"Your stomach is showing," she murmured as if the neighbors could hear.

I looked down to my pant line. I hadn't intentionally worn a midriff shirt but yeah, I'll admit that there was a little bit more skin showing than I had realized. I guessed either the shirt had shrunk or I had grown. Pulling it down, I promised to change before going out.

"Wait," she suggested. "Come here for a minute."

I walked toward her, eyebrows bent.

"Let me see your belly button."

What did she want with my belly button?

"Come on…" she implored.

I lifted up my shirt to reveal my own "innie" shining toward her.

And like a little kid on her tall yellow stool she moved in closer, inspecting my naked belly. "Are they all like that?" she asked.

"Well, yeah. I guess. Basically." I thought over the list of belly buttons I had witnessed in my day. "What do you mean?"

"Well," she confessed, "I always thought that there was something wrong with mine."

"Let me see…"

Little by little she reluctantly pulled up her flowered shirt and showed me her eighty-something-year-old belly button sitting in all its glory amidst wrinkles and reminders of having four children.

"I've always thought there was something wrong with mine," she uttered candidly.

Where would she have seen a belly button after taking care of her children? Her husband's? Was it truly possible that she had never seen another grown woman's belly button? It was a viable explanation, considering those fuller-coverage bathing suits I had seen in her pictures.

"Is there something wrong with mine?" she asked.

"No, Grandma Jule, look…" I said, standing belly to belly with her. "Yours is perfect, it's just like mine."

⌘

What is something that you find odd about yourself? Imagine that everyone you pass today has a unique oddity of their own. How does acknowledging the oddness help you to connect differently with them?

SECOND MOVEMENT: ON TO THE WEST

Connect with your Compassionate Creativity by...

27. Listening for when to stay and when to go.

Buffalo, New York to Humboldt County, California. September 2003.

People laughed when I told them I was getting ready to go to school in Humboldt County, California. I naively had no idea that this place was infamously known as the weed-growing capital of the world. Heck, I hadn't thought that there was anything beyond a little physical theater school there. If it had occurred to me that in order to get back to Buffalo I'd have to fly, I probably would have called it off, but you know those times when there is something in your gut saying, "Go!"? Even when you don't know why? Even when there are a million reasons to stay?

"I've gotta stay here and take care of my grandma," I explained to a friend.

"It could be two years or it could be twenty," he reminded me.

"Then I'll have to figure out how to take her with me."

She was my best friend, but she was sixty years older than me. Her life was coming to a close and mine was just beginning. *How could these two things be happening at the same time? Instead of going away to college, my dad stayed close by for his entire life. Maybe I should do that too?*

"Go..."

Saying goodbye to her on the porch that day was the hardest thing I have ever done, but as I began the drive in one of a two-car caravan, packed to the gills including walkie-talkies (cell phones were still a rare commodity) and two other twenty-two year-olds, I suddenly felt free. Guilt and grief and gifts fit together like Russian dolls. Right, I had always wanted to drive west. I had grown up just south of Buffalo and every time we took the highway somewhere (beyond the one family vacation to Cleveland for a Major League Baseball game), we always drove east. Now for miles and miles and days and days through Illinois and Missouri, Kansas and Texas I watched the westward-facing movie play outside of my station wagon windows. The sun setting in my face. The cornfields becoming red rock. The skies becoming grander. The land only widened as these three young New Yorkers majestically crossed the border into California and moved along into the Pacific Northwest.

In the middle of San Francisco streets I called my mom. Joyous and full of seafood, I was met with the news that my grandmother would be going into a nursing home. I had tried to broach this conversation with her that summer several times. "I am fine. By myself. In my house," she'd say. But apparently she knew she wasn't. The week after I left, my mom and brother took her to the emergency room because she was in such pain.

"Mrs. Quinn, if you can not walk across this floor to the other side," said the doctor, "then you can't go home."

My grandma had lived on the first floor of that house for sixty-three years. Her mom had bought that house. My dad grew up there. My grandpa died there. My parents lived there before they were married and it was the first place they brought me after I was born. My dad had lived there when my parents split up. My brother and I lived there every weekend. I had lived there this summer. When I saw how much care she really needed, how she wouldn't be able to live alone.

"What did you want to be when you grew up?" I had asked her as I tried to brace the conversation about why I was leaving for California to study theater.

"I don't know what you mean," she responded.

"What did you want to be? What did you dream of?"

"No one ever asked me what I wanted to be. I guess I wanted to do what I did... to be a mom."

117

I wrestled with what that meant. I had never considered being a mom to be a dream or a job. In high school or college, no one talked about becoming a mom. In fact, quite the opposite philosophy was instilled. I thought the worst thing I could do was become pregnant. Did I want to be a mom? No, definitely not. Or, I don't know. Maybe, but I couldn't think about that now.

"You need to stay here, find a man and pet him like the cat," she pleaded as I tucked her in that night. I smiled and turned off the light.

"Ya tebe lyublyu," I said ("I love you" in Russian).

These words played and replayed in my mind as I left San Francisco. The roads continued to curve north for five hours, and our walkie-talkies went silent for the first time since we had left Buffalo.

"Maybe it was wrong to leave," I thought, "Maybe I should turn around. Maybe I should just find a man and pet him like the cat..."

Out our windows we saw less people, less billboards, less chain stores, less everything that we had always known... and more trees. And they only became taller. Taller than we had ever seen. So big that we even drove through one.

Where were we going? What wild, secret place were we all about to grow up in? Was this the right choice?

That evening, after fifteen days on the road, we arrived at our destination. A painted wooden sign greeted us off the exit: "Welcome to Blue Lake, California." The population of this town was about to go from 1135 to 1138, and the population of South Buffalo was officially down by two.

⌘

How do you decide when to leave? When to stay?

What role does your Compassionate Creativity play?

28. Noticing how an opinion changes from minute to minute, while a point of view is built and articulated over several years.

Blue Lake, California. 2003 – 2004.

I woke up to run along the levee with forty other people before stretching and doing some acrobatics in the second floor of an old Odd Fellows building. This was the rhythm of my new school, called Dell'Arte International, where I continued learning alongside people from all walks of life from all over the world. Although our class ranged in age from eighteen to forty-something, we were all considered alike when attempting our latest handstand, where to place our foot during Tai Chi, or when we sang a solo in our voice class.

Once a month, we took turns volunteering at the Grange breakfast in town, serving special pancakes and local eggs with four-year-olds and elders who had lived in Blue Lake for their entire lives. I had never seen kids involved like this before. I had never seen a woman who let her hair go gray, let alone growing it out and leaving it down.

We spent our days learning from everyone in the community: *Theater of Place.* A woman came in from the Rancheria to teach us about basket making, and a couple from down the street visited to show us their owls. But we didn't do these things so that we could make our own baskets or rehabilitate birds. We gleaned everything we could from their wisdom and applied it to our own process.

Get together.
Make something.
Get together again.
Make something.
Eat sleep, breathe, and love theater.
Stories.
Perspective.
Night and day.
Day and night.

Week after week we were placed in a new group with a new assignment. From "A Time and a Place" to "Giants Walking on the Face of the Earth," every week the faculty, along with their husbands and wives and dogs and the waitress from across the street, came to our building on the corner to witness what we had made. This was never about receiving praise, and I took each criticism harshly, still believing that there was something to "get right." But we weren't getting grades; we were being encouraged to step up. To figure out how to work together, make something, and share it.

"Fight me!" said our conditioning teacher one morning after commenting that our class was "too nice." We all sat staring at him, a tall skinny alumnus the same age as some of us, standing with arms open on a blue mat ready to be tackled. "Come on," he provoked as we held our breath in suspension. Was he really serious? I felt the push and pull in my gut. In my heart. Not wanting to hurt him but feverishly wanting to take a stand. To fight for what I believed in. To hold my ground. But what did I believe in?

No matter the new collaborators or assignment, I always became the negotiator, listening and helping the group and helping to find compromises. This was an important role for our process, but it kept me safe from having to share my own ideas. How did I identify those and when did I bring them forward? And how could I fight for them if I was so afraid to fight? This wasn't about fighting over a flippant opinion. This was about developing my own point of view and finding my best way to articulate it and see it through. Firmly stating my beliefs wouldn't hurt anyone. In fact, sticking my stake in the ground would give them something to push off of so they could find their own.

I took a drive to the ocean and stood along its rocky cliffs. The western expanse made me feel so significant and insignificant at the same time. An unprecedented sense of calm, recalibrating me to what was important, helping me to reconcile being so far away from home, from family, from friends, from everything I had known before. "I am going to claim my point of view here if it is the last thing I do!" I called out to the Pacific. "I'm going to chase it with love! From the ends of the earth into the center of my bones! Day after day, path-by-path, stake by stake. Rocks and mountains and deserts and rainstorms into perpetual spring…"

⌘

How do you define an opinion? How do you define a point of view?

How as your point of view evolved over time?

29. Remembering what you love.

Arcata, California. 2004.

"I love ice cream!" he shouted from the back seat as we drove to get some.

He was four and had the best little British accent. His excitement could not be contained. Each syllable a firework exploding into the sky, he began to light up:

"I love sweets!"

"I love streets!"

"I love people!"

"I love cars!"

Eyebrows raised and tongue out, his eyes darted in every direction. His little fingertips touched everything in sight.

"I love colors!"

"I love seatbelts!"

"I love hands."

"I love..." he paused for the first time since getting in the car. Wheels turning, he searched for the next thing to love.

"I love…"

"I love… Love!"

We all laughed, looking out the windows the rest of the way there.

⌘

Write a list of all the things you love. Go on… revel it in!

What is the essence of these things?

Notice how much you currently include these loves in your everyday life.

How might you be able to include these loves more often?

30. Letting love guide the way.

Blue Lake, California. 2004.

That spring I fell in love with a man who had a four-year-old son and was going through a divorce. Before I knew it, I was up early making breakfast for the two of them in my house before going to school.

"I could get used to this," said my heart.

"But this isn't my family," said my gut.

"But it sure reminds me of my own family," said my head.

This relationship helped me to understand my parents better: their relationship, their challenges, and their great care for me and my brother. Even though they separated, their love and friendship always felt strong. I continued to feel guided by this fact.

I cared so much for the man I was dating that I urged him to put his family first:

There is a child laying between you and your wife that calls for simple care. He calls for you to love one another and he is evidence everyday that love did, does exist: in the world, in your house, in your heart. He includes half of each of you – getting along and playing in the sand and making decisions about eating Chinese food. Don't doubt his powers. His knowing. His understanding. Although there is no one who would want you to be together more than he would, he also knows what is best at the end of the day. Not sadness. Joy exists somewhere along the way in the patience of an unraveling existence together under the same roof. Everything is known. It is just sorting itself out. Slowly and carefully. Be aware of it. Let it guide you. This patience. This time. When it seems like there are no answers, there will be more questions that will bring you closer to calmness. Trust them. Let them in the front door and settle in for a while. In the meantime, try to find the beauty in the little moments of looks and passes and touches between all three of you, knowing that love will guide you step by step by step.

⌘

Think of a relationship that you are in right now that feels challenging.

See the love that is there. How can you let it guide you through this tough patch?

31. Looking to the far-off horizon even when it might seem foggy.

Fresh Water, Northern California. 2004.

That summer, the company at my school did a piece about "Tree-Sitters." Tree-Sitters were people who, day and night for months at a time, sat on a platform one hundred and eighty feet up in a Redwood tree in order to protect it from being chopped down. Enthralled by their commitment, in love with these huge ancient trees myself, and hearing that anyone could visit and bring them supplies, I gathered some food and water and drove out to see them.

When I arrived the sitters gratefully dropped their rope, and we conversed politely as I put some goods into their plastic bucket.

"Do you want to come up?" one of them shouted from high above.

No way. Climb up there? To an 8' by 12' platform built by someone else who knows when? No, definitely not. I just wanted to see if this was all true and how it worked. I could never actually go up there. I was afraid of heights and... God, no.

"No, thanks, but it was nice to meet you all... from down here."

"Cool. Cool. Well, would you mind taking away our waste? We'll send it down..."

How was I ever going to explain this to anyone back home?

I made it a point to visit these Tree-Sitters on a regular basis, both to learn about their culture and to recognize that as I moved around all day, they were still right there sitting in the same place with the same task: to watch over a tree they called "Jerry." I frequently brought some food and water, sometimes hauled waste, and always declined their invitation to climb up before happily going on my way.

That next fall when friends from the East Coast were passing through town, I took them to see the trees... Some of the tallest and oldest trees in the world. The one that they called "Jerry" was now only a tall pole reaching into the sky. Its high branches had been cut off during one of the recent court-ordered extractions, but the sitters had found a way to go back up.

"Hey!" they shouted as they saw my car pull up to the side of the road. "Welcome back! Long time no see... Do you want to come up?"

"Sure..."

And before I knew what was happening, I was hanging from a rope off the side of an incredibly steep hillside. Humboldt Bay hovered far off below. I used the help of two Prusik knots to climb up. One was connected to a harness around my hips, and the other one had a loop for my foot. Simple friction was all it took. Like and inchworm, I moved my bottom and then my top and then my bottom and then my top. Up, up, up.

This was going to take forever. What was I thinking? What made me all of a sudden say yes? I was deathly afraid of heights.

Suddenly realizing what I had done, I nervously asked to come down.

"The only way is up!" yelled a man coming across on a kind of zip line they had built between the trees.

And little by little, amidst much coaxing from the ground and above and beside me, I made my way up the rope. *I can't do this. I can do this. I don't want to do this. I do want to do this.* What took me hours to climb, took this tree hundreds and hundreds of years to grow. I felt its life and its strength, its long arc on the planet, all that it had seen change around it as it continued for thousands of days to reach further into the sky.

The awe still overcomes me now as I sit and write.

Speechless, I arrived onto the platform of Jerry and shook hands with the two sitters. They untied my rope and welcomed me into their home. I felt the strength and calm of their conviction that they would rather be sitting here day after day than be doing anything else anywhere else on earth. Because other people hadn't considered this place sacred, they had made this their home and protected it with all their life. If someone came to extract them and cut down their home, the sitters were ready to lock their hands inside of a concrete barrel and hold onto the key. Why did the logging companies and police value the life of these people, but not the life of the trees themselves?

This tree has been able to stand tall for so long because it is part of a family, a circle of trees holding onto one another's roots. If we cut this one down, all these others would fall too.

Jaw dropped, this innocent kid from suburban Buffalo now sat over one hundred and fifty feet up, suspended in an ancient tree looking out toward the fog-filled Pacific. I thought of my grandma as I felt the sun setting on the far-off horizon.

How was I ever going to get back down?

⌘

Draw a picture of your far-off horizon.

What do you see there that gives you hope, makes you smile, or allows you to breathe a little easier?

When do you tend to lose sight of this thing? Place your picture in a place where you will be reminded of your horizon every day.

32. Surrounding yourself with people who feed you.

Blue Lake, California. 2005.

"Come on, Gerlie! Get in the car! We're taking you out for ice cream!"

I've just finished a performance at school. It is my birthday, but I'm totally wiped and ready to go home.

"We don't take no for an answer," shouts the other one as they pull up to me on my short walk home.

The first is middle-aged with curly grey hair. He and I met when he was the volunteer spotlight operator for a show at my school. Since then, he has been introducing me to the taste of avocado, pineapple, and sushi and encouraging me to do away with American Cheese Singles.

The second is part of an older generation and ancient ways. Although his heart is from Mongolia, he now lives in Portland. Since the moment we met on the street during one of his visits, this man was certain that I was Mongolian too. "Cheekbones and all," he pointed out before inviting me along.

"Come on, we're gonna teach you the ways of the world!"

The two men smile a similar smile with keen eyes and

sneaky eyebrows that let you know they are up to everything good. They love life and when they are together, they don't waste time sleeping. Every moment is wistfully spent playing music, catching up, or hatching a new plan.

Tonight, they are bent on celebrating my birthday and like two excited dogs, they sit panting while they await me to enroll. There is no way I can say no to this posse. I've come to love our magical nighttime routine, and wholeheartedly come to embrace it as an integral part of my education.

"Okay, okay... I'm in."

They rejoice and turn up the music as I get in the car to be whisked away once again. At the ice cream shop, they convince me that the next stop must be our favorite beach.

"The moonlight is just right tonight. How can we resist? Let's go see the tides!"

We walk and talk and drive along the coast for hours before returning to Blue Lake to enjoy a buffet meal at the 24-Hour casino:

Three generations
Sit
Eating dinner at 4AM
Casino style
Discussing the ways of the world
Who invaded who
And why
Rewriting history
Figuring it out
Up until now

We share food
Laughter always arising
With drumming
We talk about plans
To do this or make that
Living
Selling
Helping
Dying.

What truly gets done
Is simple actually
Special really
Spending time
With endless
Swirling possibilities...

"Once a week go barefoot in the park. It will keep you centered to mother earth. Take care and don't forget me!" shouts the second from his truck as he and his lady dog companion drive off. The other guy and I wave, proudly sporting our colorful Mongolian jacket gifts, before taking our late night position on the post office steps. As the town falls asleep, we review the weekend's events and lessons.

At the end of the day
And the dawn of this new one
We say goodnight
In the rainy street
Barefoot all
I am home
And prepared for class.

"I am up here and you are down there, north is up and south is down," writes our friend once he is back in Portland. "And as Cesaro said in 250 BC: 'Always wish the best for yourself. Think good thoughts and 'be kind to those you meet on the road you travel, for we are all fighting great battles.'"

⌘

Name something or someone that has fed you this past week.

What kind of sustenance are you missing from your days right now? From whom could you ask for support?

Whom do you feed and how?

33. Seeing nothing as an interruption but rather part of what is happening.

Arcata, California. 2005.

"Who's up for a game of backgammon?"

"Sure, I'll play with you..." I replied to the old man standing up in the middle of the crowded coffee shop. My friends rolled their eyes and returned back to school as I joined the man at his table.

"Nice to meet you," he said shaking my hand, ready to get down to business.

"I don't know how to play backgammon."

"Well today's your lucky day, my new friend!"

A week later, I fell out of a tree. Yep. There I was lying on the ground of the Arcata Community Forest looking up into the towering redwood tree whose roots I had just climbed up. I had never broken anything before but I was sure that having just braced my fall with my hand, I had entered into this new territory. Not wanting anyone, including myself, to have to see its sudden deformity, I kept my wrist covered up with my wool sweater while my mind whirled in shock. Like a pendulum that swayed between the circumstances of the moment before the fall to the inevitable effects it would have on my future, pain and song constantly nudged me to return to the present.

Biding time before the ambulance arrived, my nine classmates sat as still as could be, hands upon me or along the backs of one another. We believed in the comfort of touch and we knew each other's bodies and needs well. We had spent whole hours of time giving one another massages that started on the ground and eventually lifted the person up into the air and upside down before placing them gently onto their feet anew. Imagine eighteen caring hands giving a healing touch to your entire body.

Sitting along the forest ground, my classmates also hummed melodies from our cherished repertoire. We believed in the power of shared song and sang together often. Not just while performing but we broke out into song while driving in our tour van, while walking to classes, while eating dinner. From barbershop quartets to spirituals, we sang. One of our favorites was a Kenyan funeral song. It been taught to us by our Dutch classmate who had learned it while on tour in South Africa years before. That song had traveled through many voices and places to be with us. Listening to their voices, I imagined all the people around the world who knew it singing it with us at that moment. Maybe they were.

In the days before coming to the forest, we had been studying the spirit that lives within a mask. We sat holding beautiful old wooden masks from Mexico in our hands, seeing how their carved features changed as we shifted them in different light. Sculptures that imbued a personhood and when put upon our face immediately transformed our entire body into that of another being who looked out with different eyes at a different world. We could hardly recognize one another when the masks were on, and in the moment one was removed, we somehow saw each other completely anew.

Within this work, we had each identified our own kind of spirit animal. An animal presence that shared similar qualities to that of our essence. A totem. There was a dog and a cow, an ape and an insect of some kind, to mention a few. I was a gazelle – connecting to anticipation, eagerness, vulnerability, speed, and awareness. As a next step, we collected natural materials and spent time gluing and nailing and papier-mâché-ing them into forms that we could wear upon our heads as our own masks. We had tried these out in the studio, and we ended up in the community forest in order to see how these masks would play in a natural environment. How we would transform.

Minutes before the fall, the lesson began by being told to choose and hold onto a tree. Now, like you possibly in this moment, I had some resistance to this. Why would I do this? But "Why not?" quickly won out. I loved trees, and I immediately knew which one to choose. I always identified a special tree in every place I lived and here in Northern California, my favorite tree was a redwood tree that grew inside the stump of another redwood. Its bright-green, moss-covered roots dripped down along the sides of the huge stump so in order to get to the actual tree, I had to climb up its roots. I didn't realize how high I had climbed until my hand slipped and I started falling and falling backwards toward the ground.

I never learned what the rest of that particular lesson was exactly, but rather it continued for me with a full-arm cast, a pin, and surgery. Instead of performing that Friday, my housemate drove me home from the hospital. Nauseous as could be, I was carried out of the car by my other two housemates. For the next six weeks, these three guys would voluntarily be the ones taking care of me: one would cook and clean, the other would drive me to appointments, and the third would make sure I bathed by getting into the tub with me before catching me up on schoolwork.

My teacher from Mexico City visited my bedside. We didn't speak a lot of the same spoken words, but we loved to be in one another's pure presence and longing to connect. Together we created a language of friendship through our common affinity for theater, masks and teaching and smiling, through our having known one another for several lifetimes, long, long ago.

In the show we were creating together, this teacher had been encouraging me to take my violin out of its case. I was so excited to finally be able to integrate my love for music with my love for theater. With the help of my Mexican mask, I created the character of a logger who carried his violin around all the time. The violin was part of him, an extension of him. When times got rough, he played a tune. A week after my injury, I performed as part of the show, but the violin was replaced with a large cast in a sling. I had a hurt arm so the logger did too.

My mom wanted me to come home to recover in Buffalo, but I wanted to continue to live out my newly gained freedom and independence. I was months away from graduating. At school we were learning about buoyancy; we basked in resiliency. Nothing was an interruption but, rather, integrated into our learning. Down a limb, all my others became more articulate and expansive. Going to classes with a broken wrist taught me how to do one-armed cartwheels and during these weeks, I successfully learned how to walk on stilts for the first time. Go figure that these things would be the best remedies for someone suddenly so afraid of falling.

After doing physical therapy, I would have to take a nap in my car after. Moving my hand was so painful, and pain, I was learning, was absolutely exhausting and couldn't be ignored. More painful were my doctor's latest words, which started to echo in my mind: "It is doubtful that you will ever be able to play the violin again."

For the past year and half, my body had been doing things that I never believed were possible, but it was true, my wrist didn't seem to be getting much better. I couldn't even turn my palm up, let alone wrap it around the neck of a violin. Maybe this new hand was my new reality.

As we played our next game of backgammon, my new friend massaged a place in my leg that hurt. He explained how it was related to the pain in my wrist. "An introduction to backgammon and reflexology!" I joked.

"I was thinking," he offered as he continued to desensitize, "I have a friend who is a hand therapy specialist. Maybe she could help you."

"I don't think she'll take my insurance."

"Insurance is only interested in helping people to meet a standard of function, not to return to full use and certainly not to play the violin. This is going to take a lot more than a few appointments. I'm sure she'd be happy to see you."

In a kind of barter that my friend worked out, and I never quite understood, I went into the hand specialist's office.

"You've been protecting your arm so much that the nerve bundles in your shoulder have started to shut down," she said as she broke up some of the tissue in my wrist with an ultrasound machine. "They no longer believe that they can move your wrist. Do you believe that they can?"

"Well the doctor said…"

"Do *you* believe you can play the violin again?"

"Yes, I do."

"Great… then I do too," she said as she finished up the treatment. "Everyday, you need to keep trying to put your hands in your back pockets. That's the only way we are going to get your wrist to turn over fully. Let one arm remind the other how to do it."

Three months later my backgammon buddy choreographed a dance for my thesis project, and the next month, moving through some pain, I played violin in a chamber orchestra! That summer, I debuted with a hillbilly rock band on an outdoor stage for hundreds of people dancing on the school's lawn. While I continued to obsess about what key we were in and how well I was playing, the audience had an incredible time. Walking home that night, I stopped in my tracks and made a promise to myself that playing was no longer about perfection or winning but rather about resiliently enjoying the privilege to play.

⌘

What is something that you perceive as an interruption right now? How can your Compassionate Creativity help you to integrate it into your life?

THIRD MOVEMENT: INTO THE WORLD

Connect with your Compassionate Creativity by...

34. Continuing to fall in love with the world.

Blue Lake, California to Brooklyn, New York by way of many places. August 2005.

When I finished school in California, my best friend from Buffalo came out west to drive with me back to the east. I was not the same person that he had known growing up.

"Are you a hippie now?" my mom asked over the phone.

"Compared to the hippies, no. Compared to you, yes."

I now climbed redwoods and slept outside on trampolines. I

wore skirts over pants with long knit granny sweaters that I had bought at thrift stores. I danced in the streets and swam naked in the river. I shopped at the co-op and the farmer's market. I sat in the plaza and petted dogs. I had long pigtails and preferred to walk around with no shoes. Every once and a while I let my leg hair grow out, and I occasionally took a drag off a joint.

Boxes full and car packed, my one housemate scribbled a note and left it for me on our kitchen table: "Whatever you do, never stop falling in love." He and I both had our shares of love affairs and heartbreaks in the bubble of Blue Lake. Maybe it was about time we moved along to see how the rest of the world was doing and grooving...

On the first leg of the trip, my best friend and I were singing so loud that the only way we noticed our muffler was falling off was by someone in another car pointing it out. Laughing, we called a tow truck and fell in love with San Francisco for a few days more than we had planned while our car was fixed.

In Los Angeles we fell in love with cruising down Sunset Boulevard late at night. We sweat bullets through Death Valley before we stood in awe at the edge of the Grand Canyon. Colors and layers and grandiosity. It was more amazing than words could ever have described or any photo could ever have shown.

Next we went to stay off-the-grid with my cousin in his Earthship house just outside of Taos, New Mexico. I fell in love with his way of life. Sustainable, connected to the land, he had built his home with his own two hands. Putting keepsakes into the walls and having banana trees inside fed by waste and rainwater run-off.

"I thought I would never get you out of there," my best friend joked as we pulled away and moved on to El Paso to witness how narrow the Rio Grande runs there, and how tall the fence stands between the US and Mexico.

That night, two guys that I met that summer asked if they could meet us for dinner. They were on their way back across the country too and it just so happened that they were on the same route at the same time.

On our way to dinner, I updated my best friend: I recalled how these guys were part of a class that I took on a field trip to the ocean. "We found a pile of feathers there, and I encouraged us all to throw them and make a wish. Mine got stuck and the one guy threw stones down the cliff to make sure it took flight and it did."

"This feather landed on my shoulder," he said a few days later before he left. "I thought it might be your wish, and that you should have it so that you can throw it again."

"Oh, boy... here we go," interrupted my best friend, thinking that I had a crush on this guy. But no, I wasn't ready to be in love with any more people. No. Places maybe, but not people. People were not to be trusted and neither was I. When people didn't know what they wanted, love only led to misunderstandings and heartbreak.

The four of us had a nice, cordial dinner and the next morning, my best friend and I continued on driving free and single through Texas. Having a best friend was love. Who needed another boyfriend?

We arrived in Austin and met up with some people who I hadn't seen since college (the girl who had played Anna and had taken me to a strip club years ago, along with the guy I had flown to visit in Santiago and his new girlfriend). Still on the same route, the two guys called and asked if they could join us too. Why not?

This intersection of people from different times in my life was a bit more than I could handle. When I thought no one was looking, I put my head down on the table. My mind was swirling trying to piece together the long ago past with the recent past with the current present. How people who once knew each other from one place were now in other places, with other people, and other interests. How time moves so quickly and how I felt as though I could never catch up.

The following day, my best friend and I fell in love with a burrito breakfast before heading further east. On the way we remembered high school and how we couldn't believe our two friends were moving in with their boyfriends. It felt like we had all just been teenagers hanging out and making bets on who would get married first and who would have children first. Was that time already here?

That night, we fell in love with New Orleans and met up with the two guys to listen to music. The Feather Guy and I took a walk outside along the cobblestone streets.

"I want to know you," he offered.

But who was I now? And where was I going?

"Please," he said, giving me a piece of paper with his address in Brooklyn, his parents address in Connecticut, and his email and his phone numbers.

He was kind. He was witty. He was handsome. He was present. He was patient. But I couldn't possibly let someone into my world. It was tarnished and confused and petrified to say the least.

Leaving them behind and driving through Nashville, I let it all go and picked it all up and let it all go again. Above all, I wanted to prioritize my great love affair with the glorious world around me in all its forms and figures. If I was able to do that, then maybe, just maybe, I could give this new fellow a try.

My best friend and I stopped in Cleveland to see one of our old Music Dork friends for dinner and we met her new boyfriend. He was so kind and friendly and they seemed settled and happy and happy to see us.

"I love you!" I yelled to her out the window as we drove away onto Buffalo.

"More!"

"Most!"

"Always, always. Promise, promise."

And having had quite the trip, my best friend and I arrived in Buffalo safe and sound and still laughing and having a great time.

Finally home and unpacked, I retrieved my housemate's note from the glove box: "Never stop falling in love," and out fell the feather given to me California. I gave the The Feather Guy a call and accepted his offer.

A few weeks later when I arrived to my next gig just outside of New York City, he and I met in the middle of the Brooklyn Bridge. Together we tossed that same feather from the Pacific onto the waves of the Atlantic, beginning to fall in love with one another while gratefully falling deeper in love with the world.

⌘

How can you fall further in love with the world today? Tomorrow?

How do you continue to discover the balance between your own journey, your journey within a relationship, and your journey with the world around you?

35. Doing research. Seeking out the clear, hard facts.

Brooklyn, New York. 2005.

Going from a little rural town of one thousand on the west coast to the biggest city of millions on the east coast was quite the shock. There was no denying the contrast:

As I turn the corner, leaving the dirty subway stairs behind, wondering what might be sticking to my boots, I look across the Brooklyn street. I hate that I should have to wait for a green walking signal to get across Roebling, especially on tired nights. Most nights. Instead, I look across and up to my skinny apartment, which sits waiting to crumble, atop a red-bannered awning with bright yellow lettered "Hello Cingular." A store owned by the Hasidic man who won't give me my mail. As I dodge a few cars waiting for the right moment to make a total go of it, I make myself ignore the empty chip bags and the other trash that floats amongst the yellow lines and treeless streets. Finally, I step carefully onto the broken curb, having crossed diagonally, making up at least fifteen seconds of time. I hold my breath and tippy toe amongst black bags of apartmental-garbage-tomorrow-is-Wednesday smells. Under the red banner now, just to the right, is a white door with no address and a keypad that sticks or won't work even when you punch in the correct combination. I don't want to call the landlord tonight. Please. Not tonight. I fumble through my three pocketed, brown, leather purse that keeps me somewhat in fashion and still smells of California. Finally my fingers reach the beaded chain that holds my one city key. As always, I quickly look from side to side before jiggling the uncooperative key into the bottom lock. When I open the cold knob, a dirty stairwell greets me. Black and white tiles grayed. Junk mail from years ago is smashed the corners. Closing the city out behind me, I find refuge here in this temporary home as another train departs from the station close by.

Of all places, New York was the last place I ever imagined I would be, but there I was once again, remembering old dreams in the face of new ones. Trying to put them all together continued to be challenging, and I allowed the extremes of New York to send me into my own extremes.

If I got carried away with what wasn't working and tried to figure it all out in one subway ride, I reminded myself of the facts: 1) This was my first time in the "real world." 2) Before this I became used to living in a small town community of 1000 people. 3) I lived in New York before and had a tough time and had to leave. Once clearly laid out, I saw the immensity of what I was dealing with. From this new perspective, I gave myself some time and space to grow and began to look at everything as research.

My study revolved around this: "What did I learn today? What did the city teach me?" These questions enabled me to find everything interesting and to enjoy the city immensely as a playground of learning that was full of beauty and kindness if only I was open to seeing it. New York wasn't California, that was another fact, but my research proved that New York was truly an incredible place, a testament to humanity in its own unique way.

Each night, arriving at my apartment, I put down my things, pulled up a chair, and made sure to write myself a little reminder of the day's discoveries:

I enjoy tonight
As withered and dark as it is
I drift along with it
Waiting with everyone else
Pace by pace
I find a block I never knew
A conversation I never had
A passerby who smiled
Without reason, without shame
I know the city haunts me
Challenged by every thought
Toying with the possibilities
Of what could be
And not what was.

Manhattan urges me
Pushes me forward
Now gently
Yesterday with a demanding force
Always calling
Listen to the lights
Amongst the skyline
Venture past its hidden walls
Take time to wait with the masses
And look up so you don't fall.

Mean envious city
Hold me in your hands
Without regret or longing

To place me somewhere else.

For now
Teach me solace
In big dreams
Comfort in forever sidewalks
Between buildings
And the difference
Between comparing
And simply choosing to live.

⌘

How can your Compassionate Creativity let you see everything as
great research today? At the end of the day, take a moment to write
down what you learned.

36. Learning how to communicate, especially when you think it is impossible.

Manaus, Brazil. 2006.

Six months later, The Guy with the Feather and I were in the middle of the Amazon. Having been in Brazil for less than a week, we stood at the crowded port of Manaus ready for our 48-hour boat ride along the river.

From the moment we stepped out of the taxi we stood out. Our large blue hiking bags on our back. Our white skin. Our confused eyes amidst hundreds of people who, like buzzing bees from flower to flower, went about their daily tasks between docks and boats and docks and boats. We handed our bags off to the waving man who greeted us and slowly watched our bright blue sacks make their way over and down a steep wall that held the wide river. The man smiled and waved from a tiny motorboat. A tiny speck moving in what must have been low tide, we had no choice but to descend and rejoin our bags there. We moved down the ladder, rung-by-rung, becoming smaller and smaller as the other boats reached higher and higher toward the sky. We scooted in as our boat could only fit the three of us, and only if we all straddled and held our belongings on our laps. The waves crashed as we all swayed, unsure of whether to hang onto the boat or our bags or each other.

Where were we? Why had I decided to complete my degree by travelling to an internship so far away? I could have gone anywhere, but was drawn to here. Called by the rhythms of the music and the stories of the people and the beauty of the land. I wanted to do this and we had decided to go together and explore first.

Eventually we arrived at the back of a small three-level boat. The motorboat driver said something and nodded his head before throwing our bags up into the kitchen, only to be caught by two people in the middle of slaughtering a chicken. Their hands then reached out to pull us up to their level.

"Obrigado," I said, afraid of mispronouncing it but wanting to be polite in both directions. This was one word I fully knew by heart without looking it up, but I still confused the ending. *Obrigada,* like our obliged, is thank you, and I needed to put an A on the end because I was a woman. I was the one who was obliged. "Obrigada!"

"De nada. Não tem problema!" yelled the boat driver already on his way. This phrase I recognized. I had heard it often in coordinating my internship with the theater company in Belo Horizonte:

"But where will I live there?"

"De nada. Não tem problema."

"Will there be work for me to do?"

"Sim. Não tem problema."

"Is it okay if I come a month later than I had thought?"

"Sim. Não tem problema."

"Just come," they kept saying, as if it would all magically work out. A kind of faith or laid-backness – I was learning quickly – that all Brazilians seemed to engender.

So, we had made it onto our boat and on up to the second level, the passenger level, and to our amazement, we were the first ones there. We checked our tickets. If the boat was to depart in twenty minutes, where was everyone else?

Setting up our hammocks we were interrupted by a surprised man who made his way up the stairs speaking quicker than we would ever be able to translate, maybe even after years of study. With hopes to quell our confusion and his, we handed him the tickets we had purchased at the airport. Suddenly his arms began to move through larger gestures, attempting to find the words he wanted. The ones we wouldn't understand anyway. More men, who had heard the commotion from above (the third level was for cavorting), joined us with similar and acute concern. The word they had in common started with the letter R. Riberrio or roubado or something. We grabbed our dictionary and began to flipping through. Yes! "Roubado!" I finally understood. Wait. *Roubado* equals stolen, robbed. We had been robbed?

"Sim. Estava aqui." Stay here, they said, as the boat began to move.

You know that kind of moment when you are within the absolute beauty of your dream, wind in your hair, in full amazement of the world while side by side there lives the absolute panic of not knowing what's next and if all decisions you had made might lead to a bitter end? There we were, flanked in the exhilaration of it all.

The boat began to move along the crowded port, veering between other boats of all sizes. Each one seemed to be its own fish, knowing exactly how to maneuver without any road signs or routes. A free-for-all that seemed to work and make sense. A different kind of listening. A knowing of the place and the culture and the water. All methods of communication. A negotiation between bows pointing in all directions.

Coming around a huge iron cargo ship with no windows, a long dock came into view. A long dock swaying with lines of bags and boxes and dogs and children and people of all ages and sizes. The only commonality was that of a colorful hammock slung over each person's shoulder. As the boat pulled up, the captain came up the stairs and waved his arm toward us commanding, "Você vem comigo!"

Understanding somehow that only one of us should follow, my boyfriend took a breath and gave me a look of fear and trust and adventure all at the same time. "Don't let the boat leave without me," he yelled trailing behind the captain. They moved onto the dock and through the sea of people until they disappeared onto the port in the distance.

Beyond a quick bathroom break, this was the first time we had been apart in weeks and definitely my first time alone in Brazil. My panic was on the rise only to be blown further out of proportion by the multitudes of people that now flooded onto the second level. Like bananas handing side-by-side, hammocks quickly lined the deck, each one claiming a seat for the duration of the ride. Boxes and bags and dogs were hurled just underneath. A scene of over a hundred people settling in for a 50-hour trip. All words were foreign to me, but the movements were a language I understood: kindness, anger, hurriedness, sadness, excitement, and what I imagined to be the unfolding relationships of a mother and daughter, of three sisters, of a couple, of a lone older woman and her sweet dog companion.

"Oi, tudo bem?"

I continued to remain quiet. I didn't know how or whether to answer, but had just started to learn that this was the way everyone in Brazil greeted one another. It literally translates to "Hi. All good?"

"Fala português?" (Brazilians don't write languages with a capital letter.)

No, I didn't speak much Portuguese. I ran and grabbed my dictionary, flipping through to somehow attempt to explain why I was there and that I was scared because my boyfriend was just taken off the boat and I didn't know what to do. In the minutes that followed, we did our best to understand one another. As he tried to calm me down and I tried to figure out what he was saying, two women my age joined us. (In Brazil, I was learning, conversations were always an open invitation, and somewhere along the way other people always found a way to join in whether the present conversers knew them or didn't. Calling it a culture of inclusivity is a vast understatement.)

The four of us spoke with one another about our families and where we were from. They could see that I was *nervosa* and wanted to learn why and how they could help. They saw the next dreaded moment when the captain returned to the boat but without my partner. They understood my fear that the boat might leave without him. They held my hand and rubbed my back and told me, "Tudo bem."

But all was not well. All the passengers were on board, along with a couple hundred motorcycles for transport on the first floor, and the boat that I learned was supposed to leave five minutes ago was beginning to rev up. I took a breath, not yet knowing that in Brazil nothing ever starts or leaves at the time that was originally intended. Should I get off or wait?

"Fique." And I learned the word "stay."

"Calma," and I became more relaxed.

"Ohla!" and I saw my partner running down the pier all by himself.

Out of breath, we embraced at the top of the stairs before I introduced him to my new friends.

"Oi," he said to them, "Tudo bem?" This was the first moment I ever heard him speak Portuguese without looking at a dictionary or turning red from mispronunciation.

He was confident and proud as we cobbled together the words that described his journey. We all learned how he met a man who had a hand in selling us the fake tickets. How the captain escorted that man to the police. How the policeman made the man to confess where to find the stolen money. How my boyfriend sat at a table in silence across from the man in the basement jail. How he didn't understand why the man didn't run or beat him up. How the cop returned with the money and after some banter let the man go. How my boyfriend had figured out that our new tickets were actually a hundred Brazilian *reals* less than we had paid. How he understood from the police that he needed to run back to the boat as fast as he possibly could and he did.

And thus began our voyage, crossing from these banks of the Rio Negro that met the Solimões waters and then turned into the grand Amazonas. The fact that we were the only two people aboard who didn't speak much Portuguese didn't seem to be an obstacle for a single person on that boat. Day and night, people wanted to talk with us and us with them. We played games, we drank coffee, and we learned more words during those fifty hours than we would ever learn in our entire stay in the country of Brazil. This horizontal time in hammocks gave us the foundation to speak to every new person we were about to meet over the next three months of our continued adventure.

Now, years later, I sit with a picture in my mind of that dock halfway across the world. It must be bustling with colors right now as I write, as you read, and every once in a while, when I'm lucky, I dream in full Portuguese.

⌘

Remember a time when you had to learn to communicate a new way. What strategies did you use? Whom or what helped you along the way?

37. Continuing to define what you do without pigeonholing yourself.

Brooklyn, New York. 2006.

Weeks before finishing graduate school in California, I met a woman at the Arcata Farmer's Market who was selling various kinds of leafy greens. When I told her that I was about to graduate, she looked me square in the eyes and delivered her wish: "My work is of the land so I must stay here and in one place. Your work is of the body so it is your responsibility to go out into the world and then come back and share your experiences with me."

Without realizing just how special it was, the coddled place where I had the time and space to create and learn and awake each day, immersed in an exploration of art, entrenched in a search for my own point of view, had come to an end. Twenty-two years of formal education was over, and there I was standing at the edge of the abyss that was the rest of my life.

So out I went, along with my nine classmates who dandelioned out on the wind to the likes of Korea, Oregon, Kansas, Montreal, and Amsterdam. For some this meant returning home. For some this meant moving on. For some it meant both. Whatever their next step was, everyone scattered throughout a world completely different than the nest that we had become so accustomed to in Blue Lake.

A new world that demanded a resumé and a headshot and a "day job" to pay the bills while the grace period for my educational loans came closer to running out. How could I describe to prospective employers that my MFA degree in "Ensemble-Based Physical Theater" was one that made me uniquely skilled, readily qualified, and especially marketable rather than misunderstood or a little too specific to hire?

"Why did you get that degree?"

"Because I loved every minute of it," I wanted to respond, but I didn't.

"What do you expect to do with it?"

I don't know. I never thought about that. Suddenly I was a deer in the headlights of New York City.

At times it was better to hide my theater in order to get other kinds of work or to make money. I had never quite connected making theater to making money so theater quickly and unconsciously became something that I did for free or on the side. Art felt like something that the rest of the world seemed to use up as a decoration or a hobby, something that I should do only on the side or at the end of the night if there was time or if I wasn't too tired. Being involved with theater was only something that could happen through an unpaid internship or by making a few bucks administering or by supporting someone else making theater. These were all great experiences, but none of this was how I imagined I would be giving to or living in the world.

Within theater, theater was all we ever talked about. We never discussed day jobs or money or the end of the night. We all assumed we were doing what we remembered doing together, but how was anyone sustaining themselves? Who were we becoming? How did we want to spend our time? Was there a choice?

People started dropping like flies.

"I don't do theater anymore. It's a waste of time," one friend said.

"Yeah, it's totally impossible, and there's no way it will pay the rent."

When I met new people and they asked me what I did, I wasn't sure whether to tell them I wrote calligraphy for wedding invitations off Craigslist or that I worked at a flea market on the weekends or that I just finished an internship at the United Nations. Sometimes I made conversation by explaining how I collated press documents for an Australian financial firm in Brooklyn or if I was brave, I invited them to a solo show I was working on and let them see for themselves.

⌘

How are you defining yourself these days? What words are most important to you?

How do you balance what you love to do with how you make money?

38. Telling people how beautiful they are.

Grand Island, New York. 2006.

My dad's best friend was a sweet, funny guy. He and his wife, who was from India, met at the same neighborhood bar where my parents met. I grew up knowing this couple as my Aunt and Uncle. They were fun and welcoming and part of every one of our celebrations. They were part of our family. I especially enjoyed learning about Indian culture, loving to wear colorful saris, eat naan, and learn a few words in Hindi while trying to understand why she fasted on Tuesdays.

Although my uncle was deathly afraid of flying, every few years he would somehow make the twenty-nine hour trip from Toronto to India to visit his wife's family. Lucky for him and all of us, her family would also periodically come from India to Buffalo.

In the later years of her life, my aunt's mom came for an extended visit of a few months. During this time, she wanted her mom to experience what it was like to age in America and took her mom to see my grandma who was now close to ninety and living in a nearby nursing home. Although my grandmother was fairly hard of hearing, she was still a great conversationalist when she wanted to be and always welcomed visitors. My aunt wasn't sure how the interaction would go considering that both moms were up in years, a bit hard of hearing, and hadn't ever formally met before, not to mention that neither of them spoke a lick of the other's language.

My aunt and her mom meandered through the hallway of wheelchairs to knock on my grandmother's door.

"Who is it?" my grandma shouted turning her wheelchair round. "Oh, come on in..." she continued as she backed away from the window and waved them on. When they came closer, she kissed them both on the cheek and offered them a seat.

"Oh... hello... I haven't seen you two in a while..."

My aunt quickly pulled up a chair and helped her mom get situated before going to the other side of the bed to grab a chair for herself. In motion, she pondered the best way to introduce the two women. But by the time my aunt joined the circle, she realized that the two moms were already off to the races. They were chatting away, happily exchanging words and gestures back and forth, and seemed completely un-phased by that fact that they probably didn't understand a single word that the other was saying. This joyous conversation went on for close to an hour, and my aunt was hardly able to get a single word in. She couldn't figure out what they were saying or what they understood. They just kept talking.

Eventually, they said their goodbyes, and my aunt and her mom walked out to the parking lot. In the distance, my grandmother waved out her window, grateful for the visit.

"You know," said my aunt's mom very-matter-of-fact in Hindi as they got in the car, "That Mrs. Quinn is so nice..."

"Oh yeah? What were you two talking about the whole time?"

"Well, she just kept telling me again and again how beautiful I am, and I told her how beautiful she is too."

⌘

Whom do you find beautiful today? How could you take the extra step of letting them know how beautiful they are? How do they respond? How does it affect you and your interaction with them?

39. Gaining the courage to share your story.

New York City. 2006.

"Why don't you share your own story," a teacher said to me in graduate school.

"But I don't do autobiography," I remember repeating in my mind as I marched back to my house. I wrote in journals, but I didn't want to share my dirty laundry in the theater or anywhere else. No, instead I wanted to be characters in other people's stories and go out to dinner after and talk about those. Not my own. It wasn't just that it felt too close to home, it was just that, well, who would be interested in my stories and what I had to say anyway? I wanted to create a show about disintegration and movement and new forms, not Buffalo or my grandmother.

"But isn't it all the same thing?" provoked the teacher.

"No!" Theater was a way to escape. A way to express myself, not face my own demons or share them in public. But every time I went to rehearse, there they were lurking in the room, friends and foes alike, all wanting to be part of the play. But who would want to hear these and what would it feel like to share them?

Eventually coming to my feet in New York, remembering

this conversation, I sat in a dressing room in lower Manhattan about to premiere my solo show. My boyfriend stopped in for one last "good luck" before taking his post in the booth where he would call the sound and run the video. "Why are you crying?" he said, surprised to find me with my head in my lap, "It's gonna be great."

"I don't know why I'm doing this," I whimpered. "I do theater to be with other people and play scripted roles, but now I'm going to be on stage all alone and share my own story. Why did I do this?"

And for this first performance of *Vamping,* I was on stage all alone and scared to share the play that was so close to my heart. I went about the words and moves as I had rehearsed them. Inspired by my grandmother, I spoke my first monologue from a wheelchair:

I remember a house.
Blue, with a front porch
And yellow tiles in the bathroom.
The lights in the front hall turn off at 10.
And in the morning the television turns on at 11.
I keep ice tea in the fridge
And collect buttons in glass jars.
On Friday I get my hair done by Natalie
And buy Entenmann's coffee cake
Even though it is too expensive.
I pay nine dollars to get my lawn cut on Wednesday
And I always balance my checkbook on Thursdays.
I love red lipstick.
And those Jell-O molds with the marshmallows in them.
In the back room there is a bike I never used

And whiskey we never drank.
I hate when potatoes aren't done all the way
And how the walkway gets when it's covered in snow.
Now...
Now, I am here.

I didn't notice the audience nor did I talk directly to them at all. I was isolated in my own little black box and the audience was like a bunch of flies on the wall. After the show, although finished, I felt empty. What had I just done? Shell-shocked, I looked around for my classmates I could turn to in the wings before bowing with a quick thumbs-up but they were nowhere to be found.

"How was it? Was it good? Did you like it?" I asked my mom, my boyfriend, a teacher from college. And for so long, I asked everyone else but myself. I waited for the award at the festival, I ran to reviews to hear what the critics thought. *"A high school science project. A generalized character. Social activism."* They ranted, and I pivoted.

"But theater is not just entertainment," I remember saying amidst a disagreement with one of my friends. I can't just sing and dance and call it a night. I have more to say. There's more that needs to be talked about. There's more to do. I began to believe that my grandmother's story was one that was shared by many. I remembered my friend with the flashlight and I wanted to turn it on bright and hear how others had been affected too:

There are over five million people in our country that have this disease. And there's another 10 million of us taking care of it.
That's right: For every one of her, it takes two of me.

Thing is, a nice room in a place like this costs $230 a day, which adds up to $7000 a month, $85,000 a year.
So after I finish my twelve hour shift here, I'm gonna be going home to take care of my own mother there.

The next time I did this show or any other solo work, the audience would need to be my partner and my ally. Even though I was performing solo, the theater was still a community space. A place for dialogue. No more flies on the wall; from now on, we'd all be in this together. Doing solo performance work would continue to teach me more and more about the relationship I could have with my audience. To share my stories with them and to hear theirs. To ask them questions. To hand them a photo and pass it around. To sing a song with them. To be on the journey along with them as they, too, rode along with me.

⌘

When it is important for you to share something? How can another person's perspective be helpful?

How can your Compassionate Creativity give you the courage to share your own story more often?

40. Knowing that you have the power to change the atmosphere of a room, a community, the world.

Throughout Southwestern Colorado. October-November 2006.

In the spirit of saying yes to whatever came my way next, I took a last-minute gig as one of three actors in a clown show that would tour to children throughout Colorado for five weeks. Because the show had been created and toured several years ago with different people, I simply flew in, met my new compatriots, learned the basic storyline and movements, and off we went in our van full of sets and props. Being new to this team and to this part of the country, my part served me perfectly: I played the kind of odd, alien clown who was new in town. Because I spoke in a different language, I was afraid of people and people were afraid of me. A toy duck was my only friend.

Driving through mountain passes – sometimes in snow, sometimes in sun – we performed inside tiny schools on back roads and outside others with the Rocky Mountains as our backdrop. Each audience was different than the last, but most audiences seemed to think my character's voice was pretty funny. I had invented a kind of high-pitch gibberish, accompanied by some silly movements to express myself, and I was finding ways to expand the laughter with each new show.

A couple weeks in, we pulled up to an elementary school outside of Grand Junction where we prepared to meet our largest crowd. Getting ready backstage, we heard the children begin to enter the gymnasium-cafeteria-auditorium. The sound grew from a few whispers and laughter to a dull roar of waving hands and stomping feet.

Once we gave our thumbs up, the principal quieted the audience and off we went. My fellow actors entered first but they couldn't seem to keep the attention of the audience. They yelled their lines across the stage louder and louder as teachers tried to shush their students from the sidelines. Even from backstage I could tell that this was going downhill and fast. They were losing control. For some reason the kids weren't into it. Whatever had worked at other schools was not working here.

By the time I entered, it was impossible to focus. There looking back at me was a colorful sea of constant wiggles awaiting greatness but getting quite antsy. Over a thousand little eyes darted every which way. We arrived at the part where I said my first line, I thought the high-pitched gibberish would help, but there was no chance that crowd would be able to hear it. And then, as if on automatic, I clapped three times; somehow recalling the same way the principal calmed the group in order to start the show. A ripple effect of silence pulsed through the students. I had their attention. All five hundred plus of them looked at me wondering how I knew their code. What now?

I remained still, enjoying the moment of suspension. In order to teach them to listen, I would need to learn to listen to them, too. This was a complex, reciprocal relationship. I squeaked out a little bit of gibberish along with a tiny movement, and the whole place broke out in uproarious laughter. I suspended into stillness once again, listening. Silence. Wow. This was power. This was responsibility. I moved and spoke again. Laughter again, and this time the teachers joined in, too. They couldn't help it. This kind of laughter was outrageously contagious, and now echoing from wall to wall. I think we even started laughing on stage.

The school breathed together in a rejuvenation I didn't know I had the power to initiate. And with great attention and interest now honed, we continued to be as specific and efficient as we could to articulate ourselves, demanding of ourselves the same focus we asked of them. Exhausted in the best way possible, we finished the show to the sound of huge applause accompanied by hundreds of high fives as all of the excited wigglers returned to their classrooms.

⌘

How do you listen to the needs of a room/group of people?

How does your mood or attitude affect those around you? At home? With friends? At work?

How can you use this awareness to shift the dynamic of a relationship you are in today?

41. Seeking out your best process.

Brooklyn, New York. 2007.

While in Colorado, The Feather guy and his best friend came up with the idea to start a company. Our collaboration on my solo show had gone well and instead of doing everyone else's work and not making money, they figured, why not make more of our own theater?

I drove through the mountains and thought about their proposal. I recalled the two goals I had when going to graduate school: The first was to integrate music and movement in my theater and the second was to meet people who shared a similar philosophy and wanted to work together long-term. While in California, however, the experience became about so much more. It was about being far away from home, growing up, collaborating, and making great stuff.

Before leaving school, my original dreams were reignited when my school hosted a national festival for the Network of Ensemble Theaters. Ensemble theater makers of kinds came from all over the country. This was a perfect moment to graduate into. These people were the most selfless, giving, generous, fun, loving group of people that I had ever met. They were living my dream and proving to me that having a long-term company was totally possible. And, because it hadn't been easy for them, they were wholeheartedly committed to supporting one another in any way they could. This wasn't just an organization. This was a movement. One where artists were valued as the primary decision-makers. Instead of a corporate model, these artists believed in the power of a lateral structure and collective vision that was community-based.

I wanted this for myself and maybe now this was my chance to do just that with these two guys. We had a common vocabulary from our class together that summer and they were right – our work on my solo show had been incredibly fruitful for all of us.

"Yes," I responded to the guys, "Let's do it. Let's start a company."

As soon as I returned from my tour, the three of us sat down and wrote a mission statement. We wrestled over every word, but agreed that we would take a multifaceted approach to telling visceral stories, believing that each one would warrant the creation of a new process.

We found a sewing factory in Brooklyn that would let us rehearse there when they were closed. We refinished the floor, tried our best to ignore the rats, joined the ensemble movement, raised money from our family and friends, and began work on our first official project together. We found a new play from Australia about two men in prison. I directed for the first time ever, and the two guys acted.

From that moment on, we mustered up the late-night time to rehearse and once a week we had an endless business-planning meeting. Being in concert like this put everything into perspective. It didn't matter as much what kind of work I had to do during the day to support myself financially if I had this play to look forward to every night.

Our similar passion for theater drew us together, but the ways that we each expressed that passion and where it had come from was completely different. Illuminating these differences sparked incredibly rich, creative disagreements. These fights brought about unparalleled growth for me. I began to identify what I believed in and experiment with how to articulate those beliefs to fellow artists and to audiences: I didn't want to just hear the words of the actors. I wanted to impel them to fully embody their characters. I didn't want to just see their struggle. I wanted to witness the possibility for hope, for finding joy within the hardships.

Every rehearsal continued to strengthen our budding team, our ensemble. Our moments of disagreement opened up entirely new passageways for each of us. I translated my vision into their language and they threw their understanding back to me. Together, path-by-path, stake-by-stake, we climbed the mountain, and that spring opening our new piece off-off Broadway, I felt tremendously proud of our joint process and its product.

⌘

How do you work with people who have a different process you? How do you articulate needs to them?

42. Creating life in your own way and time.

Athens, Vermont. 2007.

Entering my mid-twenties, many of my friends started getting married and having babies. These were the people whom I had just grown up with and left "the nest" with, and already, they had a new nest of their own. I wasn't judging their decisions; I was just in shock. What they were doing felt so foreign to me.

In one part of me, there was a young kid meeting up with a sense of adventure. I was just getting out of school for the first time in my life. I still didn't know what I wanted to do or how. I was okay not knowing and ready to explore the world.

In another part of me, there was a teenager with some leftover religion hanging around who was still afraid of getting pregnant as if it was the worst thing I could ever do. As if getting pregnant was something that would only screw up my life.

In another part of me peer pressure shed light on a biological clock that was ticking inside me. If my boyfriend had been more for it at the time, I might be telling a very different story here, but he adamantly knew we weren't ready for it and in my heart, I knew it too. Our focus was on our work.

Our families came together to meet one another as we passionately parented a company and brought new plays into the world.

⌘

What have you been a parent for in your lifetime?

What have you enjoyed about it? What has been challenging for you?

How has this experience brought out your Compassionate Creativity?

43. When someone is dying, go and be with them.

Grand Island, New York. 2007.

When I call her
She tells me she loves me before she knows who I am
When she realizes that it's me
She tells me to please come visit so that she can hold me like a baby
And I want to just drop everything and go...
But I can't...

Three days after we premiered our first full production in New York, I received a call that my grandmother wasn't doing well. Four hours later I was at her bedside in a nursing home just outside of Buffalo. Holding her hand, conversation no longer an option, I settled in and tried to shift my heart and mind that were so set on helping her survive to now helping her to die. But how could I encourage my grandmother to give way to her death if I wasn't ready for her to go myself?

Talking with people from Hospice, I understood that my grandmother had chosen to stop eating, and that not eating meant that her systems would be shutting down one by one. The first to go would be the nervous system, so she wouldn't be in much pain. I also understood I had the right to tell the doctors and nurses to stop doing things like bathing her or getting her out of bed. There was no longer a routine that needed to be followed here. We were all going to simply wait and listen and respond.

The next afternoon, out of nowhere, she sat up, opened her eyes and yelled, "I want dinner!"

We quickly snapped to and got some food sent up from the cafeteria. We propped up her pillow, helped her to sit up, set the tray on her lap and much to our amazement, she ate. It was a joyful moment, filled with life, with hope. But this hope was confusing. It wasn't the kind of hope that makes you call the rest of your family and let them know that everything would be fine and then return to your normal daily routine. No. We had to be careful not to let this hope-filled moment turn into that view of the future. The joy of this moment possessed another kind of hope. One that reminded us all of the possible life-giving strength and courage that is possible at every stage of life. It was the kind of hope that reaffirms the truth and beauty that no one goes quietly into the night. Whether a death lasts for a moment or for weeks (in time as we know it), there rages a great battle. A movement from one world to another. A transformation into something somewhere else. Energy can never be created or destroyed. It can only be changed from one form to another. Something like this was taking place inside my grandmother. A convergence between her and all the energy that ever was.

I had no understanding of where she was going or what she was turning into, but in the two days that followed, I was witness to the extreme violence and infinite grace that is commonly part of the end of life. My grandma thrashed and smiled and tried to take her clothes off. She mumbled and cried and laid so absolutely still and then reached for my hand. I don't recount this to scare you. I intend for quite the opposite actually. I share these details to let you know that death is just as much a part of life as doing laundry, catching the bus, or reading to your children before they fall asleep. It is not a moment to be hidden behind closed doors. Death is an ancient dance that every creature will move through at the close of his or her lifetime.

Not knowing when the moment would come but knowing it was imminent, I talked to my grandma all day, believing that in some way she could hear me. I slept next to her all night, believing that she felt me close by. "It's okay," I told her. "You've brought us this far and you can go now. Everyone will be... everything is okay."

I felt my grandmother leave the world that next morning. In a moment when my aunt and cousin and I happened to be laughing at the foot of her bed, my grandmother took her last exhale. I felt her 33,200-some days and ways swirling around us. As she released out into the cosmos, our memories turned into tears for all the more days we wished that we could spend with her.

Light came through the blinds of the window as I looked out onto my first day on earth without her. Her body was still there, but she was somewhere else. I thought of her first inhale sixty years before mine. How she was a baby once like me. Maybe somewhere out there she was meeting my dad, her son. Energies recognizing one another. Reconnecting in a new form.

In the days that followed, I wrote her eulogy:

Jule, Julianna, Julia, Mrs. Quinn, Mom, Gramma Jule
Don't be afraid to talk to her
And please feel free to
Talk about her
Tell stories
Lots of them
Remember times of long ago
As if they just happened yesterday
Or believing that they just might happen in another way again tomorrow
All of those little things
That somehow made a difference
Hold them close by
Because they are a part of you
Remember with those who know
And with those who never crossed her path
But do cross through yours
Pass on her ability to love
And her strength to live
Even when it might have been a real battle
Share especially with children
Her funny faces
And talent to make things out of nothing
The importance of watering the rhododendron in the backyard
Don't forget her overwhelming tidiness and amazing stubbornness
The possibility of a friendship not just through words
Take a ride through Buffalo and
Know that she saw a completely different place living on that same street
Realize that you can
Extend her life by fully living yours
Get together with your family and play cards where everyone gets

an honor
Those related and those who become such over time
And if some days you feel that she is too far away
Or you might be forgetting something
Cook a great big meal with at least two meats, seven vegetables,
  homemade rolls, lots of sweets and a backroom full of beverages
Or just buy tons of groceries and hope for company…
Imagine her sitting on the porch drinking ice tea awaiting you
Loving more than anything to simply be a good host
Only to finally be content by listening to your laughter while
falling asleep.

I think that a big part of me
In my little kid mind
Always thought Gramma Jule would live forever
And it's only now that I believe she truly will.

At the funeral luncheon, someone handed me my cousin's three-month old baby. People offered reprieve, but I declined. All I wanted to do was hold that new life.

"Who the heck are you?" my brother said as he passed by me. He wasn't the only one who was surprised. I had never really held a baby before, but I can't tell you how good it felt to have this little one sleeping in my arms. So peaceful. So natural. Just starting out.

"What did you want to be when you grew up?" I remembered asking my grandmother before I left for California. "What did you want to be? What did you dream of doing?"

"I wanted to do what I did. To be a mom."

"To be a mom."

Hours later, bewildered but somehow ready to extend my grandmother's life through my own, I said goodbye, handed off the baby, and stepped out of the house still teeming with the energy of family. A sky streaked with clouds and color greeted me, letting me know that I too would be a mother and a grandmother sometime soon enough…

⌘

How do you find a way to support someone when you aren't sure how?

What has been your experience with death and dying? How have these experiences brought you comfort, awe, fear, love?

44. Sharing what you believe and believing in what you share.

Buffalo, New York. 2008.

Given the choice between a one-woman show about Alzheimer's and the *Batman* sequel opening at the movie theater next door for half the price of a theater ticket, even I might choose *Batman*. So what was I creating and for whom? Disappointment and questions loomed as I persevered with my solo show. Adding, tweaking, reworking. Audience after audience. Going to day jobs. Teaching others to make theater as I wrestled with my own.

If you think I'm going to let you sit in here all day long without saying a word to nobody, you've got another thing coming. Do you think I haven't seen this before? I've been in here since the day you came in, remember, so I know you're not fooling nobody. I know you're in there somewhere, so don't give up.

Eventually I performed in my hometown of Buffalo. My first-grade teacher offered to rent a theater. My dad's old workplace gave a small grant to pay for travel and advertising. The bar where my parents had met, now under a new owner, became the leading sponsor, helping to keep ticket prices low. We partnered with adult day-care facilities, the council on aging, and neurologists. My cousin's first-grade class even did a project on elders and their artwork lined the walls of the theater.

My grandma had passed away but my grandpa, my mom's dad, committed to being there with his oxygen tank in tow. "That's my grand-daughter!" I would hear him shout before it started.

Everyone gathered and the two-week run sold out. Family brought friends, and friends brought family. And others just came because of reading an article in the paper, hearing an ad on the radio, or after seeing one of the TV interviews: *"Local girl makes good."*

On the second weekend, I proposed a "caretakers day" for half-price and people came hand-in-hand: nurses, daughters, husbands, sons.

At the talkback, an older gentleman stood up to speak. "I have Alzheimer's Disease," he said slowly with tears rolling down his cheeks, "And every single day I try to help my wife understand what it's like for me, but I have never been able to do it until now. Now I know that she can see me better. And I can see what she must go through too." He grasped her tightly as he sat back down. The rest of us remained silent. There was nothing more to say.

That night, I stood weeping at my grandmother's grave, sorry that I didn't have all these resources when she was alive. Thanking her for the gift she was helping me to bring into the world.

⌘

What is a project or way of being that you believe in?

How has it been challenging to see this through?

How has it been worth it?

45. Investing in & cultivating relationships of love, friendship, family, and work.

Saxtons River, Vermont. 2008.

Fully settled into Vermont, our theater company decided to stage a new play. Note that everything our company had done up until this point was always much more successful than we imagined and every production always seemed to lead seamlessly onto the next, so much that the built-up momentum of it all had begun to take us on a much steeper roller coaster than we anticipated, than we ever had the capacity to endure or control or plan for. Always easier to say now, of course when looking back, when desperately trying to reframe a dream...

The play was about the singularity, the end of the world. The year was 2098 and the dead were coming back and there were electric storms and all of the churches and mosques and temples had long ago been abandoned. I played Lou, a zookeeper in the Bronx taking care of the last lion on the planet within a holographic Africa. Eventually I turned into a holographic lion that guided a priest and lost refugee woman through seas of people making their way to safety.

This was a much bigger project than any of us ever realized, and we enthusiastically went for it in every way. We collaborated on the script. We built huge puppets out of old clocks. We designed video. We decided to create all of our lighting with handheld lamps. We found housing and invited and paid our actor and designer friends from Montreal, England, Chicago and New York. We hosted a radio show. We hired a local rock band to compose live music, and we booked and budgeted for a two-week tour throughout New England.

Everything was coming together, and this was going to be the best piece ever.

See, by this point I was on a crusade to create the best theater ever. I'm not sure I even knew what that meant or where that would take me, but I imagined there to be a path, and I was surely on it. It wasn't just a project. This was my life. It didn't matter how many dollars of savings I had to spend or how many midnight hours I had to stay awake, this show would go on, and it would become the answer that we had all been looking for.

So like a wild, bucking horse with creative-business-woman blinders on, I did nothing short of eating, sleeping, and breathing this show, and the way I communicated with my company members showed it. They became pawns in a kind of competition that I pressured myself to win. I became obsessed with marketing and websites and newsletter and ticket sales. My heart was in there somewhere, but it was hard for anyone to detect. I cared about the work so much more than the relationships with my company members. I wasn't grateful for what they were going through or how hard they were working. I only demanded that we all work harder. This is not a period in my life that I am exactly proud of, like to admit to, or want to talk about often, but at the same time, what I learned from this experience I brought with me into every new classroom and production and relationship.

Interestingly enough, everyone we invited to be involved in the piece had a wild and amazing time, but the three of us doing the planning amidst acting and directing and designing and booking went through a beautiful, tragic hell that I now refer to as "my most successful failure."

Audience members – from huge, old opera houses to one-room schoolhouses to university stages – might have agreed as they witnessed the huge mess and the loud noise that we threw in front of them as we explored our own sort of apocalyptic *Wizard of Oz*. Years later one friend finally admitted that he had to shower several times after he saw the piece because he was so angry and distraught.

There were also moments of absolute splendor and magic, of course. There always are: beautiful images and turns of phrases that made their way into conversations of students and families of all ages. To be honest, we didn't really know what we had done. We just did it. Like animals, with all our might. Everyone else went home or onto the next endeavor, and with a kind of whiplash, our company came out of it wide-eyed, hurt, and bewildered – unsure of where we had ended up – and we had no idea how to start talking about it with one another.

New anger mixed with remnants of care as we stepped into our new roles in-residence at the local boarding school directing high school students in *Little Shop of Horrors*. Going through the motions, we worked and loved and played side-by-side, unable to deal with the wreckage that was living between. Building new puppets and a rotating stage and choreographing dances, we fulfilled our job and buoyed ourselves on the spirit of theater now living in the eyes of teenagers experiencing their first time on stage, their first time singing in front of an audience. Kids believing in themselves and in the power of theater, of sharing stories, of making something together.

It wasn't long ago that I was them. That I was making theater for the pure joy of making theater. Before going to college and grad school, refining my technique and getting headshots. Before what I loved turned into work.

For weeks I continued to put together press packets to be mailed out to future producers. My company members looked at me as if I was crazy: "Are you kidding? We aren't ever going to do that piece again."

And I was suddenly lost, completely embarrassed. Since stepping into the real world, I had put all of my energy toward this company. I saw my whole life through its lens. We created three pieces of theater together. We raised money. We invested our own money. Our families and friends donated to our cause. They all came together to see our shows, something to gather around, and they celebrated with us. This was success. We moved out of the city and into Vermont. We were settling in. For the first time in my life I was calling it good. There wasn't grass that was greener. My company wasn't just a project. It had become my life's work, my identity near and far. These two guys were my forever comrades, my family, my home.

If I wasn't going to make more theater with the two of them, then I would have to make it somewhere else.

⌘

How do you value your relationships? At work? With friends? With family?

What have you found to be the essence of the lasting relationships in your life?

What do you consider to be your "most successful failure?" What lessons do you take with you from that time?

FOURTH MOVEMENT: MOMENTOUS LISTENING

Connect with your Compassionate Creativity by...

46. Asking open-ended questions that allow people to access their own story.

Dummerston, Vermont. 2009.

Her happiness stems from a string of pearls
Given to her on her fourteenth birthday
By her dad.
A little something
To fall back on when days get long.
You look beautiful he said
As she attempted to make up her face
In her grandmother's yellow-tiled bathroom.

You are beautiful.
Stopping mid brush stroke
Cheeks blushing for real
Looking into her own eyes
Eyebrows pondering the thought
The phrase…
Me, he's talking about me.
No one had ever told her she was beautiful.
Some people are never told
But her dad now ten years gone
Still echoes in her mind
On darkest of days.
Resonance while moping around
These words glistening around the house
Reflected back again and again:
You are beautiful already.
You don't need any more.

I decided to commemorate the tenth anniversary of my dad's passing by seeking out some kind of counseling, something which up until that point, amidst encouragement from outsiders my entire life, I had staved off. I was afraid if the dam opened up there would be no way to stop it and I would have no idea what to do. This felt like it would be worse than holding it all in. I didn't want to go back to talking about my childhood, I wanted to move on, but how could I do both?

"I want to learn from an old, gray-haired sage of a woman who will greet me kindly and offer me tea before embracing my stories and enfolding them with hers," I expressed to a friend.

"I have just the woman for you," he offered. "And she already knows you. She saw your show the other night and she was once an actress too."

I made an appointment and drove up the dirt road to her home. "There's nothing like driving along a back road for me to start a secret process of healing," I remember thinking. The woman and her two cats met me at the door. She greeted me kindly before escorting me into the bedroom she had converted for doing her work. There we sat across from one another. The space was colorful and calm and full of special trinkets from her travels.

"Tell me about you," she offered, after explaining how excited she was to work with me.

Where to start? Work? Relationships? Family? How did I want to introduce myself? Where should I start?

As I began to speak, she became an open vessel ready to take in the rivers of words and thoughts and feelings that were easing out drop by drop.

"As you've been talking, I've noticed you gesturing toward your chest. Tell me what that's about," she said. She encouraged me to talk not about 1986, but rather about the images and feelings that resided in my body in that exact moment. She was present to my presence and then so was I.

This woman was a practitioner of the Rubenfeld Synergy Method. (For those of you who don't think we need yet another method or practice or healer, I say, Why not? The more the better... that way there will be the perfect person practicing in the exact way that speaks to you just when you need it most.) This particular method was created by a woman named Ilana Rubenfeld when she realized that every time she went to therapy, she felt things physically, and when she went to do physical work, she felt things emotionally. She realized that she couldn't separate out her mind from her body because they were interconnected. Like me, she longed to listen to both her mind and body at the same time and to play out the conversations going on between the two.

As I continued my session, I laid down on a table, and this Rubenfeld Practitioner placed her hands on me. I breathed. She listened. To my words. To my impulses. To where the tension was sitting in my arms, my legs. She took her time and encouraged me to take mine. We went on a journey accessing the stories and images in my head, heart, and gut. What I'm thinking, what I'm feeling, and what I'm wanting to do.

This opened me up to understanding how my everyday mind was constantly trying to figure things out and make sense of myself and the world. But if I listened more deeply to my body, I tuned into a different kind of knowing. A faith that everything was okay. That everything was exactly where it needed to be. And rather than trying to manipulate them into something else, I could look at the pieces of my life one by one and see them for what they were in that moment. If listening like this, my body was always ready to tell the delicate and elaborate truth, if only I was open to hearing it.

⌘

How do you listen to the stories playing out in your head, heart, and gut?

What questions might you ask yourself or someone else to allow for the fuller story to emerge?

47. Leaving everywhere better than you found it.

Saxtons River, Vermont. 2008-2014.

I met him one night while he was up late feverishly working away in his garage on his newest creation for the famous Fourth of July parade. Whether rollerblading through the streets in a cardboard airplane, walking on stilts, or dancing with a life-size woman he had built, every year his creation was a sight to see. The amount of care that he gave to make something, let alone the commitment to pulling it off, was something to behold.

Years later, when I heard the news of his sudden passing, I felt horrible. He was such a sentinel in the town that I couldn't imagine it without him. I wanted to run away into sleep, but then remembered that a friend had recently introduced me to the structure of an alphabet poem.

"Write one word for every letter of the alphabet and see what you get," he said.

I remembered my friend who had passed away as I moved through the alphabet:

A beautiful comrade
Dignifying elegant furniture
Generously honoring

In joyous kites
Light
Moving news of parades
Quiet red stall
Tender upright villager
Whittling XYZ

This expression gave way to tears and which only expanded
the poem:

The most beautiful creative comrade
An integrator of hope amidst great loss
A tender upright villager
Planter of trees and ideas
Skating through streets
Stilts dresses and all
Ready always
A soft voice
Gentle hands
Discovering tables within trucks
Benches within branches
And perhaps driving them hundreds of miles
On a sweet whim
To a new home
A glorious inspiration
A man of his land
Joyous in his barn
Every time we met
A smile that sat in the corner of his eyes
Shared with each neighbor
Each child
A magical kindness
A parade of lightness

Generously now
We honor
We remember always
The most generous soul taking flight.

His wife placed these words on the back of the program at his services later that month where hundreds of people from the community gathered round to sing and remember and celebrate. Sharing together, we all learned how many other people and places were better off because they had crossed paths with this special man.

⌘

What does it mean to make your community a better place? What role do you play?

Who is someone or something you might want to write an alphabet poem for today?

48. Visiting friends in their home.

California, Baltimore, Virginia, Pennsylvania, Minneapolis, Oregon. June-August 2009.

To spend time with people
Friends
Family
Colleagues
Those you just met
Or have known forever
To be in their homes
Is unlike any other kind of travel
Not to see the sights
The greatest museums
And bridges
And capitol buildings
Or landmarks
But to witness
Someone's every day
Drives and walks
The way they keep
Their home
Their desk
Their love
Their clocks
The way they make and eat their dinner

And share it with you
At their table
It is a real honor
A blessing
An adventure
A breath of new air
And a perfect reason to celebrate.

⌘

What have you learned from visiting friends, family, and co-workers at their homes?

Whom would you like to visit today if you could?

How do you host people at your home?

49. Noticing when something has your name on it.

Portland, Oregon to Athens, Vermont by way of New York City. 2009.

Pulling out of the station, my drooping eyes were propelled open by a loud scream that emanated from a woman who sat a few seats in front of me. While awaiting take-off from Penn Station, someone had stolen her purse. Obviously in the shock of being so violated, feeling guilty for resting her eyes, the attendants half-listened to her story, maybe one that they had heard one time too many.

"Ma'am, there is nothing we can do until we get to the next station. We can report it once there, but what's gone... is probably gone." And with that, they moved on, business as usual. Really? There was nothing they could do? The shiny white-haired, woman sank into her chair shaking and crying, everyone a witness to her loss.

My eyes shifted to those around us: headphones, eyes fixed on landscapes out windows, kids mostly unaware playing with paper dolls, and me, lids heavy, awaiting my much-needed rest. I took two more breaths as I resurveyed the scene. Sometimes you need to keep your eyes closed and rest. Other times you need to be the person someone else needs you to be. There was no way I couldn't help her.

As the hours of the trip passed, we went through all that had been in her purse: what could be recovered and what couldn't. We filed the police report. We called her son (a sweet entertainment lawyer in Northampton, MA) who helped to cancel all her cards. And I listened to the significance of losing her brown, leather, hand-written address book. She had it for as many years as she could remember and it included friends from when she had taught in Alaska, distant relatives in Alberta where she was originally from, her second husband's children. We talked at length until she seemed calm, stable, safe.

Realizing that she hadn't brought up the purse incident in a few minutes, that there was nothing more that we could do, and not wanting to overstay my welcome, I offered to give her some time to herself.

After a bit of a pause she smiled first out the window and then to me. "Actually, would you mind staying and talking to me for a while longer?"

Fascinated by her dream-like history of traveling and teaching and love, I happily moved all my belongings into her aisle and we continued our conversation throughout the rest of Connecticut and most of Massachusetts until I helped her off the train in Northampton. Thanking me profusely, I assured her that it was no big deal and that I knew that she would have done the same for me or anyone else.

Two weeks later, a package showed up in my mailbox that included a thank-you note along with a turquoise necklace that she had someone make for me. "For travel and friendship," read the enclosed card.

Two years later, this woman came when I did my show near her house. She invited me to dinner at her house and showed me the pictures of all of the people she had talked about in her stories, the people included in her address book.

The next summer she invited me to her 75th birthday party where I met her son who I had spoken to on the phone, and I played violin with her granddaughter. When I took my seat for dinner next to some of her other friends, they already seemed to know all about me. "Nice to meet you finally," they offered, "You must be the train angel."

⌘

Describe an initial encounter with someone who ended up becoming a great friend?

What has your name on it today?

50. Finding a reason to celebrate together.

The Valley, Buffalo, New York. 2008-2009.

When the second Bush came through Buffalo during his second term, my grandfather was found on the roof of his house with a cardboard sign full of hand-painted profanities. Apparently when he had heard that Bush was rerouted and would be driving on the Thruway right across from his house, my grandpa was inspired by the notion of colorfully displaying his freedom of speech for all the world to see, and he was especially excited for the opportunity to give his own words to Bush himself.

Surrounded by a lawn of plastic flamingos and a window full of neon Chanukah candles (which he loved to plug in each night even though he wasn't Jewish), my grandpa wanted everyone to hear what he thought and why. Known to drive by and place placards in front of my more Republican uncle's house, Papa was always ready to debate, play, crack jokes, and tell you one more long winding story of what it was like to sail around the world as a Merchant Marine during the Second World War. Anything to keep you on your feet.

The next summer Papa was in the hospital for a week with breathing issues and quickly came to be known for his special antics. In one specific instance, he made a nurse jump in the middle of the night, when thought to be sleeping, he reached out toward her and in a frightening raspy voice declared, "Don't worry, Lady. I'm not going to die." Stunned, the nurse sweetly attempted to calm him down. But he didn't want or need to be calmed down. He was just telling his story straight and wanted her to know his vitals. He continued: "I am going to live to see our country free if it's the last thing I do... Do you know what freedom means to me?" She shrugged, not sure whether to encourage his developing manifesto. Either way, he rallied his considered truth onward and outward: "I will be free again once Bush is out of office."

That fall, Papa was the first person I called when the election results came in. He was overjoyed to see Obama win. Hanging up the phone, I gratefully celebrated that someone so near the end of their life could reconfirm for themselves the beautiful possibilities of humanity.

When it was too difficult for my grandfather to ring in that next year without his wife who had recently passed away, all of his extended family came together to ring in the New Year in a new way. No matter what part of the family you came from - old or young, near or far, left or right, it didn't matter. All generations and beliefs gathered in his house – not to watch the ball drop – but rather to join together for a jubilant, balloon-filled "Bush Out of Office Party."

My grandpa lived until about a month after Obama's inauguration. A month of smiling freedom and regaining hope on the way to his next adventure.

⌘

What would you like to celebrate this week? Who would you invite?

What's the common reason for your family to get together and celebrate?

51. Humbly recognizing your own privilege.

Throughout Guatemala and El Salvador. 2010.

In the spring of 2010, I filled in last minute as a volunteer for Central America with *Clowns Without Borders*. Roaming from town to town around volcanoes and lakes, I was one of three clowns from the United States who, along with a clown from France and one from Guatemala, performed for children throughout the countryside as "ambassadors of laughter."

Our transportation was an old yellow school bus, its Wisconsin elementary school still written on the side. This was the place most American school busses went to die; I was learning quickly upon my arrival. The roads there were filled with them.

As we played the ukulele and sang songs crossing into the long, windy, desolate land surrounding the border between Guatemala and El Salvador, out the windows we saw so many people walking and waiting - longing to be on the other side of something. Stories unfolding in steps. Eyes begging for another life. Hands empty of promise. Guns slung casually over shoulders of guards who asked for our passports, all smiling briefly as we explained that we were clowns. A quick look at our passports and we were off to the next country, but others remained waiting at an imaginary line they were not allowed to cross.

In place of songs, silence filled our bus until we reached San Salvador, the capital city of El Salvador.

Once there we were immediately put into a van with a group of people who worked for Save the Children and we were all taken into a nice apartment complex up on a hill that overlooked the city. Once beyond the maximum-security fences and gates and doors, we were politely but seriously briefed on the rules, one of them being not to leave that place unless accompanied by one of them. *Okay... A breath. Where was I?*

Swallowing and innocent, we descended into the city. Eyes gazed out the windows in witness of a poverty-stricken place. A place lined with billboards upon billboards for American Banks, ways to send money, ways to get loans.

What had I been part of for so long without knowing it? What was America? To me? To them?

While squished into the van and headed for the coast to play with kids who had been relocated after Hurricane Ivan, I sat next to a woman who might as well have been a friend of mine from childhood or a sister even. In the minutes that ensued, though we only knew a handful of words in one another's languages, we somehow figured out that we shared the same age, that we both wanted to be married and have children, and that we didn't know how those things would ever happen. Smiling, hours passed as we counted fingers, made up gestures and talked slowly on repeat in order to learn more about one another's families and dreams.

Bit by bit, I parceled together that her parents lived close by in the city and that she lived with them. She had one older sister (and maybe a brother or two, too). Her sister was married and lived in North Carolina with her two children.

"Have you been there?" I asked. This took a lot of rewording.

"When did you last see her?"

"Did you visit there recently?"

The look on her face transformed from excitement to sadness, inevitability to anger, and truth to acceptance. A rule, I learned. A law. The way things were. She hadn't seen her sister in over fifteen years. She'd never met her sister's husband or her sister's children. She couldn't visit them and they couldn't come back to see her or her parents. These were not options. But her sister did send money, and they had fixed up their house a bit. I remembered that there was a word for these kinds of houses, houses that only looked nicer because of someone else who was far away in America.

"What is it like there, Kāli? Is it really as amazing as they all say?" she asked.

I looked out the window, in awe of my privilege and the country that I happened to be lucky enough be born into. It wasn't until now that I began to understand that not everyone had the same set of givens. I held passport that would let me go almost anywhere in the world. Not everyone had access to this luxury. The reasons for this varied, and many were unwarranted and unjust. In that moment I didn't want to express my guilt or shame but rather deepen my gratitude and discover my own unconditional generosity and humility, committing to and recommitting to seeking out the fuller story wherever I went.

"It's pretty incredible in America, and it's beautiful here too," I said as her country passed us by. "I just wish that I could welcome you in my country as you and everyone here have so graciously welcomed me here in yours."

⌘

How do you relate to your own sense of privilege? How is this different or similar to those around you?

What is given, what is earned, what is deserved, what is needed?

How can you engage in a humble conversation about privilege with yourself or someone you care about today?

52. Discovering the universal language of play.

Throughout Guatemala and El Salvador. April 2010.

When electing to travel with *Clowns Without Borders*, you enter into places ravaged by natural disaster or torn to pieces by war. Traveling down these roads, you see such hardship repeated upon the faces of the people. Homeless, hungry, hurt. Such grief affecting all people. A devastation and loss so much more vast and real than would ever be reported in the news. How could you, now witnessing it firsthand, ever have the words to explain this to someone who wasn't there? How would you even start? How could you possibly find a way to get onto the next plane home and move on to have a conversation about anything else other than this?

So you get out of your vehicle and walk down the streets. You realize that the city or town might have been destroyed and many of its inhabitants might be missing, but at the same time there are people, individuals, there. Alive. Standing on the line between life and death, a sense of community can't help but linger in the air. A mother feeds a child. Two men lift up boards. Children tickle one another in the dirt. There is a want to be together. Laughing. Listening to music. Celebrating something. Anything.

Your colorful clothes and red nose set you apart and draw a

crowd, but that isn't what keeps them watching. It's the continual surprise of being in the presence. A performance based on being affected by every sound, movement, and pebble placed on the ground. Everything an offering, an opportunity, for play. A universal laughter erupts when you unexpectedly trip over your own foot and end up being okay. All of your actions illuminate again and again a buoyancy that we all love to watch. A resilience that we all long to somehow find our own capacity for.

A kindred spirit who simultaneously embodies qualities that everyone recognizes: the innocence of a child, the gut of a dog, and the wisdom of an elder.

After the street performance, a young boy runs up to you and tugs on your shirt. Translated, he asks if when you get to the next town, you could please help his cousins put a violin together. They've been wanting to learn how to play but only had the pieces of the instrument, sent long ago by mail.

In the next place, deep in the jungle, you give your final performance. Afterward, a small family of three generations comes up to you and offers up a violin case cradled in their arms. "Yes," you nod, remembering the boy who had wanted you to meet them. To help them put it together.

You move together to a nearby pavilion and through joy and anticipation they open the case. How long had these pieces been waiting in their home? You cradle the new instrument in your arms as they hand you one peg and string after another until they are all balanced along the bridge. You pluck the strings into tune as the family claps and claps in amazement. You imagine the place across the world where the violin must have come from. You remembered your first violin teacher back home. You remember your fear in saying yes to this trip.

The afternoon sun beams to the song of a child's smile as he places the bow along the strings for the first time, his family suspended in pure delight.

The sound of the violin and laughter echo as your boat makes its way back down the river to the next place.

⌘

How did it feel to imagine walking through the world of this story?

How and when do you play? How do you feel when you play?

How can you find ways to play more often?

53. Beholding every life as its own arc.

Saxtons River, Vermont. 2010.

I sit holding my friend's apron in my lap. A nearby note from his fiancé reads, "May you cook the most wonderful meals in it." I remember the beans he soaked overnight in our house in California. I remember walking to school kicking stones and writing poems about love. I remember landing a pose on his shoulder as his wife in a play. I recall the time he jumped into the bath with me and my broken wrist to ensure that I bathed. I considered him to be a brother, a provocateur, a fellow clown. I visited his parents in Riverside. Their dog named Canela. Their fruit trees lush. Their home a place of forgiveness and pride in being family.

I remember after the news of his death, I talked to friends from around the world throughout the night and into the next day. I remember once evening came being encouraged to take a walk. I felt scared to go out into the world because that's just what he did. I stood at the doorway pondering how life could just be cut off like that. Gone. I took one step out, breathing. Afraid. One step at a time, I meandered about my tiny Vermont town. I crossed over Main Street with tears flowing from my eyes. I didn't know where I was walking, but I was walking. Moving. Alone in a new world. Everything different now. The grass was greener. The streetlights felt brighter. People gardened in slow motion. Did they see this new world too?

As I made my goal a playground in the distance, the sun began to set. The metal chain of the swing was cold to the touch. The wind shifted my hair along my face. My eyes were out of tears. My heart was heavy in my chest. Angry. Solid. Rock. As I pulled back to swing, my gaze turned up, greeted by a full rainbow sailing across the eastern sky. A family laughed as they crossed the field below. Looking back up, the swing released forward and a sense of calm washed over me. My ravished mind focusing only on the swing. *Squeak, squeak, squeak.* Back and forth. Forth and back. My questioning ceased. "Every life is an arc," said the rainbow. "We just don't know what part of the arc we are each in."

I sit, holding his apron in my lap. I remember how much I miss him still.

One grief brings up all grief that ever was. Yours and the world's. So be with yours now. No one else could ever know what yours is like. Hold it. Caress it. Love it. And let it transform you. Lets its shards reflect your own bright light back to you and, like a lighthouse in the middle of the deep, dark ocean, circle your light round for the world to see. Calling your flock to harbor. All will be well. All is love in your arms.

How does Compassionate Creativity help you to see every life as its own beautiful arc?

54. Moving through life as a clown.

Saxtons River. July 2010.

"You're a what?!"

When I say clown, what do you think of? Big red shoes? Birthdays? Scary make-up? Laughter? A character that has lived in every culture since the beginning of time? A necessary ingredient to keep the world spinning?

About to land in Central America for the first time, I quickly filled out my passport information. Getting to the part that asked for my occupation (similar to my latest experience filling out tax documents) I stopped, thought between what I believed versus what would be accepted, and decided to go with "theater artist." This only made it more difficult and took a lot of explaining in order pass into the country: "Help me to understand. Do you paint the scenery?"

A week later when I passed into El Salvador with my three new clown compatriots – ukuleles and dance combinations in tow – the driver simply told the border guards that we were *payasos*, and on we went. Same word on the way back: *Clowns.*

Clowns. We were clowns. I was a clown.

When I said so on my way to Montreal for an audition for Cirque du Soleil a couple months later, on I went with no questions asked. North of the United States and South of the United States, a clown was something that was understood. A clown was even considered a position of honor. Of respect. The one who brings the laughter.

After crossing three international borders as a "clown," I felt I had earned the title and could back it up with these experiences and other resume bullet points as needed. Yes! I was a clown, and I could educate all of America one cocktail party or networking event at a time.

That summer, after my friend died, I was scheduled to do my newest clown act as part of a nearby circus. When someone dies, I wholeheartedly believe it's a reason to cancel most things, but when I picked up the phone to call it off, I realized that I needed to do it. That it was the best thing I could possibly do. I got out of bed and took out my violin and reluctantly began to play.

I remembered the last time I played; it was at a town square in the jungle of Guatemala. I found the clown nose that my friend had made for me out of a gourd he found in his family's backyard, and I looked at the last text he sent me: "Make sure you are in joying all the love that you are being given." (I'm not sure whether the "in" part was a typo or not, but I do know that to enjoy something, I need to be "in" the joy.)

A clown lives with a vulnerability that comes from his or her commitment to being absolutely in the present, playing with each moment as it arises. No past and no future. Only a continual presence. Ready to be with whatever is happening and play with it.

With a buoyancy, a resilience, that we all dream of having the capacity for. Letting everything exist at once. Not an either/or but both and all. Joy and sorrow. Hope and fear. Love and hate. Funny and serious. Black and white. Stripes and polka dots. Here and there.

Being a clown wasn't a job or a label or something I would ever be able to explain. It was a way of life. Although buried deep down at times, it was always a part of who I was and what I believed in: playing through life one moment at a time compassionately and creatively. Acknowledging the loss AND somehow finding the joy.

⌘

How does this definition of clown connect to you?

How can you bring out this clown part of you more often?

How does it have an effect on those around you?

55. Letting everything become your teacher, especially children and animals.

Throughout Vermont. 2008 – 2014.

One of my best friends in the whole world is my friends' daughter. She was the first baby that I was really close with, even before she made her appearance into the world. And because she lived nearby, I had the amazing gift to witness her growth day after day after day.

When she was two-and-a-half, she had her first sleepover at my house. We had a great time playing inside and out and eating watermelon on the porch. When we were finally going to sleep, she came and crawled in bed with me and said that she wasn't having fun anymore. That she was scared. Because I knew that I could talk with her about anything, I asked her what was making her feel so afraid, to which she responded quietly, "I miss my mom and dad. I never slept without them before."

"That's true. This is a big step for you. Is there anything I can do to help you to feel better?"

"You already did," she smiled before falling asleep close by, "I think I just needed to say that out loud… Goodnight."

A year or so later when I was going through a challenging

time, unaware if she knew or not, she looked up at me with her same smile, "You need to get a balloon and put all your thoughts on it and let it go down at the river."

Yes, of course, I thought. The perfect ritual! And out I went.

Shortly after I left Vermont, she and her mom and dad moved out to Colorado and lived another half of her lifetime before I saw her in person again. So much time had passed that I wasn't sure if the seven-year-old I was about to see would remember me or not.

When I drove up to her circus camp, she immediately ran toward me and took my hand, "Come on! I'm going to teach you how to ride a unicycle."

And before I knew it I was up and riding round in circles as she helped to steady my balance. "Great job, Kāli. I've missed you too. Remember the time we ate watermelon on your porch?"

⌘

How can you see everything as your teacher today?

What great lessons did they impart?

56. Embarking everyday anew with experience in tow.

Saxtons River, Vermont. 2010.

It was an incredible world out there, but without a company, it wasn't the same. Without a company it was everyman for themselves. Project after project it was a hello and a goodbye.

At theater festivals, I felt like the divorced one coming to hang out at the party.

"How's it going with your company?" people would ask.

"Great," I would respond, hoping that they didn't ask what our next show would be. I didn't want to tell them that we weren't talking about it. That we were hardly talking at all. That something had been lost and that I didn't know how to find it.

A year and a half later, I called together our first business meeting since that notorious summer. Reluctantly, the three of us pulled up our seats.

"I don't know what there is to talk about," one of the guys said. I knew that there were things to say, but wasn't sure how to start. I mentioned a lingering website and a bill for our monthly newsletter and then we all surrendered to apologizing and admitting that we all didn't know what to do next. We decided to keep the company as a producing company that any of us could use with the permission of the others.

To finish, we agreed to sell the veggie oil bus that we had bought and taken on that tour. It had been sitting empty in the parking lot not running for years, always epitomizing for me our unrealized dreams each time I walked by. I wanted so badly to move on and forgive myself, or the theater itself, but I still couldn't seem to let go. I didn't want to have a company. I wanted to have an ensemble. A family. A commitment. I didn't want to move along from role to role on my own. I wanted to walk with this same crew into every theater over time, growing with them and reminding each other why we started in the first place. Who we were then and who we were now.

Watching the bus being driven away by someone else, I started to realize how much the three of us had grown up together. Not only as artists but as human beings who, because of relating to one another, learned to believe in themselves and could now state their artistic point of view clearly and directly without apologizing for it. Three people who now saw the true value and delicateness of relationships. Three bold and gentle hearts needing to flow with the momentum of it all while knowing that there would always be parts in and out of their hands. Three people who lived this joint dream to its greatest possible potential. Yes, there rode the decade of our valiant twenties, being carted away by a brave, young kid who was eager and ready to fight the good fight that we had just seen through.

In the dust that settled, our new, individual dreams were now uncovered and begging us to gain the courage needed to drive separately forward into a new world. This was our place of parting... *and* our starting to see who we might each be out on our own.

The experience of having a theater company in tow, an evolving and dissolving memory, we each rowed into new waters. One of us returned to New York and moved on to Boston. And me? By way of New York City and Rochester, I would eventually be held in between the other two... flying solo in the palm of Providence.

⌘

How have your dreams/passions evolved over time?

How can your Compassionate Creativity help you to refresh these dreams in some way today? What learning from the past would you like to bring along?

57. Remembering that you must choose to create. No one is going to do it for you.

Saxtons River, Vermont to New York, New York. 2010.

Three weeks before my second solo show went up, I had nothing. Or what seemed like nothing, and I was at my wits end. Throughout the past year I'd been gathering beautiful, ancient household objects from thrift stores and barns throughout Vermont:

- *An old wooden ironing board (one of the neatest pieces of architecture I have ever seen)*
- *1 little blue suitcase containing an old red rotary phone (Heavy)*
- *1 larger tan suitcase*
- *1950's dress, apron, and jacket*
- *A clothes-line (the kind with the metal wheels)*
- *A coat tree or two*
- *Little wooden chair*
- *A slide projector (that worked!)*

And in order to ensure that I'd actually make it, rather than just having these objects gather dust, I entered my dream of a new show into a solo festival in New York City, describing it thus:

A fifties housewife alone. Neighbors ready to help. Circus. Fiddling. Time-travel. A road trip to everyone's dream world and the struggle when they are all forced to come back to reality. Told through everyday objects and breath-taking physical feats, Delusions of Grandeur is a beautiful, quirky story that questions the will to go on and the fear of joy when faced with unprecedented grief.

The idea was interesting, but when I went to play with it in the studio, it stayed an idea. It didn't want to live and I couldn't force it. And yet, the tickets were already being sold. We all had this show on our calendar, but if the audience only knew...

I'm not a person who writes a script chronologically A-Z and then performs that exact alphabet. As you've probably already realized from reading this book, I'm more of a collage artist. I research images, colors, time periods, and music. I write a little. I play with objects. I improvise different characters. I scribble exciting discoveries on Post-it notes and see how they might connect. Eventually I see one of them as an M that could go before a Z and happen sometime after an A. And although I had begun to accumulate some great Post-it notes during my process, something just wasn't working. It wasn't coming together. Every time I tried to be the housewife or create a scene with her neighbors or fiddle a tune, it just didn't feel right. No matter how many hours I spent trying to figure it out, the ideas remained separate, disconnected: 1950s. Housewife. Violin. Objects. Each an overwhelming island unto itself and I was drowning in their murky waters while madly trying to swim between them, the festival sitting on the horizon.

One night I came to a standstill. Sitting amidst the rubble, I debated whether to cancel the show. What would it mean to take it off the calendar?

In the same moment, one of my company members popped through to see how it was going. "Well, the truth is…" he shrugged (realizing I really didn't have much to show for the amount of time I'd been spending in the studio), "The truth is… you are obsessed with these objects. Every shop owner in a forty-mile radius can attest to that. So why don't you try to write a jingle for each one? That seems like something one might do in the 1950s."

Part of me wanted to scream after him, "Stay! You do it! You write the jingles! Help me!" But this was my show. A *solo* show. And it was already after midnight. Why was I doing solo work again?

I took a breath and embarked on his recommended train of thought. Attempting his suggestion without judgment or attachment, I looked at the objects and started to spout jingles for them. Whatever came to me. I rhymed. I laughed. I felt ridiculous. But what did I have to lose? I discovered a jingle for the red phone as I dialed some numbers. I created an award-winning caricature commercial for the ironing board, and soon after arrived a radio talk-show ad for the suitcases. As I repeated the themes of my new melodies, I began to lose track of the time, and although it was the middle of the night in 2010, I was engrossed in an afternoon during the middle of the last century:

In a time in between wars
Before Velcro on shoes or blinkers on cars
Let alone Hula hoops, Dr. Seuss, or the pill

When segregation was legal and Stalin fell ill
The first eight McDonalds were built with such care
Seat belts were invented and smog filled the air
Lego peace symbols were built by Playboys
Betty Crocker and Barbie sang Elvis with poise
Taking remote control of a new color TV
Choose Ed Sullivan, Sputnik or Howdy Doody
With microwave supper and office cigarette in hand
Suburbia opened its doors alongside the famed Disneyland.

My shoulder held the phone to my ear and I listened, wrapping my fingers in cord, holding the receiver with my other hand. Who was on the other end and what were they trying to tell me?

In all of my ditties there seem to be a common veneer. A sarcastic tone. A raise of the eyebrow. A shrug of the shoulders. Something that was being referred to without actually being spoken out loud. Some kind of secret. And guilt. Yes! I rummaged through the 1950s research that had been rolling around in my mind for months. I looked to my Post-it notes:

"Always greet the members of your family when you enter and always bid them goodbye when you leave."

"I'm still alive and on channel 5!"

Father Baker's Infant Home, Lackawanna, NY

"Your one goal in life is to have a family. You keep the house running smoothly with style and ease. You believe a woman's job is to take care of her family. You throw one hell of a Tupperware party." (The Good Wife's Guide in Housekeeping Monthly, May

13, 1955)

What was happening in Buffalo at that time? *Father Baker's Infant Home!* I ripped that post-it note off the wall. The pinballs started to bing. Father Baker's: An orphanage. "If you don't behave, I am going to send you to Father Baker's," even my parents threatened decades later when I was a kid. Father Baker's: A place where girls from all over the country were sent to have a baby out of wedlock only to return home without a trace. With a secret. Father Baker's: A place I drove by all the time. A huge basilica just down the street from Lackawanna Steel. A neighborhood once booming with workers. With nuns. A secret.

Lord, forgive me for I have sinned.
And seem to keep on sinning ever since.
I just knew I liked him.
And he liked me.
And he made me feel so special.
Like I had this special secret.
Now I do.
Oh God, do I ever.
I'm so sorry, Mom.

I started to see all that was there. A nurse. A girl. Roommates. Fear. Joy. Forced to return to reality. Babies. Children. Grown-ups. Separation. Heartache. Snow. Secrets upon secrets upon lives that would be lived in all directions. Never turning back. I started writing:

Whatever it is that's been growing in there...
It's been moving around and talking to me now.
Real quiet... Late at night when everyone else has gone to sleep...

It's been telling me things.
Like "Don't worry. "
And "You're not alone."
"Not any more."
It says it's real happy in there.
Inside me?
That's disgusting!
I don't even know what's in there besides my dinner…
Then, when I think I must be dreaming…
It comes straight out and asked me, "What's it like?"
What's it like out here.
And I didn't want to answer.
I never talked back to it before.
Besides, why should I be the one telling it about the world?
I've never even been to the other side of town before now.
Where have we been?
What have we done?

Nothing but bad things lately…

But it keeps asking.
Night after night.

When I woke up, I saw how the story could fit together. The islands merged further. A new Pangaea. I talked to myself out loud on the way to rehearsal. I was in the thick of it now… "Hi, my name is Lila," I kept saying in this angry tone. But who was Lila and why was she so angry? It was as if she was introducing herself at an AA meeting or something. A funeral. Or… a concert? Yes! Totally! What if she was a kind of rock star wannabe character who played the violin?

I ran out of my car and into the studio. How was Lila related to the girl in the infant home? Was it her mother? But did her mother keep her? I improved further:

"It's real nice out here," I said.
"It's real nice outside in the summertime. No snow.
The birds sing sweet in the morning.
And people are nice too. Usually.
They like to help each other.
And teach each other things.
And eat together.
This world is so big and I've only known this tiny piece of a tiny piece of it.
But I want to see it. I want to see it all.
Meet every person.
See every place...."

And then she asked me, "Would you take me with you?"
"Of course," I said, "Of course I will."

I picked up my violin (which, mind you, I had brought to every rehearsal wanting so badly for years to include it in my theater but couldn't figure out how). I held the violin close like a baby and began to sing a song that hung on one of the post-it notes, Hobo's Lullaby by Goebel Reeves:

Go to sleep you weary hobo.
Let the town pass slowly by.
Listen to the steel rails hummin'
That's a hobo's lullaby.

I quickly searched to see what other verses people had sang. Two weeks later, I shared my findings with the audience as the end of the performance, accompanied by layers of layers of violin harmonies, generations and generations coming into view:

Don't you think about tomorrow.
Let tomorrow come and go.
Tonight you have a nice warm boxcar.
Safe from all that wind and snow.

⌘

What was a time when you didn't believe that you could make something but somehow you did? What was the turning point?

What do you consider to be your art these days? How do you continue to practice it no matter what?

58. Inventing your own specialization.

New York, New York. 2010-2013.

"You are going to get a call in five minutes. Tell them yes."

A month later, thanks to my mentor and colleague and friend who was unavailable for the job, I was on the nineteenth floor of a building in Midtown Manhattan training an Off-Broadway company. They were a lovely group of people who were open to play during training week but when they went into rehearsals, there was a different ethic. Now fixed on the task and deadline of presenting a show, there was a seriousness and rigidness that I hadn't experienced with them before.

Everyone had an assigned role and not just in the script. In addition to the actors, there were directors and designers and a stage manager. As a creator of my own work, working in ensemble-based practices, I was used to being all of these things at the same time. In the processes I had previously worked in, as an actor it was okay to give the director your idea. It was normal that the stage manager would warm up with the cast, but here, when I asked for ideas or invited the stage manager into the circle, everyone looked at me like I was speaking a foreign language.

My role for this particular show was to be the Assistant

Director, a role that is a bit challenging to define. You don't want to do too much but you don't want to do too little. Sometimes it just involves watching until you are given a task and then you jump to it. My main assignment became to figure out how to stage a man being pulled out of a well. The director had no idea how to do this and was happy to leave the room and hand this part over to me. I was so excited to work on this with the cast.

I came in with some exercises that we would all play together to incrementally discover ways that we could pull the man out of the well. I started by asking the cast to create a soundscape of noises they associated with the man trapped in the well. They reluctantly started to make sounds but quickly one of the men raised his hand and asked what this was about, where this was all leading. I explained that I knew, but I didn't know. In that moment, it became apparent to me that not knowing was not okay in this rehearsal room.

"We only have three weeks to get this three-hour play together," said the director.

Oh right, I thought, *This is all about being efficient.* That day I took one of the brooms from the corner and started to help the stage manager clean up. She looked at me as if I was an alien and took the broom from my hands: "Thank you, but I don't want your help. It's not your job."

But in the theater, didn't everyone help with everything? Maybe not. In this room, everyone focused on what they were assigned to do, and everyone trusted one another based on the assigned roles. No one made suggestions on someone else's territory. I perceived limitations in this. It wasn't the atmosphere I preferred to work in, but how could I thrive in it? How could I learn to be the expert of my assigned task? How was I going to stage getting this character out of a well? If I came in with authority and presented my vision, I had no doubt that the actors would fully commit to making it happen. But without collaboration and play, how was I going to figure this out? This was new.

I cut out pieces of paper and moved them around as if they were the actors, but this didn't help at all. I wasn't a choreographer. I didn't want or like to set things on people. I wanted to facilitate a process for them to discover it for themselves. To know where the impulse came from. To have a stake in the process.

That night after rehearsal I stayed in the studio for hours. I became all the actors experimenting with ways to pull the man out of the well. I stacked boxes. I pulled on ropes. I rolled around on the floor. The next day I came in with a plan. If I believed in it, they would too.

The scene became a great success. It was imaginative and cinematic. When I saw the audiences on the edge of their seats as they watched the ropes being pulled in all directions until a man finally emerged from the well, I was proud.

"Do you want to work on another show this season?"

"Yes, and I would like to be the Movement Designer," I said without hesitation.

That night I went home and wrote out my responsibilities as a Movement Designer and emailed the director to let him know what he could expect from me in that role: physical conditioning, building ensemble, constructing a movement vocabulary, character physicality, broadening the actors' ranges, helping actors to sustain characters over a long period of time, creating innovative movement sequences, and consistently using language that encourages company members that physical work is not a separate component of the process, but rather a necessary part of the whole that only leads to a more dynamic piece for the audience.

And as a Movement Designer, with as much or as little time that I was given, I travelled around reintroducing the spirit of play into the plays.

⌘

What is your specialization? What does it lead you to do?

How can you find ways to share this role more often?

59. Considering that something that ends could be a success.

New York City to Vermont and back to Hamburg, New York. December 2010.

Later that winter, I decided to end my relationship of close to six years. The one with the feather. The one that started with a wish and turned into a company.

I often wonder how I left the driveway that snowy afternoon. *What was it that actually made me get in the car and go? How did I leave that relationship of six years and keep leaving?*

We had recently moved back to New York City from Vermont. We were both reconnecting to our career paths and it brought us to a real crossroads.

"I fell in love with the you that was so many different you's," I remember him saying, "But if you've figured out that you want to just be one of those you's, then go for it. That's not what I want. That's not who I am."

So we went on dates for two weeks. We talked things out and mutually decided that we weren't sure about our next step together or otherwise, so we thought we'd try something new. Being apart. We thought that this would teach us what was best.

Everyone was so upset that we had broken up, which didn't help. It was close to the holidays, and everyone thought it might go the other way, so there were a lot of questions. People wanted to know whose fault it was and why, why, why, we would do such a thing.

But when something ends, there is never any easy way to explain it. The two people within a relationship are the only ones who can know all of the details. The layers. The stickiness. Exactly what led to what... and even then, there is my story and his story and then the truth (or something like it).

I would tell people that we weren't giving up. That we were truly calling it good. That this parting was a great thing that we had ultimately decided together. That there was no drama. That it wasn't anyone's fault. We had, in the simplest terms, had a good run with many beautiful ovations and encores, and we were now closing this show and seeing what wanted to happen next. It sounded simple, and although amicable, the months and years that followed would not be easy.

The relationship wasn't him or me. In that moment we met long ago, we had begun to create a third thing in the middle. In the space between us. We were both in our early twenties. I was leaving California and he was passing through. I was the assistant for a summer workshop and he was a student. By the time we both returned east, we were in love and moved in together within months. The relationship then took on a life of its own and had been evolving ever since. We created a theater company, became part of each other's families, traveled together, shared finances, had two cats. When we went separate ways, the relationship didn't stop. It fractured into many pieces, and continued to live on in our hearts (and all those who knew us). Each piece reflecting different ideas of what was, what is, and what could have been. A prism of hopes, joys, disappointments, possibilities.

Looking back to that moment in the driveway, what got me to get in the car and go was reconciling with the fact that this relationship wasn't a failure, but rather that it was a grand success.

⌘

What is something that had a good run in your life and then came to a close?

How can you remember that time fondly today?

FIFTH MOVEMENT: AN INTERLUDE FOR LOVE

Connect with your Compassionate Creativity by...

60. Receiving the love that you are given.

Hamburg, New York. 2010-2011.

I arrived to my mom's house on Christmas Eve with my most important belongings in tow and stepped into my childhood room. Since I had been away, this space had become more of a storage room than a bedroom. I couldn't quite tell what was mine or what was other people's stuff: my grandma's, my dad's, my grandpa's. This was "drop-off-and-move-on-without-looking-back" space.

I cleared a space for my suitcase and plopped it down on the futon. There waiting for me was a package from my dear friend and colleague who lived in Oregon. She was the only one who I had really updated along the way of this break-up, and I recalled at one point she did ask me for my mom's address.

Inside the box were a card and a Christmas present. "I hope that this can help you as it has helped me throughout the years," I read before unwrapping the present: a book by Pema Chödrön called *When Things Fall Apart*: *Heart Advice for Difficult Times.*

"Wow. Here I go," I thought, "Things had fallen apart and this is surely the beginning of a whole new chapter."

As I gratefully flipped through the book (which I would read and reference and recommend hundreds of times over the next few years), these words jumped out: "When the lake has no ripples, everything in the lake can be seen. When the water is all churned up, nothing can be seen."

Everything was churned up alright. Murky and confused. I wished I could be anywhere else: fast-forward or rewind, but not here. *What should I do next?*

"Don't make any major decisions three weeks before or after any major transition," I recalled a teacher/friend saying years before.

I shut the book, lay down on my bed and stared at the ceiling.

"Listen to your body," chimed in my teacher from Vermont.

I inhaled – afraid to listen, afraid of what I would find. I closed my eyes and exhaled:

"Why did I do this?" asked my head.

"I don't feel so good…" ached my heart.

"Don't worry, everything is going to be okay," said my head.

"Everything *is* okay," responded my gut.

"Really?"

"Really."

In making theater, I always started by naming the knowns and unknowns. Here is what I knew:

- *I would be in Buffalo for two weeks.*
- *Next I would go to Rochester to work on a show for the semester.*

I would stay in a room that my friend from college was offering me, which happened to be around the block from the house of the bat incident many years ago. *What I didn't know, or rather wanted to know, was:*

- *What I was going to do after that.*
- *How I was going to continue to make money.*
- *Where I was going to or wanted to live.*

How it was going to be, surviving in the world for the first time ever on my own.

First things first: I would be in Buffalo for the next two

weeks, and this house, this room, was going to be much more of a home base from now on. *How could I make it my own again? How could I make it feel welcoming?*

I loved setting up spaces and always nested quickly in places all over the world throughout all of my touring. How could I do that here? The space felt cluttered and heavy and abandoned. The wallpaper was the same Notre Dame wallpaper that I had chosen in the eighth grade. The glue stain reminders from that high-school project still remained in the same spot on the yellow carpet.

Like this space, my insides felt cluttered. A very churned-up lake. Feelings and times were fragmented and separated out into boxes and randomly placed on dusty shelves. I myself wanted a new, clear start. *If I transformed the space, how might it help to transform me?* Yes, my room was about to be the only room in the house that had clean, white walls.

I told my mom what I planned to do, and she excitedly agreed to help and offered to buy a new rug too. She gathered her old wallpapering supplies from the garage, while I cleared all of the stuff into her room.

"What do I do next?" I asked her remembering that she had her own wallpapering business for over fourteen years.

"Start peeling," she smiled, "Like this…"

The actual walls of this room hadn't seen the light of day in a long, long time and getting them there wasn't going to be an easy task, but little by little the Fighting Irish turned into pink flowers which eventually revealed patches of light green paint.

This process continued every day for over a week. I peeled and remembered. And remembered and peeled. This was the room that held me when I got in trouble and was grounded. It was where I first practiced violin. It's where I had my first sleepovers. The dresser drawers held hundreds of collected rocks. This was where I grew up.

When I got to the part behind the door I discovered some mysterious pencil lines. This wasn't something I recalled doing, but apparently I had measured everyone in the house: our hamster and our dog Beckett (on four legs and two), my brother, myself, my mom, and some of my babysitters and friends. I wondered where they all were now. What they were doing and how they had grown. As I kept peeling, I noticed that high above the rest was one more line labeled "My Dad." Yes, my dad was 6'4" and there was the proof.

I remembered dancing on his feet and sitting on his lap. I wished he could be here now to help me figure out what to do next.

"It's better to have loved and lost than never to have loved at all," he had quoted Tennyson to me once, long, long ago.

Remembering all of this made me feel angry and happy and sad and lost and found all at the same time. On the way to becoming clear, these walls and waters were sure becoming messier.

Once I got to the closet, I came upon a box full of cards and letters. I took a break to read old birthday cards, letters, and thank you notes given to me by friends and family from throughout the years. Every word was a comfort, an embrace as I continued to paint the walls white. A blank canvas. An old space made new.

Boxes cleared and a new rug in, I laid out my most essential belongings along the floor. Carefully choosing between what wanted to stay, what I wanted to take with me, and what I was ready to throw away, I cobbled together a kind of altar of my most precious things: little reminders of who I am, where I've been, and what I care about. This colorful collage of gifts and trinkets, rocks and seashells, notes and memories has traveled with me ever since, and when I look at it, I feel full of all the love I've ever been given.

⌘

How do the words of an old friend still resonate for you today?

How could keeping a folder or creating a space of these tokens help you at times when you need to remember all the love you have been given?

61. Witnessing evolution.

Rochester, New York. January 2011.

After dropping my stuff off at my new place in Rochester, my housemate and I agreed to go sit at our tree... the one we all used to visit and climb in and sit below while moving through college. The place I went to be quiet. To feel at home. To feel the world pass by and wonder how I wanted to be a part of it.

"I'm back!" I was ready to call to it. "Thanks for holding down the fort!"

But as my housemate and I drove round the bend, we didn't see the tree. Silent, we stepped out of the car and down the hill. Its once high limbs lay along the ground in every direction. My heart beat heavy.

"Let's not let this mean anything," I said.

"Let's let it mean everything," my housemate responded.

Later that night, settling into my new abode in this old place, these words made their way to the page:

A late night drive
The falling snow
Illuminated streetlights

Old one-way roads
A quiet campus
Winter breaking
Once a student
Now a teacher
Returning
Arriving.

Through the signal
A sight to see
A change in shape
The aged vision of glory
I remembered
Now with branches askew.

Jaw dropping
Pedal stopping
Down the slope
There she sits
One love of my life
A few perhaps
The place we'd perch
Redhead and goose
A boy called JB
Climb
Rest
Or take in the world at war
Beside a riverbank.

Wind
Breath
Now split in two
Due to such magnificence

And horizontal weight
There she lays
Lies
Heavy
Covered in new snow
An angel
With the same angles
Lowered simply to the ground
Halved.

When and how
And bless the one who decided not to
Whisk her away from here
To leave a gaping landscape
Where once stood a majestic beauty
Arms outstretched for all
Night and day
Spring and fall.

She must have become too tired
Of holding herself up
Who doesn't?

One day
Not long ago
She gave in to taking rest
Upon the earth
Her mother
Years and years gone by
Roots still intact
Now serene
A moment of silence

For a different position in space.

We get out of the car
Walking closer
Breathing this in.

All akimbo
Surprised
Unbooted feet sliding toward her
A gasp
Our smiles.

A dinosaur
A grand ship
A woman legs crossed.

A tree
The tree
Our tree
Fallen
Now ready to grow leaves
Of a different sort.

⌘

Where are the special places you go to feel at peace? How have those places changed over time?

Tell the story of a time when you unexpectedly saw something in a new form. How did it mark a change in you?

62. Creating and articulating your boundaries.

Throughout the Northeast. 2011.

People in the theater, or so long as I've experienced it, easily fall in love with each other. There is such passion seeping out of every corner. And when someone is authentically being himself or herself, it's hard not to fall in love with them. When someone genuinely cares and invests time into getting to know you, it's hard not to be attracted to them. But, are you actually falling in love with the other person or rather with the rare feeling, the connection that lights up in you when you are around them? Am I in love with this person or am I in love with the theater I'm making with them or both? Very tricky territory with many possibilities to act on. Many choices. It's one thing when you're in school, but it's another thing when you are a working woman.

This was the first time I was single in the real world and in the professional world of theater. Before this moment I had become accustomed to showing up to work with my partner or knowing that my partner was at home. Either way, I had a partner, so having a romantic relationship with someone else that I was working with was never part of the equation, and I simply focused on the work at hand. The conversation stopped there. By being partnered straight out of graduate school and throughout my twenties, I now saw that there was a whole other interesting and complicated layer that I had been missing out on and had never taken into consideration.

I felt like I suddenly had a neon sign on my head that blinked "Single" and attracted all sorts of new insects and critters. Was I making it blink? Did I have control of it at all? People's motives quickly became questionable. Did they hire me because they liked my work or because they were attracted to me or some of both? What did they expect out of this relationship? What did I expect? If I got a late night drink with them at the conference did that mean something other than a good networking chat? The waters only became murkier and messier.

For someone who genuinely loved everything and everyone, this was going to be an important boundary to learn to identify and articulate; otherwise I was inadvertently going to hurt people or end up being hurt by them. How could I express how much I loved working with someone, but that I wasn't and was never going to be in love with them? How could I be excited and passionate without having that misconstrued for something else? How could I hug the lighting designer at the end of the night without everyone starting to question my motives? What kind of reputation did I want to have and how was I going to work to protect it and myself?

⌘

What is a boundary you would like to set for yourself in some area of your life? What steps do you need to take to make that clear for yourself? For others?

63. Looking to be surprised.

Rochester, New York. February 2011.

When I took the day off to rest, I started to feel all the things I hadn't been feeling while I was at rehearsal. Suddenly I became highly aware of my loneliness, and I wasn't quite sure what to do with it. Rather than isolating myself, I decided to take a drive and see what happened:

I sit bayside
On the Great Lakes
Playing hooky
For some rest and reflection
Only I would decide to go to the beach
On one of the coldest days of the year.

Footprints on the lake
Trees bare
A little sun peeking through
As the snow still falls.

I am reminded of the winter of my heart
A much needed hibernation
That at the moment feels like
One level above hell
But I'm not falling

Where is the net coming from?

Don't ask so many questions
While being given so many offerings
In a time of such need
Such loneliness.

A man sits along in the booth across from me
Glasses on
Watching the Packers
And reading a book entitled
"The Times are Never so Bad"
Ice fishermen cuss at the bar.

As a woman sings the national anthem
The man in the booth speaks
"Are you from around here?"
"No. You?"
"No, not really."
"Can I join you?"
Moving plates
Two hours are what follows
Sharing stories of separations
Beginning around Christmas Eve
A number of siblings
Ways to write
The end of the pier
Another much welcomed surprise
To the waiter too, I'm sure.

We talk and talk
Not just about the weather

And he obligingly pays both checks
A mozzarella stick halved
A cold walk to the car
A breath of this life
Not seeming quite as cold
As before the tackle-and-bait menu.

A hug.

The word "magical" surfaces.
Yes, agreed
Happiness does exist around every corner
If only one is open to it
Which is especially difficult
And more special somehow
In the dregs of this winter
In Western New York.

⌘

What is something that surprised you today? This week? How did it wake you up/shift your perspective?

64. Assembling your own identity.

Rochester, New York. March 2011.

"Are you bi-sexual?" my mom asked over the phone after I referenced a friend who happened to date men and women. I didn't realize that becoming a single woman in my thirties would open me up to all sorts of new questions. At first I took some offense, but then I was grateful that my mom felt open enough to ask straight out. We had always had an open relationship and could basically talk about anything.

"No, I'm not," I responded. "Why?"

I recalled the time I cut my hair short before going to college and some people assumed I must be a lesbian.

"Well I'm just trying to understand it. How could someone like men and women? It's one or the other, isn't it?"

I didn't know how to explain sexuality; I only knew my experience of it so far.

"Well..." I said slowly to buy myself some time. "Did you like dad because he was a man or did you like dad because dad was dad?"

"Both, or I don't know... what do you mean?"

When there aren't defined categories, the world can get complex, but it also gives each individual a freedom to define themselves from inside instead of the outside and then articulate and express their own choices in whatever way they'd like. My mom's question helped me to wonder: How much of my identity had I taken for granted along the way? Had I ever actively decided to like men or did it just start happening at some point? Was monogamy something that I believed in and wanted or was it something I followed along with and accepted to be right as part of the status quo? Now out of the safety of a relationship, what did I actually believe in and want to actively decide on? What did I want to experiment with to better understand myself?

I hoped that someday there wouldn't be any categories and that people would just happily love people and everyone would be accepting of everyone else's current choice.

A couple years later, in exchange for help with a show, I spent time with my friend's son.

"He doesn't get along with everyone. If you have to bring him right back, it's okay."

Driving to the Children's Museum, I noticed that this kid was really into Pokémon. I didn't know much about Pokémon but I figured I could build our connection by fueling his enthusiasm with some great questions.

"What's your favorite one?"

He answered quickly with a name I didn't understand even though he proceeded to spell it quickly three times.

"Okay... Awesome! What's his power?"

"Kāli," he answered when we got to the next stop light, "Pokémon are genderless. Duh..."

Whoa... This ten-year-old just casually used the word genderless!!!

The world sure had come a long way. Now if only the computer would stop wanting to replace "themselves" with "his" or "her," we'd find our own Compassionate Creativity, let everyone be who they want to be, and happily skip along...

⌘

Remember a time when someone asked you a question about yourself, and you took offense. What insight might their question have raised for you?

65. Being kind and patient with yourself.

Rochester, New York. February 2011.

I receive an email from a friend in New Orleans: "It's been a really hard time for me and my family," he explains. His grief opens me up to my own, all of the changes over the past couple months. They have started to add up and weigh me down. Wanting to cheer up my friend, I cheered up myself up too:

Although welcoming a grand transition
My heart is heavy too
Confused
Bewildered
And so the new work begins
Sits waiting for me at the end of task-filled days.

I'll remind myself now as I remind you
These times are not meant to be easy.
Change and resistance always want to be friends
And nothing feels like it is enough.

Although microscopic at points
I'm sure moving pieces are still uttering "Onward ho!"
While beginning to release some of this to the gods.

I encourage us not to make do but to let be
Not inhaling pent up and staying at home there
Rather exhaling and stepping outdoors
Simply healing.

They might seem hidden right now
But otherwise little boxes with secret surprises
Do exist around every corner especially for you
Seek them out
Smiling hands and funny faces saying
"Don't worry baby
Be happy.
It's gonna be alright."

Listen closely here:

You are enough, my friend.
You are enough.
You are enough.

And you, you are pretty damn amazing.

Just make sure that you are continuing to offer yourself
The same kindness and patience that you always offer to others.

⌘

In what way can you give yourself some extra kindness and
patience today?

What surprises do you notice when you give yourself this gift?

Please feel free to share this poem with someone today.

66. Creating your own day of rest.

Hilton Head, South Carolina. February 2011.

"I have always been fascinated by the Jewish Sabbath," I thought as I drove from Atlanta toward the Atlantic.

Sundown Friday to sundown Saturday as a separate, sacred time with no work. *Sabbath,* like the word *sabbatical,* derives from the Hebrew word for *hibernation.*

With a couple days in-between gigs, I stopped at a friend's empty condo in Hilton Head. Along these new shores of South Carolina, I spent a solid twenty-four hours hibernating from technology. These were my Sabbath provisions:

- o Only spending money on perishables and experiences.

- o No use of major machinery (cars, cooking, etc.)

- o No looking at screens of any kind.

- o Only communicating with people in-person.

- o Only understanding time by the sun in the sky.

I proceeded to rent a bike for the day and biked along the Atlantic toward the Hilton Head lighthouse where I ended up parasailing with a family I had never met, and joined a kayak tour through alligators. Although I noticed my impulses to take photos and share my experiences with people who weren't there, I didn't. I felt afraid not having my phone with me, but quickly realized that I would get along fine (I had lived a wonderful life in the days before cell phones!).

When I returned to the condo, there was only more time in the day. I wrote letters to people I had been meaning to reach out to for years. Some I later sent and others I didn't.

Here is my final reflection at the close of the day:

I sit here now
My mind a house
Full of old used things
Amongst the living
Experiencing every moment
Some 800 feet above water
Meeting a 1955 Rochester graduate
In a next-door rocking chair
A hot dog under a tree
Spending time with myself
Open to others
Not buried in a screen
And so I reflect
I write
Lucky and grateful
For one of the longest
Fullest
Easeful
But in ways difficult
Days I've had thus far

There needs to be this 24-hours
Experiencing human interaction
Reconnecting
Going with the flow
The joy
The fears
That readiness
A love of life
This gift to myself that
I keep giving to others.
Happy New Year.

⌘

What would your "Sabbath" provisions be? How could you experiment with these provisions – even for an hour? How does this shift your relationship with yourself and the world around you?

67. Appreciating the people in the room.

Rochester, New York to New York City. March 2011.

It was the biggest relief to have my solo show presented as part of a theater's season for the first time. Being presented meant that my only role would be to show up and focus on performing the play. The rest – booking the space, getting the press listings, and selling the tickets (which I was used to doing too) – was all up to the staff of the theater that hired me.

Graduate school feeling like eons away, my company folded and my relationship ended, this was also my first time ever on the road by myself. Independent, I arrived in Midtown Manhattan, unloaded the suitcases one by one and carted them up the ramp and onto the stage. Everything had its position, its perfect place. I felt the light on my eyelashes, and I was home again in the theater. I was ready for my two-week run, ready for my breakthrough, and ready to get reviewed by the *New York Times*.

When doing a show, especially in New York City, one can easily become fixated on hitting it big by getting butts in seats and good reviews. The usual guidelines are as follows: You need to do at least a two-week run so there are multiple opportunities to see it and gain momentum. On the first week, you give away tickets to friends and critics. You hope that they spread the good word and write good articles so that your second weekend is full. Then, if you are lucky, the show is extended or picked up by another theater or agent. There is no such thing as making it. You merely ride out each wave of success for as long as you can and then you do it all over again.

That afternoon upon leaving the theater, I found out that somewhere along the way someone at the theater had dropped the ball and the press releases went out too late. Ticket sales were low for the beginning and end of the run and no critics had reserved tickets. Beyond the people I had contacted, no one knew about this show. It's hard enough to get people to come when it's one of a thousand shows playing that weekend. It's a lot harder when it's not even listed.

I hastily made my way out to a friend's vacant apartment in Brooklyn. On the train, I brainstormed all of the press contacts I could email and call when I arrived at my stop, but by the time I got there, I had to give over to the fact that it was just too late. The show went up tomorrow and whoever was going to come, was going to come. There was nothing more I could do but commit to doing the performance. Whether for audiences of forty or five, no longer could I focus on what the reviews might say or how this gig could lead to the next bigger one. These two weeks couldn't be about the people who weren't in the room. It had to be about the people who were.

The next night I set out my make-up and costume pieces in a dressing room that accessed the stage by climbing two stories down an old fire escape behind the stage. Before leaving, I caught a glimpse of myself in the mirror. Alone. Ready. I never meant to do solo work, I thought, but here I am.

This is who I am. This is all I have for you.

After each performance, I invited the few people out to a bar and opened the conversation up to their feedback, to their own stories. Some of the people I knew, others I met for the first time. Some of their suggestions I took, some I pondered. Others I put in my back pocket as an idea for a future show. Every night I rode the subway home, and sitting among the other late-night passengers, I made changes to my piece, finding little ways to make it better, to try some new things out.

On the second weekend, a girl I had grown up with showed up in the audience. She brought her best friend and each of their five-year-old sons. My friend, now fifteen years older than I remember her being, explained how she currently lived in Florida and that this was the first vacation she had taken in a long time. "Wow," I remember saying, so surprised to see her after so many years, "Thanks for coming. How did you happen to be in New York at the same time?"

"We came to see your show," she replied, "I wouldn't have missed it for the world."

This was the most beautiful kind of breakthrough that I could have possibly had.

"Thank you for being here." I have now said to countless

surprise visitors like this throughout the years, "You have no idea how much it means to me that you are here. You are why I continue to do this work. Thank you."

⌘

Who believes in you? How do you know they do? How does their support help you to believe in yourself? How can you thank them more often?

68. Befriending your fears.

May 2011. Buffalo, New York to London, England.

As soon as I drive down the highway or turn on the television, I am bombarded with more reasons to be afraid… Huge "bears" on the front page of every newspaper and billboard screaming: "Oh Shit! Run!" or "Let's go get 'em!" and I just want to say *no, please no, stop. Please.* We've paid in centuries of pain by reacting hastily to every *Oh Shit Moment…* This will not help anyone or anything. I can't fight or flight my way into healing or peace, no. Fight or flight only elicits more fight or flight. War will not bring about justice. War will only teach and preach more war. And if there's a war going on outside of me, you'd better bet that there's one going on inside of me too. How do I begin to look at my fears and take responsibility for what I can?

Fear
A funny thing
Eh
That
Taking us unknowingly by the hand
Leading us somewhere we didn't
Nope
We didn't quite want to
Want to go

Or perhaps
Maybe
Making us sit down
Down
Down
When we had meant to stand up
Up
Up
Convincing us outright
To run away
Far far away
From the one we love
So sorry
Or to battle a country we had thought as friend
Too bad
We can
Yep
Unwrap it like a candy
This fear
Give it a taste and go on our way
Yum
Yum
Or turn it into a ball of
Of
Of
Twisted rubber bands
Overlapping
Colorful
Beautiful even.

Oh the stories we can tell ourselves
Tangling us with tension all the live long day

Long
Long
I'm afraid you will leave me
Also scared I'll get sick
Then what
Whispering
I wish I wasn't alone
Or that the garbage truck didn't come
Or that detour
That president
That
This
That
But no matter what or where or how
Yes
Yes
Yes
We can calendar
And tailor
And tuck in
And be on time
We say yes
And I do
And go team
And then go
And then go.

But when do we sit
Looking straight into the
Vast or the little of the I don't know
Before
Aw man

And oh shit
And wait what.

Panic ensues
And we fall in love with the freak out
Out
Out
The pattern
And how could she
And why would he
And then what
What
What
What if
Or if
Or if.

Okay calm down
Turn on some music
Have a glass of wine
And welcome this thing in
This fear
Good evening gorgeous
Greet it at the door with open eyes
Joke and give it a wink
And converse
Freely
About the tricks of the trade
And at the end of the night
You know
I know you
So

What do we have to lose
And so and so
And so.

I am terrified of being up so far off the ground. Up in the air. On a plane. If you didn't already know this about me, you would learn quite quickly when convincing me to go to the airport or when giving me a major pep talk in order to get me to my gate. Sure, you might quote all of the statistics, how much safer we will be up there than here in the car and all that, but I've heard it all before and it doesn't really help. There is no such thing as fearless. With life there will always be death and I could stay in my room and hide out or I could continue my great love affair with being alive.

In every world traveler lives an agoraphobic homebody
In every well-known performer such unrelenting stage fright
In every tightrope walker or skyscraping window washer a fear of heights so vast.

And yet
And yet
And yet.

There also lives a love so great
For the world
The audience
The sky
That they merge their love and fear into wonder
Somehow managing to majestically soar on.

⌘

What are the things that you fear?

How can your fears remind you of what you love and cherish?

69. Finding your own meaning of home and how to create it wherever you go.

London, England. 2011.

I awake, hazy, still jet-lagged, to a kitchen where the woman doing dishes wears a t-shirt that reminds me she was also "Born in Buffalo." I eat breakfast with my aunt, drink tea, and catch up. We talk anew and reminisce.

I visited her here in London many years ago, and I remember riding along the Thames and realizing that I was meeting my aunt for the first time – in the place that she had chosen to live and be and work and love. Walking on *her* streets. Having *her* show me about. Free, excited, light.

My aunt is a teacher. She has lived in London for twenty years working with deaf children and their families. Now, mind you, this is nearly just as long a time as she spent growing up in Buffalo. Her voice now lilts with upward inflecting sounds. It is really as if she has become British herself. She now throws things out in the *rubbish*, puts groceries in the *boot* of her car and she and her beautiful, Tai Chi, printmaking *bloke* who I am honored to call an Uncle – own a *flat* in North London along the River Lea. They've built a grand life with friends and dinners and travels and seashells in the bathroom.

My aunt is playful. Singing when biking under bridges to hear the echo, making up stories about things when I ask questions she doesn't know the answer to. Open to hearing about all. Taking photos. Even ready to sport a clown nose. And without knowing it or needing to prove any kind of point, my aunt reminds me again today about where we are from: Buffalo, the people, the snow. That our beginnings stay with us... Not to weigh us down or to run away from, but rather as a beautiful springboard from which to wander the world and a gateway that welcomes us back.

Every year since she's left, my aunt flies from London to Buffalo for weeks at a time. She visits every household, plays cards, and runs the children's games at the annual family picnic. Sometimes her visits are the extra excuse to get people together for pizza and wings. Today, loving Buffalo while walking through London, she welcomes me into her other home... smiling, and sharing the sites with me once more.

⌘

Where do you consider your home to be?

What makes you feel at home there?

How do you take these qualities with you when you visit or move to new places?

70. Moving forward, onward.

Cromer, England. 2011.

So there I was, standing at the back of the crowded room against the bar, listening to the sweet, endearing reception speeches. My college roommate from freshman year had just gotten married to a wonderful man, and I had come to England to be her maid of honor for a simply perfect wedding. While hearing the reflections, my mind couldn't help but drift off to the relationship I had just ended. I looked out the window to the ocean. As I watched the waves crashing to the rocks below, my regrets started flooding in one by one, and I began to question every choice of the last six months, trying to figure out how things were better now, how I was moving forward.

My thoughts were suddenly interrupted when a random wedding guest ran up to me and starting hitting me in the back of my head. "Lady, lady," he whispered, "Your head is on fire!"

And thus it was. As my mind was busy pondering what might have been, my hair started to un-bobbypin, making its way down to meet a candle on the bar and burst into flames. Unsurprised that my angst-filled, burnt-out thoughts turned into smoke, I didn't panic. I was more embarrassed than anything. The last thing I wanted to do was to disrupt the reception with this silly incident, so I tried to draw as little attention as possible as the man helped me to put out the fire.

The only one who seemed to notice was the groom, as he was the only one who had been facing in our direction. "Are you okay?" he said after finishing the speech and making his way toward me.

"I am going to smile right now, let you know that I'm just fine, and ask that you walk away. We can both pretend that nothing happened and I will go up and give my speech, okay?"

I made my way to the front of the room, and ignoring the fact that the back of my head might very well look like a singed little dog, I focused on my amazing friend and her amazing love and had everyone raise a glass to the newlyweds new movement forward together.

As the rest of the night progressed, many nice conversations included the other person raising their eyebrows at some point with a "Do you smell that?" or "I could swear I smell something burning again. Do you?" I managed to excuse myself or tilt my head downwind of them and continued to enjoy the party.

The next morning, I woke up to the hideous smell of burnt hair, which reconnected me to my lament. Drowsily I made my way to the bathroom and because there was no one there to ask for advice or listen to my fuss, I simply started to cut. Inches of hair fell onto the floor. Once I was sure all the burnt parts were off, I picked up my regrets, tossed them into the garbage and I looked in the mirror. A fresh start. A new look. I raised one eyebrow: "Hey baby, wanna dance?"

Chin up and bags packed, my new doo and I boarded a plane destined for Rome.

⌘

What's something that you can't quite move forward from right now?

How can your Compassionate Creativity help you to navigate forward?

71. Discovering the quiet of your mind.

Rome, Italy. 2011.

Tired, overwhelmed, and in awe, I arrive in Rome. It wasn't the ancient city it once was, but rather a bustling modern city with cars zooming between tall buildings, piazzas, and the ruins of the Colosseum.

I check into my hostel and lay down listening to the sounds of this new place. I'm afraid to turn off the bedside lamp. I stare at the zigzag light it splays along the walls and listen to the city below. I don't know what to do, so I open my notebook and write:

Eyes floating like goldfish
Saying who knows what
Blinking for air
Thinking aside
Exhaustion dwells here.

Time goes like watercolor waves
Suspended like prayer flags
For a bed of her own.

Love happens just as life does
In spurts and sparks

And moves and moves
Constantly shifting
Redefining
Rekindling anew.

Eggshells cracking
Letting go of the reins
She winks to the world
Disassociates
Turns off the light
And readies for slumber.

The ticker of her mind
Goes through its usual motions
Check-lists
Would haves
Should've dones
Better ifs
Gears and cranks and locks and keys
Anything please
Some one or thing to rid her of the present chatter.

Wishes and wants
Travels and round the bends
Insects and darkness.
Patterns on the ceiling
Shadows along the wall...

The next morning I wake up afraid and ready to explore. This would be my first day out by myself in a place where I didn't speak the language. "If you feel overwhelmed, go into a church," a friend advised me before travelling.

After twelve hours, over 1000 steps, twenty-plus gnocchi, countless statues, 786 photos, and many retreats into the most incredible churches, I returned to my hostel, proudly shut the door and put the key on the table. What a beautiful city! What a beautiful world!

Readying for bed, I set my suitcase down on the table, I knocked my key onto the floor and out it went under my door.

"Oh shit!" I had locked the door with that key from the inside. That's the way doors worked here. Had I seriously just locked myself in a room and thrown away the key? I freaked out. There was no one else on this hallway. I would be lucky if the woman would come back at all the next morning, and I had to catch an early train to Tuscany for work. There was no phone, no internet, and I was on the sixth floor.

"If you feel overwhelmed, go into a church."

I look around the room. There was no church and sirens whizzed down the street, but I remembered the new feeling I found in all those churches today.

Everything is calm.
Everything is sacred.
Everything is sanctuary.
I am a church.

I grabbed the bedside lamp and put it on the floor. I saw the key about a foot away. I looked around my room. I saw a dresser, a bed, my bag... a hanger! I grabbed it, maneuvered it under the door, and wobbled it toward the key, but it didn't quite reach. *Dammit!*

I angrily stomped around the room. I looked out the window.

If only someone could see me now and get a good laugh.

But, no, this wasn't funny. This was serious. I took a breath and began again.

I am a clown. How do I play? How do I have the faith that everything will eventually connect?

I elongated the metal of the hanger with a pen cap and held the two together with a hair-tie. I tried again. *Yes!* The cap caught the edge of key. I gently slid it far enough under the door to be able to slide it the rest of the way with my finger and... Success! I once again held the key in my hand. I unlocked the door and stepped out in the hallway. I gave the wall a high-five, shut the door, locked it, and left the key in the lock ready for the next morning.

A celebration dance ensued around the room before I rechecked the key, laid my head down on my pillow, and full of gratitude and freedom, peace and quiet, I turned off the lamp:

...Oh how the inner-workings
Finally give way
And the earth spins round
Ever so gently
Tucking her in.

⌘

How do you find peace and quiet?

What do you do when this is challenged? How do you reconnect?

SIXTH MOVEMENT: A KIND OF PROVIDENCE

Connect with your Compassionate Creativity by...

72. Remembering that everything is a process, especially letting go.

Hamburg, New York to Providence, Rhode Island. 2011.

A good friend urged me to choose a word for my coming year. This came from a tradition each of her family members take part in on New Year's Eve or on their birthdays: "No matter what circumstances you end up in, this word will be with you. It will help to guide you this year," she explained to me over the phone, wanting to find something that would be consistent for me through so many impending changes, "You will find so many ways to relate to the word you choose. It will be a reminder of what's important to you, of what you originally intended for this year to be about."

That night I paged through the thesaurus.

After much deliberation, rather than continuing in Rochester, I decided to take a job in New England. *Decisive? Inhabit?*

This would be the first fuller-time work I would ever have. The first time I would teach for an entire semester. Three courses. The first time I would move somewhere for a job. *Commitment?*

This would be the first time I would live out in the world by myself. The only people I knew in Providence were the colleague who had hired me and his wife. The only time I had been there was to visit them and teach a workshop. *Ready? Open? Roost?*

"I'm still thinking of words," I wrote to my friend, "Inhabit, breathe, nurture... I want it to relate to staying in one place. Being strong by myself. Being clear, open, listening, articulate. Forward-moving. Letting be. But settling on just one word is tough."

She emailed me back with a little suggestion: "SETTLE."

Settle? I cringed at the sight of it. I hated this word. I mainly associated settle with *settling for* rather than continuing to pursue. I didn't want to settle at this point in my life. No way. This was not the end. It was the start of a new dream, a new way of being. "Settle" was most definitely not going to be my word.

I looked through the list of the definitions and found myself resisting every one, but when I got to the second-to-last line, I paused. Number thirteen read: *"To come to rest, as from flight. A bird settled on a bough."*

This image resonated with me. It was exactly what I wanted. This new place, Providence, could be my bough and making friends with the other definitions of this word, SETTLE, might help me to do just that…

1. To decide, arrange, or agree; to settle on a plan of action:

Even though the job was only for one semester, I decided to rent an apartment for a whole year. I rented a truck in Buffalo and shoved all of the important things that I would want to have with me at my new home. This place could, at least, become a base. A place to go from.

I unloaded the truck and began to take things out of boxes. Some things wanted to be put up on walls. Other things wanted to be put right back the box.

2. To gather, collect, or become fixed in a particular place, direction:

Over the week that followed, before starting my job, I drove around New England collecting the rest of my stuff. For five years I had lived between New York apartments and my ex-boyfriend's family's homes in Connecticut and Vermont. Although we had broken up nine months ago, we hadn't yet spent the time deciding who would keep what.

I went to Vermont on my own, found the last of my things there, and brought those things back to Providence. *Check!*

On the eve of a possible hurricane, I went to Manhattan and

met my ex-boyfriend at our apartment that was now his apartment. We agreed that some of the furniture and our two cats would now be my responsibility. Carrying each item down the six-story walk-up was no small task. Some things we carried together and others we took on our own. Maneuvering down the first flight of stairs, I was so glad to have that item back. During the second, I imagined how much easier it could have been if I could have driven by while he threw everything out the window. By the third, I wanted it all to be magically beamed up to its perfect new placement in Providence. By the fourth, I wished that I never had to see that item ever again, that I could just delete it from my life. By the fifth, I never wanted to see him again. But the time I got to the ground level, putting each item in my car, I was reminded how much I loved him still. Up and down, this cycle continued as we laughed and joked endeavoring to squeeze another wing chair down the stairwell and onto the street as the cats meowed.

Getting along this well brought about my ultimate fear: I thought that I wanted to get back together.

3. *To become firm or compact, as the ground:*

With trailer in tow, I followed him up to his parents' house in Connecticut where some of my belongings were still stored in the basement. The route there was a familiar one. We had done it together often, sometimes several times in a month. I remembered how much I loved his parents. I loved getting Chinese eggplant take-out with them and talking to his step-mom until all hours of the night. I loved squishing into their waterbed and watching murder mystery shows together or rooting for the Yankees. I loved their African

Grey Parrot and their old black lab. Over the last six years, these were the people that picked us up from the airport. They were my holiday plans. They were my home base, not Providence. What had I left? What had I done? How was I ever going to leave again?

4. To place in a desired state or in order:

As we were dining the weather warnings became more severe, so we decided that it was too unsafe for me to return south just yet. His parents went to take care of the house in Vermont while we hunkered down in Connecticut.

It was just like old times. I felt safe. I felt cared for: a dream and a curse. The cats smiled as we all nestled in together.

5. To become calm or quiet:

I think it's important to mention that I didn't intend to ever revisit these details of this particular story. I meant to tell you about my grand arrival into Providence: the great start of my university teaching career, learning what it meant for me to settle. But my meandering memory has led me here to the depths and truth of this time in my life. The in betweens that I usually don't talk about.

While typing, I've fought with myself to keep going. I'd rather do anything else to procrastinate writing or remembering this because, although years have passed, this story still hurts. This moment exists in my raised shoulders. It rumbles in my gut. It rolls down my face when I least expect it. It affects everything I do, every decision I make.

I don't tell you all this to gain any pity. No. I offer this tangent as a reminder that everything doesn't rebuild or reframe easily or by itself. That time somehow helps but doesn't, won't ever, erase.

6. *To become clear by the sinking of suspended particles, as a liquid:*

Love lives forever. It twists and turns and toils. It cries and smiles and often reaches out before its ready to fully live again. But broken hearts only break more hearts, so instead of rushing on or lashing out or blaming something or someone else, we must take care and listen to what our wounds are wanting to teach us. We must take heed, slow down, and bathe in these waters of our sorrows.

With this in mind, I have continued to type and type away... reaffirming my belief that expressing these words is the only way. I don't want to be a slave to this story any longer. I want to wear it as a jewel.

7. *To sink down gradually; subside:*

The next day, the power went out and we were forced to look at each other and talk. About the possibilities of getting back together and the possibilities of not. We were caught in this back-and-forth limbo until the storm eventually subsided. Our hearts still at odds, it was now Monday, and I was due in Providence.

8. *To appoint, fix, or resolve definitely and conclusively; agree upon:*

With hugs and tugs and cats and couches, I backed the trailer down the driveway. I wished. I knew. I didn't know. I waved, I took a breath, and I drove off.

The hurricane had taken its toll. Everything had been lifted up and set down in a new and unfamiliar place. I navigated through downed power lines and broken limbs and broken street signals. The cats cried from the back seat as sea gulls soared across the clearing sky and more and more people returned to their regular schedules.

9. To apply oneself to serious work:

Cats introduced to their new home, still windblown, I went to introduce myself to my new co-workers and students: "Hello, Everyone. My name is Kāli Quinn. Like you, it is my first year here in this place. I am excited to start teaching you Clown and Mask this semester." Excited? Sure, excited *and* terrified. But what was the worst that could happen? I would fall flat on my face and they would ask me to leave?

10. To pay or close an account.

That week, my ex-boyfriend would be passing through Providence on his way to Boston. "Can I stop by?" he messaged.

"Yes! Of course!"

I answered the doorbell feeling strong and independent, proud to share my new space with him. The cats couldn't have been more excited to see him. We all sat together on our old furniture now set up in a new place. Had it all been magically beamed up or was there a weekend layover that still needed to be discussed?

We walked to dinner down the street from my house. We had great conversations about new ideas and dreams and upcoming projects, about moving forward. Drinks and desserts adding up, he offered to pay the bill. Was this a date? Or was this the new version of being best friends?

We went home, put the futon together, and then decided to sleep side-by-side in my bed anyway. How do two people who have been partners in everything for six years ever transform into being anything else?

The next morning I invited him to go with me to the opening of the season at my new workplace: "Do you think you could you come back for it? It's two weeks from now."

"No," he said, "I'm sorry. I can't."

And with that, he left, and we haven't seen each other since.

11. *To take up residence in a new country or place.*

Driving home from school that week, I turned off my GPS and took a new route each day. I was going to have to become familiar with this place, these streets, this new home. As I stopped at the light along Roger Williams National Park, turning to my left, I read one of his quotes painted on the window of the museum: *"Having made covenant of peaceable neighborhood.... unto me in my distress, [I] call [this] place PROVIDENCE... a shelter for persons distressed for conscience."*

12. *Settle into, to become established in; to settle into a new routine.*

When opening night arrived, I got dressed up and went to the show by myself. I watched the play aware of the empty seat next to me. I drove home and felt the empty car around me. I returned home, unlocked the door, and settled into bed… a bird upon a bough between two purring cats on Hope Street in Providence.

⌘

Think of a project or relationship that feels complicated right now. How can considering the relationship as an on-going process be helpful for you?

What is one word that reminds you of your intentions within that relationship? Look up the word and let its multiple definitions surprise and inspire you over time.

73. Honestly asking people how they are doing.

Hamburg, New York to Providence, Rhode Island. April-September 2011.

On my thirtieth birthday, just before deciding to come to Providence, my mom threw me a surprise birthday party. She invited many people that I hadn't seen in a long time – friends and teachers from high school, family, family friends. "Oh my God," I kept saying as I went around hugging each of them. I couldn't believe that we were all in the same room and how much we had all grown up. How much had changed and how much hadn't. The big events were readily reported on: people had gotten married, had children, gotten this job or that, moved here or there. These, the tangible check marks of our twenties. The check marks of success, of moving along, of being taken care of. *What* people were doing, but what about *how* they were doing?

"Oh, I don't have to worry about her anymore," remarked one older family friend reporting on her niece, "She just got engaged."

Although perturbed by this statement, especially having chosen to recently disengage from my long-term partnership, I understood where she was coming from. Her niece now had solid, committed companionship. She wouldn't be out in the big world alone. And it is, of course, always easier to see one another's top headlines without considering the process that it took to get there, the details of the fuller story...

My mom came to help me settle into Providence. We moved furniture around and hung pictures on the walls. After class, she took me out to dinner with hopes of me connecting to my new neighborhood. She stood in line with me at the DMV and listened when I cried, handing in my Vermont driver's license: "I loved being a citizen of that state," I confided, "I felt proud to be a Vermonter. I walked down the street and people said hello, asked how you were doing and expected you to answer."

But I didn't live in Vermont any more. That was another lifetime ago.

"This is my new life, my new place, and it is going to be great," I kept repeating to myself as I drove from school to home. I had a great new job, a great place to live, but... but what?

After my mom left, I spent a lot of time alone. I had never been this alone before, and I wasn't sure how to deal will all of my grief that was surfacing now that I had the time to see it. I panicked. What was I supposed to do? I wasn't really one to watch TV or join a bowling league. I had always made my friends through making theater, but now I was making theater with students. Even though some of them were my age or older, I wasn't going to hang out with them outside of class. They were students and I was the teacher. They were the ones with the dreams. I was the one with a career. Or at least that's how I tried to make sense of it all at the time.

"I'm afraid," I reached out to a colleague dropping me off one night after a function at school. "I'm not doing so well and I don't know what to do."

"Why don't you call up that guy you said you met last week and ask him to go to dinner or something?"

I thanked him for the ride, got out of the car and unlocked my door. This wasn't about finding a quick date or getting into a new relationship. That wasn't going to fill this gap and if I tried to make it so, which I surely would from time to time, it wasn't going to work out so well.

We live in a headline culture. One that celebrates *what* we've accomplished and doesn't necessarily care *how* we got there. Doing stuff equals having things to share at the next dinner party, and doing more equals doing better. If my headlines weren't getting married or having babies, then I was going to focus on my work.

So I filled every waking moment with more jobs. I worked for a school in Italy doing stateside recruitment workshops in South Carolina and Atlanta, and I directed a show in Mississippi. While directing, I flew to a board meeting for the Network of Ensemble Theaters in Philadelphia, and after directing, I visited colleagues in New Orleans and then drove north to through Chattanooga to audition people for the school in Italy.

These experiences made interesting headlines, and people gawked from afar via Facebook. Traveling around the country and the hospitality can be great, but it can also be completely un-grounding: not knowing where you are going to sleep next, being with and for an audience of hundreds and then being completely alone in a town where you know no one. Up, down, up, down. Refiguring out anew where to eat, where to put your toothbrush. There was no succinct schedule from week to week or day to day. Everything was new, new, new.

"Yes, I know my new headlines are good," I said to a friend I hadn't talked to in a while, "But you should flip back to the classifieds... There is more to this story."

Now don't get me wrong. I loved doing this work, but I was becoming very, very tired due to the fact I started to give more and more and take less and less care of myself. I would give 110% to my students and audiences and then flop into bed. I know that having a project to focus on is healthy for me, but having fifteen when I'm not taking care of myself isn't. The more we do, the more we need to take care of ourselves, not less.

Why is it that we glorify everyone else as perfect and yet never can begin to give ourselves even the littlest room to grow? I too tend to look at others and assume that they have it all figured out: their headlines are good so they must be too. But have I asked for the fuller story? Have I offered to share mine? Sometimes I spend an entire meal or weekend with family or friends and I never really see them. Do you know what I mean? We are all there, but we are so caught up in what we are doing that we don't find the time to look one another in the eyes and see how the other is doing. What they might be needing support on?

We leave with the sound bites without ever honestly

connecting. To empathy. To compassion.

If you were to really ask me how I was doing and await the full answer and I was willing to give it to you, I would eventually skip over *what* I was doing and tell you *how* I was doing. But if I told you the truth, I'd be afraid it would scare you off...

Although I am in my thirties, I too am still figuring things out. Sometimes I feel sad and I don't want to get out of bed. Sometimes I get so nervous before teaching that I have to convince myself to go to class and push myself to walk through the door. If I told you this, maybe you'd think I'm crazy and want to send me to the next therapist. Sure, that might help, but what I really want is to hear that you relate to some of what I'm experiencing. Then maybe, just maybe, we would both feel less alone and less weird... giving way to our natural movement through life knowing that it's beautiful and challenging, and that up and down and all around, we are creatively making it all up as we go.

⌘

Honestly, how are you doing?

What are the five words you would use to describe your current state of being? How can you let these parts exist without needing to make sense of them? Do you have a drawing or movement for each one?

How can you ask someone else how they are doing today, encouraging their full response? How can you connect to what they are sharing?

74. Viewing everything as a relationship.

2011. Providence, Rhode Island.

"Let's start off by walking," I say to my first class in Providence. "Every once and a while let's each make sure to move through the center of the room."

Like the chaos of a city street, we move. We walk.

Next, I add the following context: "We each have something that we really want to give to each other. How does this change your breath, your direction, the pace, how you are holding your body? Does it affect whether you make eye contact or not? How does it change your overall outlook?"

Next, I add this layer: "Now every person also has something that you want... So you want to give them something, but there is also something you want from them. Both things are happening at the same time. A kind of magnetic pulse of give and take with each new person you pass."

"As you go, without analyzing, simply observe what dynamics seem to develop or repeat within each relationship you pass, saying 'Interesting... when she does this, I do this. When I do this, she does that.'"

"Notice how with each new pairing, as contact is made, a unique relationship starts in that instant. A fluid thing, constantly in motion, with each person having an equal effect. A give and take. A rubber band of ideas that commences a push and pull that will go on forever. The space between the two is alive and dynamic, creating a complex third entity in the middle, the evolving relationship built and cared for by both people."

This is the start of my first attempt to teach a semester of clown. Next we will try the same exercise with an object. With space. Then with an audience. Then an idea.

Everything is your partner. Give and take.

Everything is a relationship. Always evolving.

Not just in trigonometry.

We are in a continual relationship with everything.

⌘

What are ten things that you are currently in relationship with?

How would you describe the current dynamic of each? Are you pushing, being pulled, or moving together?

What is the third thing in the middle that you are creating together?

75. Recognizing when you are being curious and when you are being skeptical.

Providence, Rhode Island. 2011.

In-between teaching classes one day in Providence, this conflicted kindergarten teacher made her way into my notebook. She speaks about her most challenging student who also happens to be her favorite:

That way he was
His hand on his face
Sitting quietly
Looking up
It was unnecessary
For him to be there like that
Intimidated
Feeling bad
What did he do wrong
A little kid
Hardly six
What a sweet young thing
So he didn't know
That it wasn't right
To empty the classroom fishbowl of water
Ever so quietly during naptime
He was curious

Brave
Resilient
Not wanting to know
And wanting to know
At the same time
What would happen to the fish
If it would float in air
How it breathed
What color it might turn out of water
If it could fly
Or live on land
He wanted the fish to be free
Rid of the confines of the bowl
Him of the classroom
Of walls and schools
And cars and family
And that war
That people were talking about
He wanted freedom
This other thing
That everyone kept mentioning
And he learned about in the Constitution
But he couldn't find it
What did freedom smell like
Taste like
Maybe I will take the fish
Straight out to the ocean with him
Out to the sea
Yes
A joyous return
To the womb.

As a kid, I was consistently curious: "What does that sign say? Why does it take that long to cook that? How did you get that name?" And in my eyes, my dad knew eeeeverything. During the Bills Sunday football game, he would have to beg me to wait for half-time before I rallied on, asking more questions about offsides, other rulings, or the history of football. I loved asking questions more than the answers themselves. I loved that each answer led to another question. I was in love with the unfolding of the story. Coloring in the whole picture.

When he didn't know how to answer my question, he would remind me that he "knew everything and a little bit of nothing." From there, whether it became an elaborate myth about where the stars could have come from or looking up facts, we continued into the depths of conversation that sprung from the initial question.

I still love asking questions, but I constantly have to check myself about sliding into a tricky territory of questioning. There is a difference. Questioning makes me want to be somewhere other than where I am. There is an agenda to get there. If I question, I assuming what the answer will be and skeptically start backing away. Once this doubt train starts, it is nearly impossible to turn around. It a dark spirals down, down, down, right where I aimed to go in the first place – to be proven right, shut the door, and walk away.

Asking questions, on the other hand, encourages me to openly gain more information. To be in the space of finding everything awesomely interesting. To enthusiastically open doors, only to open more doors. To create more space.

At first, my new students were curious. They were asking

questions and we were building trust, but then they started to become skeptical. They started to question what I was teaching them because it was becoming harder to place the work of clown and mask into resume bullet points. They didn't want to play to play; they wanted to understand how that play was going to reap dividends in their future career. I understood their fears and resistance. I too had continued to ask these questions in my own journey as a student and as a professional.

In response, I tried to convince them to come to my side of the river: I knew the work of mask and clown and devising were so important that I couldn't explain it. It had always been part of me. I tried to win them over with my enthusiasm. I created more ways to play, but it wasn't enough.

Then I tried to go to their side of the river and get them to cross to mine: I focused purely on technique. I found scenes that included mask and we studied the clowns of Shakespeare, but I was trying to be something that I wasn't.

"You have to wake up every morning and ask yourself why you are doing this," an older theater artist said to me long ago. "Otherwise, one day you'll wake up and have no idea who you are or what really matters and you will question it all."

I wanted to teach these students to be present. Can one teach that or just remind someone of something they've known but somehow forgotten. Something that through years and layers and life had somehow gotten covered up. I wasn't teaching, I was reminding. I was facilitating something that had always been in process. I was helping to jiggle the light bulb that had only become loose over time but it still works perfectly if we take the time to remember it. And once that light is shining again, it can't be stopped. It is bright and beaming and humming and buzzing with delight. It is radiant. There is no other light like it.

Then I realized there were no sides, and that might have been what was so intimidating to all of us. Being present and playing was of course the same thing that I was wanting so desperately to learn myself. Ironically, when being present is your job, it's easy to be less present in other places in your life. Like in medicine – when it is your job to take care of other people, you take less care of yourself.

Did these students want to be present and play or did they want a job where they would be present and play? How would it be possible to do both and teach both?

⌘

What is something that you have been skeptical about that you can regain a curiosity for? What are the open-ended questions you might start asking?

How does this state affect your outlook and your relationship to the situation?

76. Deciphering which part of your dream to let go of and which part to strive for.

Saxtons River, Vermont. New Year's Eve, 2011.

I stood on a bridge in Vermont and wrote down all of the things I was ready to let go of. One by one I ripped them from the page and began to throw them to the wind. I watched them falling into the river, and I smiled through tears saying this:

Thank God for you. For helping to shepherd me to here. You have no idea how much you affected all the joy and the ground I stand on today. Thank you. What an awesome success it all was and will always be. Living our lives apart was the best decision we could have made... just as valuable as our decision to be together in the first place. I continue to celebrate us with you from here.

As I walked away, I realized that I had forgotten love. I forgot to let go of the love. I turned around, wrote the word love on a piece of paper and tore it off. I held it in my hand, but I didn't want to let it go. I didn't want to let go of love completely, only my love for him. And the other things... Vermont, getting married, having children... I wanted to let go of doing those things with him, but not let go of them altogether.

I look forward to seeing who you become and how you achieve all the dreams you've always wanted.

And in that moment I began to separate out my own dreams from the dreams that I had interwoven into a shared dream with my former partner. I threw our love into the river. I watched as the pieces of our dreams floated downstream, and then without looking back, I stepped away, committing wholeheartedly to moving forward and striving for my own dreams once again.

⌘

Remember a time when you were part of a shared vision. What dreams from that time are still at the heart of your own vision? If needed, how can you reclaim them as you own?

What is a ritual you would create to let go of something?

77. Grieving when and how you need to.

Just south of Charleston, South Carolina. February 2012.

Last year when I called up a friend to see how she was doing and if I could take her out to dinner, she said, "Not this weekend, thanks. I am grieving." I had never quite heard someone use this phrase before. She explained that a good friend of hers had passed away and, although the death was a long time coming, my friend needed to take her own time to begin to process her friend's life and her own loss. Wouldn't it be amazing if we could call into work or to school or our family gathering and acceptably excuse ourselves by simply saying: "I can't come. I need to take some time to grieve today"?

Reminiscing about my friend that had died and thinking of my brother's band-mate who had passed away, I sat at the famous Angel Oak that stretched out along the ground for blocks. I remembered my friend Michelle's word of the year ritual and my special tree now fallen in Rochester. As the sun set just south of Charleston this story, called *Our South*, converged:

The moss hung naively
Simply flirting with the ground
Tendrils smiling to have made their home

So high up in this place
This tree just south of Charleston
A meeting place for many
For them.

After the longest pause:
"I have one word for you and it is: Trace."
"Okay. I'm listening."
"That's it. I think that's your word for the year."
"For the whole year?"
"Yeah. It will evolve with every situation. Lead you through
wherever you may need to go." A breath. "Cari, I don't know if I
can come back again next year..."

And without a sign of anything else, she walked away.

This place.
The place they all used to gather
Now everyone else had moved on
Or so she thought
And why couldn't she?

"Trace."

The branches
The dark lines of the bark
A bit of earth to pick up
Sort through
Going back in time
The way they'd all heard that night
A quiet wind passing through
Alone
Needing answers

Stillness
Reaching out
The words they'd never forget.

Recalling his tracks
That mirage of hope
Listening
For anything
A trace
A punch of presumable lasts

Here years later
The tree
The cold
An itch
Then many
Eyes wide
Covered by small iridescent beasts
The company of tiny spiders
What strange gifts the universe gives
Release
Refuge
Palms turned up
The lines of a hand
Two
A missing so strong it could scream
His drumsticks
Heavenly dust
New life
Afraid to move.

How a day can melt by in one place or many
With thousands of thoughts or hardly any

How time would suspend always when reminded of him?

Truth becomes dusk
Shadows bowing to sunlight
Always
Forgiving the day
Only a trace of light.

A fading farewell
A breath
The tree
Spiders vanished.

Standing up
Some rain
Some tears
Her feet secured
Roots
Ready
Not ready
Heart turning
Shifting
A chirp
A glance
A step
The rhythm of letting go.

⌘

How do you take the time to acknowledge the things and people
that you might be missing?

What might you make with your grief today?

78. Including everyone who wants to be involved.

Columbus, Mississippi. February-March 2012.

"How many students can you take?" the head of the department asked me.

"I'll find a way to work with whoever shows up."

"No audition then?"

"Nope. Just an invitation to join in."

Little did I know when I was invited to Mississippi to create a play with a group of students there, it would end up being one of the most incredibly rejuvenating six weeks of my life. The community could not have been more welcoming, kind, understanding, and enthusiastic ready to join in, teach me about their town and introduce me to southern living.

"Hi Miss. You doing okay today?" a woman asked me as I walked into a store in town.

I had never been greeted like that before. It changed me up. I couldn't just answer "good" and move onto buy groceries. Did she really want to know if I was okay? We proceeded to have a conversation about who I was and what I was doing in town. She had lived in Columbus, Mississippi her entire life and loved it there. She gave me tips on where to eat lunch and my options for church on Sunday. I hadn't gone to church on Sunday for decades, but I didn't tell her that. I just listened in awe of her friendliness.

When I met the ensemble we gelled the first night. They were so hungry and excited to play, and so was I.

"During week one," I explained to them, "We will continue to play and become a strong ensemble. This will be the most important element of our process. During week two, we will use these masks to create characters. During week three, we will find the relationship between the characters. During week four and five, we will see what world these characters live in together, and then we will discover what story wants to be told within this place."

We took a photo of our group at the end of the night and you would have thought we'd known each other for years. It still hangs on my kitchen fridge.

When the students learned that I had never heard of most of their favorite culinary delights, new treats started showing up each day. After rehearsal, each night we would stay in the theater sharing in the magic of sweet tea, telling stories about ghosts and Elvis.

"The dorm you are staying in was a hospital for soldiers during the Civil War," one of the students explained to me. "They say that there was one special nurse who died there after her lover died at war. They say she takes care of people who stay there as she waits for him to come back."

That night I went back to my room, realizing how long the bricks of that building had been there and the years of experience those walls had held. I was in a completely different part of America than I had ever experienced before.

The students bought me a copy of the *Southern Belle Primer* so that I could read up on silverware choices and religious options. While eating lunch, people I just met asked to pray for me. At first I felt nervous, but then I thought, why not?

"Hold my hands then," said one of my new friends, a former student who now worked at the school.

I had no idea that she was going to pray for me right there and then and I wanted to run away, but why? A few prayers couldn't hurt. In fact, maybe I could benefit from them.

By week two, I was going to yoga classes and making friends at the green smoothie café downtown. And new people started to join in our rehearsals: one guy's fiancé, another girl's mom, students who had heard about our developing show while in class or at the cafeteria. We began to collect a kind of following, and the theater, like when I was in college, gave people a place to be if they wanted or needed it every night from 6:00-10:00. Every person was kinder than the next and full of great input and feedback. And our already established crew was excited to invite them in.

"Who wants to have a Valentine's Day gathering after rehearsal tomorrow night?" I offered to the group at the end of week two. While out buying paint for the set, I had collected a bunch of free paint samples and thought it could be fun to make them into Valentines. The next night we all huddled in the costume shop with glue sticks and a special chocolate Coca-Cola cake sharing stories about love.

At the end of week three, I started getting nervous that we might not meet our deadline and decided to come in with a plan for the rest of the show.

"What if he grows up and then comes back but they don't recognize him and then…"

They did their best to rehearse my plan and put it into their current logic, but we weren't quite there yet and I could tell that people felt rushed. They started to back away. I had created an entirely different atmosphere in the rehearsal room without naming it. So far I had been facilitating a collective collaboration, but without acknowledging the change, I started telling them what to do without giving them a choice.

In this moment, I found strength as the "authority" in the room to admit that I didn't know what to do next. "I'm not sure of where to go from here," I said to the group. "Can I have three *what if's*?"

I listened to their ideas and then chose one of them as a way to proceed. This led to the next step within our show and continued to remind me that I wasn't alone. There were twenty-some other hearts invested in this show.

"From now on, at the end of each rehearsal, we will take ten minutes to put our playwright hats on and name what new things we know. If someone disagrees with one, we will leave that idea open and continue to play with it the next night. If we come to a consensus, then we a will stick that stake in the ground and move forward with it being definite thing. It will be *locked-in*." They seemed excited about this. "Then we will name the things that we want to know next. I will plan the next night's rehearsal based on finding ways to discover answers about these new things."

The next night, Paige, an older student who had hurt her foot the first week and had been rehearsing in a wheelchair ever since, finally started to get out of the chair and move around on her feet. When we got to the last ten minutes of rehearsal, one of the things that came up was the wheelchair.

"I missed it," said one student.

"I agree," said another.

"Yeah, my character was in a wheelchair from the start and without it, I felt like I was a different character," said Paige.

"It's become part of the Queen's identity," I commented. "Do we want to choose to lock it in or let it go?" Unanimously, the group decided to lock it in.

The following week, I understood how much people's movements would be enhanced if we had music with which to score the whole piece. This was the last layer needed to bring the audience into our atmosphere. There would be no words and great music! But this was going to be difficult to create with the time we had left.

I assigned the ensemble to bring in recordings of music that they associated with our piece. "Epic music would help to bring out the epic that lives within each of you," I explained. That night I planned to go straight home to do some research, but at the break that night, the fiancée of "Casey Boy Casey" (there was also a Girl Casey in the ensemble), a long-haired blonde girl who always sat in the back with a mischievous yet friendly smile and airy voice, approached me with her computer. "Ma'am, I have all the music right here. It's all set to go."

"What? Really?"

"Look…"

It turns out that for several weeks, amidst sketching the actors' movements for fun while watching, Arianna had been pasting together her favorite music to underscore our piece.

"Most of it comes from video games," she explained.

"Sure, let's try it. Why not?"

From that moment on, Arianna inched closer and closer to the front row as we all discovered little by little that she had a hidden talent and knowledge for sound design. We agreed that her choices were just what we needed. Not only were they the perfect length, but they also created an emotional score that we all related to.

When we couldn't figure out the ending, more people started coming to rehearsals, especially video game fanatics who heard about the music Arianna was using. Every person in that room had a personal stake in the story because they had made it themselves. Our play was about a witch sister who felt betrayed by her sister and decided to seek out horrific revenge. This resulted in a child being born and cast out of the town for over ten years. During that time, everyone wanted to punish the one sister, treating her as evil.

But it wasn't that easy. Sure, we could have made another

play about good and bad, killing off that sister while the rest lived happily ever after, but that would not have been true to our process. Our time together was so inclusive: about people joining, being a part of, opting in. We couldn't just leave that other sister in the dust. What would that teach our audience? What kind of cultural narratives would that perpetuate? Understanding this was a complex responsibility, we continued to be unable to agree on an ending.

Finally, the night before we opened, doing several improvisations between the characters to let our ending play out in various ways, we realized that ultimately, our play was about forgiveness and that forgiveness wasn't an easy thing to do. Within our story, we had been trying to reconcile how the one sister could possibly forgive the other. But like love, forgiveness doesn't have an equation. The reasons why someone is finally able to forgive can be incomprehensible. A long, beautiful, complex process.

We ended our play like this: Everyone but the two sisters goes into the castle to celebrate the return of the prince. Before walking away, the one sister offers her hand to the long-time rejected sister, inviting her to join in the celebration, and as they start to walk together in the same direction, the lights go down.

If our audience left asking how one sister could possibly find it in herself to forgive the other sister, that would be amazing. That was not a question we could answer but we could end our play by starting there.

We called the play *When Night Falls*. There were no words, only movement, and an incredible soundtrack. If any one of the voices in the room hadn't been present on any one day for the past five weeks, the audience would have witnessed an entirely different story.

The opening night was incredible. The actors were so excited to let more people into our house to see what we had been cooking up. Families and friends, neighbors and store clerks piled in, some having driven quite far, and like a sporting event, they sat on the edges of their seats and watched the action. The students' fully gave over to their story and embodied and shared every move. They believed so wholeheartedly in what they had created and the audience's silence as the lights went down before they burst into applause was a testament to the ending we had discovered together.

I went backstage to congratulate the ensemble and together we walked out to see that the entire audience had stayed for the optional talkback. I started by asking them to put into words what they were still remembering from the piece. The responses moved from "a baby" to "sisters" to "reconciliation," "community," "love," and "forgiveness" and people stayed for an hour to talk about what those things meant for them.

⌘

When have you felt included? Excluded?

How is it challenging for you to include other points of view? At home? At work?

When has including another point of view been extremely beneficial to your process?

79. Sensing the presence of absence.

Providence, Rhode Island. 2012.

On the thirteenth anniversary of my dad's death, instead of filling the empty space, I began to leave room for his absence. I even bought an extra ticket for him when I went to the symphony for the first time in Providence.

A little, a lot, a little
Trickling down you to me
And the conversation creeps on
Catching up to your age, your height
A thousand stories more
And onto the refrain.

You lift
Wait
You lift-ed
Tenses still distraught
Fingers drawn to your mouth
A rocking chair with squinted eyes
Plants holding on through haze
Lifting one leg to cross them
Charismatically so
Writing on a yellow pad.

When a teenager
Limbs akimbo
Something like me
Holding her breath
Placed herself gently on your lap
Head on your chest
A heart still beating
Two in fact
Smiling
Smil-ed.
A reckless glow
Ready to be held
Or held down for an eternal game of Tickle Tiger.

It's all good rhymes with this sucks
If you dare to flip over the coin
And you are not a butterfly
Or simply upstairs.

Unnerve me, Domino Pusher
Take another swig
Glove compartment's the home
For you to follow me round
Filling delirious windows of time
Complicating metaphors for reason
And time to truth
When death equals death
A pure end
A friend
A pushing off
A drawer
A pen

A book
Open only to parentheticals.

So this night
I sit in Providence
Paused, hungry, tired
Writers reading
Five minutes into ten
Your old friend from Urbana
Mumbles drunk in the aisle behind
And next to me a chair
Considerably filled with your absence.

Would you be like that friend now
Or something like him
If you still walked the earth?

Exponentially so is usually how on we go
Animals don't like change
Another fact
A piece of research
A thumbnail in the wall
Reconciling.

You didn't see it out
Profile nose photo predictions have gone awry
My gestures reach far beyond yours
I sit
A bottle of beer
A smoke
A girl
A dog
A car

A time where we didn't talk
A love letter
Qualitative.

Running blades of grass through my fingers
Ingesting the news of your death that day
Waiting
Waiting
Jaw dropped
Waiting
Waited.
Waiting still
Finding everyone other than you.

My body
Now a woman's.
Wanting sex
Forgetting love
Day into day
Another bath
Believing that childhood was a only grown up's dream
And still being sorry I couldn't float in your arms in that pool.

Although the promised volume awaits you
You will not show up here
In this chair
Beside me
Whispering what to do next
Or next
Or never
Instead you revolt as the earth
You appear as the sky
And you have evaporated completely

Into nothing
Except what's written on my bones.

So cottage gutters up
Another summer upon us
You fall upon
You fell
You fell upon the road.

Without you now
Days have complied themselves into thirteen
Wind-soaked years.

Missing (in the generalized sense of the word)
Cooperates like Jell-O on a windowpane plate
Unsorted laundry
Secret ingredients
An odometer replying
Only dust and bones
Just dust and bones
Dust and bones
Come home
Go home
No home.

Recalling the last words I added
I love you
Exiting through the back hallway that day
Echoing now too within the soles of my feet
While walking back and forth alone.

A lot, Dad
A lot.

⌘

Who is someone you miss?

How can compassionately allowing the space and time for their absence bring you further healing?

80. Celebrating milestones.

The American South and Italy's Cinque Terre. 2012.

When I was in a relationship for all those years, I never considered inviting my mom on a trip, but now, why not? I had the space, I could use the company, and my mom was fun. When I asked she was ready to fly down and meet me partway and get in the car and go. It was like old times and new times.

Understanding quickly that our eating and sleeping rhythms were quite different, we worked out a great schedule where my mom would wake up early and be able to take her own time getting ready and reading the paper, and I would stay up late and have my own time doing work or talking on the phone to friends. She helped set up for my show in Myrtle Beach, she watched me teach in Atlanta, and she met all my friends and colleagues along the way. In between, we drove, we laughed, and we saw the sights. We rode bikes along the Atlantic and explored Savannah.

By the time we pulled into Atlanta, I realized that I was, in fact, on tour with my mother. One night I came home from a late workshop, and there she was already asleep and all ready to wake up and get back on the road. During this new time with her, I realized how much I didn't know about her, how much I had never even thought to ask. I knew she liked oysters and drank coffee and loved to laugh. I knew that she had worked hard to manage her own businesses for fourteen years wallpapering and painting and ironing linens. I knew that she races and earned medals. I knew that she was always there when I got off the bus from school. I knew that she had her wisdom teeth out right before she found out she was pregnant with me, but what was she like before she had me? I understood my childhood from my perspective, but what had it all been like from hers? I knew that she loved me because she showed me and told me all the time, but did she know how much I loved her too?

Sometimes I would become frustrated with her, but then I would notice that the reasons why were the same things that I found frustrating about myself. Sometimes this made me more frustrated. Sometimes I became so impatient with her, but then I would be reminded of how beautiful she was, how she gained so much joy from the littlest things. How important it was for her to take a photo of every state sign as we passed it and every heart-shaped thing that she noticed. Her favorite thing was going out in the morning, exploring the new town, meeting people, and giving me the full update when I woke up. One night while I was at rehearsal, instead of falling asleep, she stayed up late dressing up and taking pictures of herself in all of the masks I bought to do the show! These photos are priceless, and there might even be one of both of us making faces next to one another in dog masks: her, the young and chipper one and me, the old, wrinkled one.

When we arrived in Mississippi, I didn't want her to leave. I had become accustomed to her companionship. "What if for your birthday this year, you come to Italy? When I'm done with my work, we can take a trip together."

"Let me think about it..."

Three months later I was picking my mom up in the Rome airport. Stopping in Florence and Pisa on the way, we took a train to the coast. There, we swam in the Mediterranean during the day, we walked the famous Lover's Walk at sunset, and we got dressed up and clinked glasses in a new village every night... gratefully celebrating the completion of my mom's sixtieth year on the planet and the newly forged pathways of our relationship.

⌘

What are some milestones that you've celebrated with your friends and family?

What's a upcoming milestone? How can you create a new way to celebrate it with the people you love?

SEVENTH MOVEMENT: ANOTHER KIND OF PROVIDENCE

Connect with your Compassionate Creativity by...

81. Listening for what keeps showing up.

Providence, Rhode Island. July 2012.

Jet-lagged and up early, I found myself sitting in one of the benches in the Quaker Meeting House. This place kept coming up in conversations since I moved to Providence and it being my first day back in America, I thought, why not?

I knew that we would all sit there for an hour in silence unless someone felt moved to speak. Then they would stand up, offer a message, and return to sit for more silence and reflection.

I had tried to sit and meditate for ten minutes before but never for a whole hour so this was going to be interesting. At first I was fidgety and felt out of place. I looked toward other people for "how to do it." Some people had their eyes closed. Others sat looking around. Some kids laid in their mother's laps. I folded my hands in my lap and tried to leave them be, but then I started biting my lip. I couldn't stop moving or thinking. I thought about my trip to Italy and my time with my job. I thought about my ex-boyfriend and wondered what he was doing right now and if he'd ever talk to me again. I admitted that I missed him still. I tried not to think about it or him but it only made me think about it more. I thought about letting go and how it wasn't easy. I felt sad. I felt the edge of my sandals along the floor. I looked at the patterns in the wood and counted the panes on the windows. I wondered what my dad would think of this place, if he knew about the Quakers. I wondered what other people were thinking or feeling or dealing with. I wondered how much time had passed so far. I started to breathe and release and let my body catch up to my mind...

...

...

...

And how was I going to know when it was over?

The two people sitting at the front, which I later understood were different people each week, shook one another's hands. This gesture started a contagion of everyone shaking hands and saying good morning to one another. Giving peace at Catholic mass had always been my favorite part. Connecting as a part to the week. Greeting people who I didn't know. I loved this then, and I loved it again now.

But it wasn't over yet.

"If there is anyone new here today," we invite you to stand up and say your name and what brought you here today.

A few moments went by. Was I the only new one? I stood up.

"Hi, my name is Kāli and I came here today because..." Why did I come here? I could feel myself turning red... "Because I travel a lot for work and this was my first Sunday in Providence, and I've wanted to see what it was like."

"Welcome..." all the voices said.

"Thanks."

From there, everyone proceeded to go around and say their own name, first and last, aloud. There was no singular minster or priest. There were committees like Peace and Social Concerns, Hospitality, Funeral and Burial, Education, Communication. There were business meetings. Some of the people were Jewish, some Christian, some gay, some from across the world. All ages. They believed in non-violence. They "held each other in the light." They sat together on benches facing one another. They reported on *Joys and Sorrows*. They called each other and were known in the world as *Friends*. To me, and in all due respect, this felt like the spiritual version of an ensemble theater company.

I would go to this meeting as often as I could for the next two years. I would get used to sitting quietly for an hour. Sometimes it would go by quickly and other times it would seem like forever. Sometimes one person would stand up and say something, sometimes five would, but it never turned into a conversation. These were simple offerings of things that were on people's hearts. I got to know some of the people better by talking to them when we shared food downstairs after the meeting. But the others I only knew by the offering they shared when they stood up. Driving through Providence I would see one of the people and think: there goes "[First name, Last name]," they were the one who reminded me to do or think about "X" or ask questions about "Y."

If I was in Providence on a Sunday, this would be the start to my week. If I was elsewhere, I'd see if there was a meeting there that I could visit.

⌘

Sit quietly for five minutes simply breathing and letting your mind slow down. What does this time teach you?

Notice what keeps showing up in your life. What meaning do you make of this?

82. Finding success in every moment.

Providence, Rhode Island. 2012-2013.

My mom finally convinced me to try online dating in Providence. This was a hilarious few weeks, which contained about a thousand more stories (as you might imagine). The best and most relevant are the moments when I tried to explain to the guys I met, all of whom were in fields other than the theater, what I did for a career:

Case Study #1: I explained that I had just returned to town after a "gig" in Vermont to a guy who was a PhD candidate in Economics. Hearing this, he stopped in his ice-cream-eating-tracks and looked at me in disgust as if I might be a stripper. We turned around, walked back toward our cars and quickly parted ways before I could tell him about theater and how I played a stripper when I was twenty.

Case Study #2: The first couple of dates went well, but then I experienced three weeks of silence before the sweet, environmental conference planner texted me out of the blue: "I realized Im not ready 2 date yet. Please dont take it personally. Nice 2 meet you and thx for teaching me so much about puppets."

I brought these findings to my housemate who had also been starting to test the waters of the Providence dating scene.

Although she no longer worked in theater, because she had attended the same graduate school, she understood my line of work well.

"So at what point do you mention that you've been a clown?" I asked.

She immediately ceased her dishwashing and turned to face me: "NEVER." And then, somewhat jokingly, she proceeded to give me a list of words that I should absolutely not mention for the first six months when dating any man. These banned words included both clowns and puppets along with masks, acrobatics, and the Alexander Technique. But without these things, what would I possibly talk about?

This was my first time mingling with people outside of the theater scene. I was learning that what was normal to me wasn't so normal to other people. I needed to find ways to translate my ways of being into something that other people relate to. Not just for the sake of having a successful date, but rather to be me and move through the world as I wanted to, without feeling the need to prove, apologize, or demand that someone understand.

Here is the evolution of my response to someone saying "I can't wait to see you on Broadway":

"Yeah, me too! Thanks!"

I nodded while thinking, "I'm never going to be on Broadway," before I changed the conversation.

"I actually don't want to be on Broadway," but I then needed to explain myself further by having a huge conversation about commercial, mainstream success and the inner-workings of the theater world as I understood it.

I smiled without a further response but felt okay about it. I knew I was on a different path of my own, and I liked the view from there.

I thanked the person and found how my path was similar to the path of that person's and then started to connect from there.

Case Study #1: We had a beautiful conversation about while growing up, his parents took in foster children from throughout the world, and I shared with him about my travels.

Case Study #2: I had an intriguing conversation about the tiny house that he lived in, and yes, that fact somehow led into me informing him about the wonders of puppets.

It's endlessly intriguing to me what the world asks of us and what people want to call us. I remind myself as I remind you: Bus driver or psychologist, lover or painter, retired engineer or brother, let the roles be specific and infinite – both for yourself and for all those you encounter along the way. Find your center and expressively move from there, finding the amazing successes in every moment.

⌘

Be on the hunt for successes today. Why do these things feel successful to you?

How does this shed light on what's most important for you to accomplish in each moment?

83. Showing up.

Providence, Rhode Island. September 2012 – January 2013.

When I was asked to create a new show for kids with my sixteen graduate students, I was thrilled. This was exactly the kind of work I wanted to do with them and it was the work that I wanted them to have under their belts before graduating.

Before the beginning of the semester, I asked each student the following questions so that I could understand where each individual was coming from and from there, plan the curriculum for our ensemble:

What is most exciting to you about this project?

What is a burning question that you are asking yourself at the moment that you'd like to explore as part of this piece?

What kinds of stories do you get excited about sharing with a family audience?

If you could share three themes/lessons with a family audience what would they be?

How would you like the audience to describe this piece when leaving the theater?

What is most scary to you about this project?

How would you like to challenge/expand yourself by doing this project?

What are other skills that you would like to offer our project?

How have you spent this past summer?

The students' responses ranged from being excited to work with an ensemble, to learning more about clown and mask, to composing music, to performing an imaginative, funny, compassionate, enlightening piece for kids. Simultaneously, they admitted that they were unsure how on earth they were going to fit this show into their already packed schedule. I also learned that they all had fears about creating something without having a script and that the process might not be enjoyable. One person even commented that they weren't excited to the project at all.

Reading this, my own excitement level dropped, and like them, I became scared too. My greatest fear as a teacher was facing resistance to doing the work. People who were in theater usually loved doing the theater. How lucky we were to have the time and space to play for work!? I was still reeling from creating a play in Mississippi where the students were so enthusiastic. Like that project, I knew that creating this new piece in Providence was going to take all hands on deck. If one person didn't want to be there, it could really derail the entire process. How was I going to show up?

The first day, I wanted to show them that if they committed to it, this class/process could be much easier and more enjoyable than they thought. I facilitated some group play and they were off to the races, making amazing connections with each other and creating some intricate scenes together. But at the end of class I could tell that there was still a reluctance to the project as a whole. They didn't believe in it. In terms of the amount they had to do to graduate, this play was low on their list of priorities. This was not the way to create a play.

Over the week that followed, I pushed ahead, but there was always a certain amount of resistance in the room. If I had been teaching them about being present for the last two years, how could I go on ignoring what was so apparent? How could they show up if they felt that they hadn't had a choice in the matter?

At the beginning of week three, I started out by naming the resistance in the room. They were surprised that I noticed, and that I was willing to talk about it. They didn't realize how much of an effect their "not wanting to be there" was having on the atmosphere of the room, on their classmates, on the process, and on themselves.

I continued by explaining my plan: *We are going to take three weeks to look at what it means for each of us to wholeheartedly show up no matter what. Whether we prefer to be here or somewhere else, every class we need to find a reason to be present for the entirety of our class time together. At the end of the three weeks, you will make a choice of whether you want to continue to be in the piece or to be in the audience.*

They all gratefully agreed, and for the next three weeks, we noted the moment when we walked through the door as a choice. No one was forcing any of us to be there. We were all actively choosing to show up. This changed the dynamic of the room completely. We were all able to present in a whole new way. We created songs and talked through our own experience of childhood and about what our education was like. We played with childhood stories that still resonated strongly for us to find the essence of why they were so powerful. The students merged these discoveries into the creation of their own characters and storyline. We were able to accomplish a lot in a short period of time because of their level of focus, commitment, and enthusiasm.

At the end of the three weeks, I had each student write to me articulating his or her choice of whether to stay or go. No need for any explanations, but rather a simple, straightforward gesture of taking a step toward the show or taking a step away from the show. This was a scary moment as a teacher and director. Would I have anyone left? Would I have a show? Would I have a job?

Eleven out of the sixteen students decided to join in, and together we continued to create an amazing show. We shared our work-in-progress with the marketing team and the rest of the school before taking a few weeks off for the holiday. While planning how to finish the show in time for us to move it into the theater, I received a call that the show needed to be canceled. The theater needed to have sold more tickets by that point and they couldn't risk losing money. This was unfortunate, but I understood. The hardest show to sell is one that no one has ever heard about and our show was exactly that. A new show.

If the show didn't go on, I would have three extra weeks off and the students would be set free to work on their other projects. This was appealing but unheard of. These students had just started to trust me. To trust the process. To see the beauty in making their own show. How could I ever show up to class and tell them that it was called off? I wanted to run far, far away from it all.

"You can cancel a show but you can't cancel curriculum," I thought, wanting to understand what the alternative could. The show was made. If it couldn't play at the theater, where could it play and for whom? I thought back to school tours that I had been part of in California and Colorado. I thought about how much those experiences taught me about the power of theater. I made a proposal to the school and theater staff that we tour the show to nearby elementary schools for free.

They accepted the idea, but I still needed to figure out the best way to introduce this change to my students. Elementary schools never seem as glamorous as the mainstage at first, but I knew that they wouldn't regret this experience if I could only get them to commit to this new plan. "Bringing a show to people in their place is totally different than asking them to come to you," I explained, "And in these schools, this will be the first time many of these kids have ever seen a play." With some reluctance and some excitement, we all moved forward.

Two weeks later we nervously opened the show to an auditorium of over three hundred wiggly second graders. "This is the most honest audience you'll ever get," I told them, "Listen to them and they will listen to you. You are doing so much more than putting on a show right now."

The curtain opened and all eyes were on the character of

Jakob, who was going to sleep the night before his first day at a new school:

The stars are out,
The sun's gone down,
It's time to go to bed.
So close your eyes,
Turn out the light,
And rest your weary head.
I know you're scared
Of what is to come
But son, just take it from me:
The world can seem
Such a scary place
But I know that you can be
Strong, funny, smart, and kind
You know how to use your mind...

The audience was up for the ride and my students rose to the occasion. I had been struggling for months to get them to use more of their physical and vocal range, but this did it. They inherently understood that in order to captivate the kids, they needed to use bigger gestures and fuller voices. And that day I saw the best acting I had ever seen my students do; they felt it too.

...First days of school can be frightening, it's true.
But when you get there, all you have to do
Is smile and be friendly to all that you see
Say, "My name is Jakob, I'm proud that I'm me."

"That was incredible," said the student playing Jakob, after giving high fives to all the kids on their way out. As he gained his breath, tears came to his eyes, "And I remembered why I chose to do theater in the first place."

"Me too," I thought as I hugged him and thanked him for showing up, even when he didn't know why or how he got there.

⌘

What is something that you have a difficult time showing up for right now?

How can your Compassionate Creativity help you with this?

84. Recognizing whether a decision is active or passive.

Throughout my travels. 2011-2013.

I sat around the table with sixteen theater artists ages 29 to 60, half men and half women. I half listened to the meeting and half started to wander, to wonder. Only one of these people had children. Intriguing. I would have thought that more of these people had already become parents. At lunch I learned that most of the women always knew that they didn't want to have children. Did I?

I returned to the meeting and doodled in my notebook. I thought about how I felt when I held my cousin's baby in my arms. I thought about my friends who were already having their second child. I thought about all the mothers of the world and wondered how they did it. I did shows about having babies, but what would it be like to have one myself?

I can imagine
Cleaning up after a small child
At the end of the night
Draining
Heavy
Spent
Picking up
Every tissue

Cup
Toy
Juice
Blanket
Quietly as a mouse
Lucky
Calm
Grateful
Honored
Fulfilled
Rest to rest
To sit
In the silence
And listen
To their growth.

Throughout my life so far, I had done a lot of amazing things, but I had always had a challenging time making decisions. Like water, I said yes and flowed down one hill until it led round into another. Like a sniffing dog I went to Brazil and NYC and Vermont and showed up wagging my tail, but what was it all amounting to? Who was I? What did I actively want to pursue? Where did I want to be instead of just ending up? In that moment, time began to shift. I suddenly saw the possibilities of my thirties flying by with more great work and people and places, but without actively pinpointing what was important for me to accomplish with that time. What would I regret at sixty if I hadn't done it?

Having children was the first thing that came to mind. It was true (and still is), but as a woman who had been wholeheartedly committed to her career, I didn't know how this dream would ever have a chance of becoming true unless I specifically named it as an aspiration and considered it to be part of my life's work.

"I want to have children," I admitted to one of my colleagues at the dinner break.

"Well then, what are you waiting for?" she joked.

⌘

What is something you dream of accomplishing within your lifetime?

How do you passively or actively pursue this dream?

85. Being a tourist in your own neighborhood.

Providence, Rhode Island. Fall 2012.

When traveling, everything was constantly new and exciting and had an extra shimmer. I noticed details on railings in New Orleans, the way people talked in Mississippi, the way the food tasted in Tuscany, and the way the Susquehanna flowed through Pennsylvania. I was intrigued and easily fell in love with what made each place unique. I took photos and shared the greatness of each place with friends who might never get to experience it. But when I returned home to Providence, I looked out through a different lens. I noticed the snow still lingering at the end of my driveway or I swore as I tripped over the same old pothole three blocks from work.

"Happy hour time!" announced a colleague and friend sitting across from me.

"What?" I didn't understand what she meant. We were in the middle of a project. Sure, we worked remotely and had a flexible schedule, but we couldn't take a break now. There was so much more we to had accomplish.

"It's five o'clock," she said expecting me to know what was next. "We'll do more tomorrow but now, we are going out!"

We proceeded help each other pick out outfits and do our make-up before heading out to a fun bar she had heard about. There we met other single, thirty-somethings taking a break after work. Some drank a little. Some drank a lot. The ones I wanted to hit on me didn't; the ones I didn't want to, did.

I suddenly felt like I was back in the hallways of high school that I had always tried to avoid. I didn't want to go back to work, but I wanted to find a balance. First things first: if I was going to spend time in a bar, I at least wanted some good music and intergenerational camaraderie. I did some research. On Wednesdays there was a Bluegrass night at a bar downtown. It had regulars of all ages and you could dance and play pool and dogs were allowed in too!

If I was going to continue to live in Providence another year, rather than just being based here, how could I start to live here? How could I begin to seek out the special experiences that were available in this place? What was unique to this place? Where were the celebrations and how could I take part? Here is a sampling of what I've found so far:

1. A Portuguese restaurant in East Providence serves a homemade buffet on Monday nights. A sixty-year old performer will sit on your lap and sing love songs in Portuguese. I recognized some of the words from my Brazilian travels: heart, vagabond, understand, speak, and upon leaving, when I said "obrigada" (thank you) a man heard me and offered that I sit with his family the next time I come in.

2. Nearby is the Bowling Academy. This is a special duckpin-bowling place. Ten pins, a little ball, and three

chances to knock them over. There weren't many of these left in the country. When my colleague got a spare, she won a huge bowling pin water bottle that she still proudly sports when she goes to work out.

3. On Thursdays the Extraordinary Rendition Band practices near the hurricane barrier while people fish nearby. There are no auditions for this group. The street/marching band welcomes everyone – even a violin player like me!

4. On Tuesdays a small, local sandwich shop called Geoff's offers buy-one-get-one-free sandwiches. My second time in, I turned to the girl behind me in line and asked if she wanted to split the deal with me. "Sure! Why not?" she responded. We started talking and decided to sit down and eat together. Come to find out, her sister lives in Blue Lake, California (the town of 1000 where I went to graduate school).

5. After eating sandwiches, you can hike up the hill and watch the sunset from Roger Williams Park before continuing up to Hope Street to the Ladd Observatory. That spring the astronomers helped me see the rings of Saturn and the Galilean moons of Jupiter.

How had I never saught out these place before? How had I never noticed the roses blooming through the white picket fence in my neighborhood or the stumps that someone had made into chairs? This was an amazingly beautiful place. Providence was no longer just a house on a street that I would just drop my bags off before heading to another gig. Taking time off work to go out and explore let me see this city anew, while learning to call it home.

⌘

How do you feel about the place that you live?

If you were visiting for the first time, how would your perspective be different? What three special things would you make note of and want to share?

86. Finding someone who will help you to be accountable for your dreams.

Marlboro, Vermont to Boylston, Massachusetts. 2011-2013.

"What is your declaration for the year?" my friend asked me once again at New Year's. "Remember the people last year who said that they were going to move to a new house and start a farm? It's being held at their new place."

I remembered the previous year when I joined the circle of people gathered in a house in snowy Vermont hours before ringing in the new year. As my friend facilitated a life coaching session, we listened to one another and reflected on each person's strengths. I was amazed by the amount of trust and sanctity of the space they held together, especially because some of them had never met one another before. The workshop concluded with each person declaring what they wanted to manifest in the coming year. Every person who spoke was nervous. They knew what they wanted but they were so afraid to say it out loud. I heard pieces of my goals in all of theirs, but didn't know what to say. Maybe time would run out and I wouldn't have to say anything? No, in the kindest way, they weren't going to let me out of there until I spoke up.

"I want to be in a committed relationship with a partner..." I began to say as they all nodded and smiled with their eyebrows raised. "Who I am also in a physical ensemble theater company with."

There I said it, let's go home! Nice to meet you all!

"But how will you know it is a committed relationship?" asked my friend who was facilitating.

"What do you mean? It just is," I responded as I started to pack up my things.

"I understand. But how will you know it is a *committed* relationship... Would you be engaged? Would you be married? Would you be living together?"

I shrugged my shoulders.

"It's important to get specific," nudged my friend further.

I didn't know. No, I didn't necessarily need any of the things he said, but I didn't want to be in just another relationship. *How did I define commitment?* I rolled my neck and scrunched my nose; ready to hightail it out of there.

"How will you know?" he repeated as the others supported me at the edge of their seats with wide eyes, biting their lips and holding their breath. Every pore of their body was saying, "Go on, you've got this."

As I squirmed, digging deeper for my answer, the door of the house opened. In ran a big, fluffy dog whose tongue came straight to my face.

"We would have a dog," I said, laughing. "We would have a dog together. That's my definition of commitment."

That year, I didn't exactly reach my goal. I took care of my two cats and dated some nice people, but there was no ensemble theater company or puppy commitment in sight. Sometimes I beat myself up for not having succeeded, but overall, having said what I wanted helped me to be more clear with my choices and continue to clarify if that was exactly what I wanted.

The following year, I returned to the group. Some of the people were the same, but most were new. "This year, we are going to stand within our visions," announced my friend excitedly. "We are each going to take the time to imagine ourselves in the moment of fulfillment."

"Here we go again," I thought. Deep down I knew, but I was afraid to voice it.

"Sometimes," my friend continued, "It's not that we are afraid to fail, but rather we are afraid of what might happen if we actually succeed."

I started writing and was amazed by the specificity that emerged:

Calmness
Green
The first time seeing things in bloom here
An open space
Where dreams run around
A start
A shiny wooden floor
A fireplace
A deep breath
Shared

A hand in mine
Laughing
Playing
The dog, my cats
Our place
Values aligned
Smiling in nooks and crannies
Embracing head, heart, and gut
Our place
An adventure
Readying for a party
A potluck
Where people could stay
All ages
Music
Celebration
Great exhales of joy
Bringing with us
Dancing for all those who no longer live on earth the way we do
We can
Inviting neighbors
Home
A day so energizing
An intersection
Integration
Intergeneration
City at bay
A campfire
Hosts a blessing in full view.

Now that I had envisioned having my own home that could also become a retreat center for creative practices, I was overjoyed. At the same time, I was terrified. How was I ever going to accomplish this? What a responsibility came along with being clear about I actually wanted to do.

⌘

Stand in your dream and write for two minutes.

Who can you express this dream to? How could they help you to be accountable?

87. Occupying the center of your own universe.

New York, New York. March 2013.

"Here's the thing," said my housemate from California, "You just gotta get in the pool."

"What?" I asked, hungry for some good dating advice.

He went on to tell me about his previous weekend when he invited some friends to celebrate his birthday in one of his favorite places in New York: a bar that was at the edge of a swimming pool. He and his wife arrived first, jumped in the pool, and talked to other bar-goers while awaiting their friends but when they finally showed up, they stood on the deck.

"They didn't feel like going into the pool," he explained to me, with a lingering twinge of disappointment. "I had made the invitation clear. This was a pool party. Come on!"

But no matter how he tried to coerce them, his friends stood there. They had already decided that they were going to sit on the sidelines. About to give up and begrudgingly relocate, he paused for a moment. "I wanted to be in the pool. Why would I leave because everyone else didn't?"

He immediately released his friends to do whatever they

wanted to do and jumped back in the pool like he wanted to do. He ended up having a great night with other people who were already in the pool.

"What I'm saying is this: don't sit at home and wait or be swayed somewhere that you don't actually want to go. Go to the places you love, get in that pool with the other people who are choosing to be there, and rock it out with them."

I started to realize how much time I was spending trying to get people to go in pools that I was excited about going in. But rather than expend so much energy trying to convince them how cool that pool was, why didn't I use that time to get in and enjoy the pool myself? If I knew I wanted to be in that pool, then what was stopping me from jumping in?

I liken this to making art and knowing its importance in the world. As artists, if we spend all our time trying to convince people how amazing art is, then how much time and energy are we taking away from actually making our art and letting it speak for itself?

⌘

What is a pool you want to be in? Who have you been trying to convince to get in with you? Why is it important to you that they come?

How can you get in the pool yourself and see what happens?

88. Choosing when and how the show will go on.

Lewisburg, Pennsylvania. April 2013.

A bunch of enthusiastic undergraduate students came out to the audition for *Masks, Movement, and Mayhem*. This was more of a workshop, really. I wanted to be able to take everyone who showed up, if possible, but I only had eighteen masks. Perhaps some could be writers and documenters and assistant directors? Every who wanted to be in, I wanted to keep in. The only confines we had were that this was going to be an hour-long production with masks based on themes of power and subversive laughter.

In order to learn about one another, I had the group arrange themselves in the space based on questions about age, where they were from, the places they'd been, the foods that they liked, and what they thought the most powerful age was. Whenever they arrived in a spot, they had conversations with the people near them, discovering the similarities and differences with one another. We concluded with a storytelling exercise where everyone shared a story: *describe a time in your life when power was taken away from you or when you realized you had great power over someone or something.*

This process began to create a group vocabulary of stories, patterns and themes, along with the trust and responsibility needed around sharing true stories and the difference between oral and written storytelling.

The stories told ranged from the college process to a lonely birthday to making a Bat'Mitzvah in Sudan. The essential themes came down to times when we feel a loss of control, when we feel abandoned, when someone or something is taken away, or when we don't have the same opportunities as someone else. I excitedly took this fodder with me back to Providence to plan our rehearsal process that would begin the following semester, months later.

"We don't know where we're going, but we know we are on our way there," commented the set designer.

When I returned, each student chose a mask and began to create a character by finding how they moved and how they felt when they put on the mask. Through moving and listening, they discovered what that character loved, feared, hoped for, and got angry about. We interviewed each character to learn more details, and then we let all the characters loose to interact.

"Be in 70% character brain and 30% playwright brain," I would say to them as they played. We looked into what status their character held within the group as a whole, and what made their character powerful. The characters broke down into four groups: *The Jackets, The Builders, The Demons, and The Forgotten.* As these groups played together, we found that they always explored the dynamics of giving versus taking and unison versus chaos.

Over spring break, I encouraged the ensemble to explain our process to their friends and family and to listen for what they chose to share and how and why. Then they interviewed their friends and family about power. When we returned and shared our findings, we all paused when we heard responses that came from two people in Nicaragua:

"Power is the state of having and giving what you have to others."

"Power is the ability to be loved. The more you're loved the more powerful you are. People that can engender love and are loved by others are powerful. If a person is loved and respected, they have more power and influence over others. Humans are connected by love."

We talked about and read these quotes often, as we discovered the story that we wanted to tell. The characters were all part of a village that was founded on love and sharing. The villagers played together in unison and they had no concept of winning or losing, but rather played together as a way of living. When winning and losing was introduced by one of *The Demons*, *The Jackets* suddenly became greedy, *The Builders* only focused on doing work, and *The Forgotten* were forgotten. Eventually *The Forgotten* find a way to remind the village of where it came from… as the heart of the elder in the village began to break, one child brought her back to life by singing her the song of the village. Then, together, the old and the young showed *The Jackets* and *The Builders* how ridiculous they had become by imitating their sounds and actions. When this was brought to light, everyone began to laugh except for one *Jacket* who started blaming *The Demon* for everything.

The chair of the department called me during the final week of rehearsals to deliver some tragic news: "I just wanted to let you know that the kids might be down today. We just found out that a theater student who graduated last year was found dead in New York City last night."

I took a breath and, remembering my own classmate who had died in New York City two years before, I went into school early. The Theater Department was a somber place to say the least. The students flooded in and were at a total loss. Teachers and students sat together crying, trying to understand what had happened. I listened to the conversations and learned about the girl who passed away... how she was a powerhouse of a performer, how she had an electric personality, how she just graduated, how much she would be missed. I sent out an email: "There will still be rehearsal tonight at seven. I will completely understand if you don't feel up for it, but please come if you can. We will take it one step at a time."

That night, everyone showed up. After acknowledging all that was going on and letting the older students tell the younger students about the girl that had passed away, I let them all know that it was not imperative that our show go on that weekend, that it was our choice.

They looked at me, stunned. "What do you mean we wouldn't do it?"

"I just mean that it is our choice. I don't want to assume that we will do it. I want us to make a choice together, taking into consideration whatever feels best. This experience is part of our process now."

They all took a breath. Deciding was harder than assuming, but it was a good reminder to all of us that nothing is more important than taking care of ourselves.

Together, they decided that they would take care of themselves by doing the show and that they would dedicate it to their friend and classmate. The group only became more supportive, more committed, and more generous with one another, and the show was only a beautiful extension of their care for one another. That weekend, the students opened the show with a level of commitment and ferocity that I had never seen before.

And how did it end? What did that *Jacket* do with *The Demon* who had come into the village and introduced winning and losing and more and less? As *The Jacket* began to hurt *The Demon*, he saw himself and so instead, he threw him out of the town. As *The Demon* walked away and everyone else started to play once again, a child ran to *The Demon* and invited him to stay. The curtain went down as the whole village taught *The Demon* how to play.

"I've never experienced a play really being a play," commented one man during the talkback. "You were all so genuinely playing with one another. Thank you for making this."

That night, I wrote this:

When I devise a piece of theater with a group of people, I feel like we are changing the world. How? By operating under a different way of working that is "un-systematizable." Instead of saying here is your part or role and this is how you are expected to fill it, we are saying: "Who are you? What can you bring? What do you want to say?" This can be a huge paradigm shift for students and professionals (in all fields). A flip of the coin. The act of introducing something new. Instead of telling someone what to do, we are giving them permission to allow themselves to do. To create.

To be. There is no audition. Anyone who wants to be in that room can be in that room. Day after day we each actively choose to show up and participate. Invest. There is no cast in this devised piece. Little by little we create an ensemble. I do not tell that ensemble who they are or even how to talk with one another. What drives the group to become an ensemble is each individual's level of involvement, and how each individual articulates themselves within the process. At the first rehearsal we make a set of agreements: ways to work. We create a common language through physical play, by titling our discoveries so that they can become tools with which we create. A way of communicating with one another about what we want to have happen again. And how. To remember something that might have excited us. A group memory. We make observations. We witness one another. It is the responsibility as the facilitator of a devised process to cultivate ways of ensuring that everyone can be heard. An act of introducing someone to their own voice. To nurture that voice. To find various ways for everyone to be present and at their best. Their essence. To acknowledge one another. And to consistently encourage a space for people to listen to each other, even and especially when there may be disagreements. To navigate these moments peacefully and productively. To discover ways to move forward without forcing an outcome. To establish group ritual by recognizing the repetition. The patterns. The tendencies. To have your finger on the pulse of the moment. To allow the work and play to teach us what wants to happen next. To always remember to start exactly where we are. To meet each another there. To invite an audience in and wholeheartedly share these discoveries and possibilities with them.

This, my friends, reflects the kind of world I strive to live in. This is power.

⌘

When was a time when you forced yourself to go on? How was it different from a time when you chose to go on?

What are your special powers? How do you share them with the world?

What's the kind of world that you want to live in?

89. Letting health and humor go hand in hand.

New York, New York. April 2012.

"When was the last time you laughed really, really hard?"

What if this was a question asked at the beginning of every doctor's appointment? And if there hadn't been any laughter, the doctor would write a prescription for it? At the follow-up appointment, the patient would deliver their newest jokes and the whole facility would shake with comfort.

"But why did you laugh?" I ask my students after we observe another group performing.

"Because it was funny."

"Okay, but dig deeper... Why was it funny?"

Almost always, the answer comes down to a break in expectation. This is at the heart of clown. A clown, like any person we know, develops their own unique rhythm, their cycle. They wash dishes in their own idiosyncratic way: grab sponge, put soap on it, scrub plate, scrunch nose, shake sponge, put plate in rack. We get to know this person through these actions. Just as they do, we begin to expect them to do it this way every time, but then suddenly, something happens – a plate drops. And with that person, we inhale and suspend, "Oh shit!" What are they going to do? How are they going to react? We are still inhaling, awaiting how they turn the "disaster" into a success by way of many other disasters. Witnessing how that person navigates this "Oh shit moment" inevitably reminds us of our own beautiful shit show, and we exhale into laughter. Laughter is the play between not knowing and seeing the truth. Not believing and then realizing.

The clown revels in these moments and always finds a way to play and celebrate. It isn't as easy for us. There is whole other psychology going on. However big or small the catalyst, when faced with fight or flight as humans, we aren't just dealing with a bear in the woods. We can't just run for safety and move on. As humans, there is always more to our story, a story that includes our relationship to our past and to our future and to our present.

"What are the five things that you need to be you?" I give my students as a homework assignment. "These could be people or places or things or ideas. You are not going to have to share these things with me or anyone else. Just think about what they are for you and note them."

During the next class, I ask them to imagine that those five things no longer exist and move for two minutes within that space. *Who are they then?* When I ding a bell (that they associate with all of their greatest qualities from an exercise we did previously), the students suspend.

"Although you might want to move on, remain in this moment and breathe." I can feel people wanting to quickly shut down and move on. It was scary to be in that place of uncertainty. Of having a new identity. "Now," I say to them gently, "Remember some things that you love."

"I love when my brother calls me."

"I love the sound of a trumpet."

"I love the smell of rain."

Little by little, at the same time as their hearts are heavy, they begin to smile. Sometimes tears roll down their cheeks.

"And what do you find funny?" I ask them.

Chuckles start and release and gratitude for the present begins.

My dad wrote it best years ago: *It seems like something will be lost and that all things will be dreadful from now on. There is only one thing that could be lost that would justify such a sentiment: your sense of humor! It is the only thing that you should guard with your life.*

⌘

When was the last time you laughed really, really hard?

What happens to your state of being when you begin to remember something that you found really funny?

What is a relationship in your life that could benefit from some humor?

90. Calling on your people when you need their help.

New York, New York. April 2013.

In the world of theater, colleagues quickly become your friends, your family, your tribe. It's not just another professional network. It's a series of interconnected relationships that you'll have for the rest of your life. When you don't know what to do at the holidays, these are the people you'll drive to watch movies and share dinner with. They are the people who you will talk to on the phone for six hours learning more about where they are from and what they are struggling with and how. These are the people who will send you the perfect card in the mail just when you need it. These are the people who will show up when you are sick.

With news of an impending surgery, my friend and his wife decided that it was time to ask for help. He had been dealing with cancer for over five years. "We're ready," they said to me, "Although afraid to tell people what's going on, we need to. We need help, and we are ready to ask for it."

Six weeks later, a Broadway theater donated their space on a Monday night, and several performers from across the country came together to share their acts. Family, friends, classmates, and strangers filled the audience, and we all experienced a magical night. Sure, the original intention was to raise money, and we did, but it became so much more than that. I've never been in a room that was filled with so much love and commitment to the present moment. I can still feel the joy and power of being together. I can still see the smile on my friend's face.

By being who they are, near or far, these are the people who will remind you what you love and how to continue to create and play. They too know that in this world, it's not easy to prioritize these things, but that valuing compassion and creativity is absolutely possible and awesomely worth committing to.

⌘

Who do you consider to be part of "your tribe"?

How do you support them or reach out to them and ask them for support?

Is there someone who could use a little extra support from you today? How might simply reminding them of your friendship be amazingly valuable for both of you?

91. Giving yourself a three-breath buffer zone.

West Seneca, New York. May 2013.

My cousin's son was four, the quintessential age of curiosity. For every moment I spent with him, there was a new question. A cute little voice full of inquisition and intrigue:

"What are we going to eat for dinner?"

"Why did my dog do that?"

"Where do you live again?"

"What's foggy?"

I tried to answer his sweet questions as best I could, feeling a responsibility to explain things carefully – after all, some answers could be such a precious start to how he understood the world. Every explanation gave way to the snowball rolling down the hill of his developing consciousness.

His second-favorite way to pass the time was to be turned upside-down, especially through a maneuver I had figured out once when he took my hands and started to walk up the front of my body. We usually did this move over and over until my arms would finally beg me to request a break.

"What's a break?"

"Listen, let's just take three breaths together before we do the next flip, okay?" I had no idea if this would actually work, but I started the count.

"One…" And with quite the serious look in his eyes, he inhaled, the breath filling his entire little being. "Two, three!" And he was upside-down again before he knew it.

A few days later, we were at my family's cottage finishing dinner:

"Can we go out and play now, Auntie Kāli?"

"Not yet. We need to be calm first so our food can digest."

"What's calm?"

Oh wow. This was a big one. To give the first-ever definition of the idea of calm? The pressure was on as he made his way over to my lap looking up for the answer. How would you describe being "calm"?

Works like peace or quiet only elicited more questions. Stillness triggered him back to his understanding of foggy from days before. He was really taking these moments of learning to heart.

"Sure," I pondered, "Foggy is kind of like calm…"

His eyebrows solicited much more clarity.

What other foundational words did we share in common? What was already within the range of our accrued vocabulary?

I started in, with the hope of connecting the dots:

"Remember the other day when we took three breaths together?"

"Yeah..." he said smiling, recalling the moment before turning upside-down.

"Well, the feeling you get when you take those three breaths, that is calm.'"

After a little pause, which included a tip of his head up toward the sunlight, Jakob responded quietly, "Oh yeah... I remember. Okay, Kāli. Ready for calm?"

"One."

"Two."

"Three."

⌘

How could taking three breaths between tasks help you today?

How does the simple reconnection to breath and calm affect your thoughts? Emotions? Actions?

Do you have another practice that you use as a "buffer-zone?"

92. Letting art be a vehicle for learning about everything.

2011 to 2013. Rhode, Island to Connecticut to Massachusetts.

"Notice whether you are tending to make eye contact or avoid eye contact as you pass people," I say to a group of undergraduate students studying science and technology as they mill about the room together. "Either choice is totally valid and perfect." What is key is the new awareness of what they were doing, that they were making a choice.

"Now exaggerate whatever you are doing. If you are making eye contact, seek out eye contact with everyone. If you aren't making eye contact, then avoid it like the plague."

Next I ask them to playing the opposite choice. Then I switch them back and forth between eye contact or not. When they switch, I ask them to notice how their breath changes. How each choice affects the shape of their body, attitude, sense of humor or level of comfort. No one answers these questions aloud or stops and asks for clarification. They simply play on, letting their own perfect interpretation guide them.

"Now you can shift between making or avoiding eye contact at your own will." They interact with different people. Some make eye contact for a moment, some continue for a longer time. Some stop and stand across from someone. Some cover their face or crouch down as they move.

To get a better idea of what the room looks like by this point, imagine a bunch of people running about every which way. The buoyancy and spark is undeniably palpable. With the help of the constant input and reactions of others, each person is going about the exercise, the choices, in their own unique way. They are not trying to do or communicate anything. They are simply playing from one instant to the next. No one can predict or discuss what anyone is going to do, so everything is a discovery. Every moment and movement is new. Everyone is awake and responsive. And this is all usually accompanied by some laughter because expectations are constantly being broken. There is no agenda, just two choices. The spirit of the room is freedom.

This doesn't look or feel like your everyday university class, let alone the usual business or medical training session. These grown-ups appear to look more like a group of children on a playground. But these students are invested in an integral process of re-learning: remembering and reconnecting with Compassionate Creativity. Of the joy that comes from freely interacting with other human beings. Without needing to speak or to prove themselves, we begin to see authentic relationships and reactions. They are present and playing.

I don't teach them how to do this. I remind them how to do this. It's natural but has been covered up by years of who-knows-what. Now that they remember, I can't stop them. They are in the flow of play.

If you tried to figure out what story they were telling, you'd be missing the point. They aren't trying to construct stories. They are simply interacting. *So I'd ask you then: what are the stories, the ideas, and the dynamics that YOU see in this play?*

Suddenly, I suspend the group in the middle of their play. They are out of breath. They were in another place and time or story. I ask them to notice how they feel differently than when they first walked in the room and to name what shifted for them.

Next, I ask them to "Google" in their own minds the image that they found themselves creating with their classmates in that very moment when I suspended them. To be an observer of their present play. What did their movement or interactions remind them of? There is no right answer that I am looking for. I am interested in their interpretation. To notice the narrative that they were automatically starting to write. The rules of the game that they were making up for themselves. They are human after all and these kinds of connections just start happening. I ask them to listen for them.

I ask them to make connection to their areas of study or their lives: "Where do they see this similar dynamic playing out?"

Out of breath, they shout out their answers:

"It's totally like the positive feedback loop I've been learning in biology," one student responds.

"Yes!" another one yells, "It's just like metabolism!"

"For me, its gravity toward a central mass!"

"Oh, I thought that we all intersecting vectors on a graph," someone else chimes in.

"It's like we are hydrophilic and hydrophobic molecules..."

In order to learn more about these interpretations, we proceed by exploring one at a time. We title our play *Digestion, Geometry,* or *The Breakdown of Water,* and as they continue to play forward, each person translates what they were doing into this new lens.

Prior to this moment, the students had generally been perceiving these ideas and theories as things outside of themselves. As facts or diagrams to memorize in order to pass the next test. But now they had experienced for themselves what it was like to *be* the stomach, the cell, the tree trunk, and the force of gravity. And by doing this, they made new observations about water, about their body, about the universe. And most importantly, they saw themselves as part of the equation.

"I could be more like water next time I call my mom," one girl remarked, as we all applied her learning to our own.

In a short time, these students had gone full circle. By moving on their own path, having an awareness of their choices, playing out those choices, and relating to one another, they realize that the dynamics of the things that they had been studying were not separate from themselves. They were able to put what they were learning about inside their textbooks into the context of their own lives and relationships.

"Thanks for teaching me about metabolism!" I say as some of the students pass through the door.

One kid turns and looks back through the crowded hallway: "Thanks for teaching me more about myself!"

⌘

What are the seemingly disparate elements that you bring together through your creativity?

What awesome adventure can your creativity take you on today?

93. Pinpointing what you need to be consistent in your everyday life.

Concord, Massachusetts. June 2013.

Arriving around 10am, dressed in a skirt and a shirt that covered my shoulders (as had been asked of all women present), I learned what to do by following along through the very deliberate tasks with which the other twenty-seven people were already engaged.

I quickly witnessed that amidst the friendly atmosphere, every moment had a ritual to it, an associated meaning. Helping to dismantle the previous sweat lodge, I moved with others ceremoniously in a counter-clockwise direction. On every circle round each of us removed one new branch from the dome, and through this dance, the old lodge became a pile of sticks.

We all gathered round. "Each one of us will share what we are praying for today before we move on to building the new lodge."

Pray? I wasn't sure what to pray for or how to pray. I sat in silence at Quaker meeting, but I wasn't praying. Or was I? I remembered being tested on my memorization of the *Our Father* when I was in third grade. I remembered staring at the intricacies of the Ukrainian Orthodox rendition of the

Virgin Mary hung on my grandma's wall as we knelt down quietly at the edge of her bed before sleep. I remembered women swaying as they prayed in Hebrew when I went to Jewish services with my friend in college. I remembered getting nervous in Mississippi when I was doing that show and someone asking me if they could pray for me while we were eating lunch. I remembered a line that I wrote in my solo show when the young girl has to bury her best friend, "I never knew what praying was until that moment..."

My montage caught up to the present as I began to hear people throwing their prayers up to the sky, held by the generosity and support of the circle. In this moment, playing felt free. It felt both momentous and purposeful, but at the same time was just another part of the day. Before I knew it, it was my turn.

"Letting go!" I offered from my heart as my feet sank deeper into the ground and my face felt the warmth of the breeze.

In the holes in the dirt that were left, we soon began a long process of constructing our new lodge. While a drum beat in the background, people took turns two at a time standing across from another, slowly bending the wood along their back until they met in the middle to create an arch. I watched in awe as multiple arches began to form a beautiful dome-like structure of about ten feet in diameter.

As I sat down to take it all in.

"Let go," said my heart.

"Be free," said my gut.

The man playing the drum caught my attention. He was

raising his eyebrows. He was motioning for me to take a turn continuing the beat. Me? I wasn't sure I was up for such a task, but before I knew it, without skipping a beat, the drum was in my lap and I was the one playing. *Beat, beat, beat.*

"Whatever you do, keep it consistent. Got it?" I nodded my head concentrating on my current rhythm. "You're doing great," he added as he walked away.

Sitting cross-legged on the warm ground, one hand steadied the instrument from underneath, while my other hand loosely held the drumstick.

Beat, beat, beat. I gently bounced the drumstick head along the stretched leather of the drum face.

Beat, beat, beat. My back started to ache under the responsibility set forth.

Keep it consistent? Oh, God.

Up and down went my arm, searching for the most efficient way to continue. Remembering to breathe, the rhythm began to match the rhythm of my heart, my thoughts.

Beat, beat, beat. Over an hour passed. As people bent the wood of the lodge, I bent my ideas and recognized my fears.

How many beats had I hit so far? How long could this go on? The original drummer was nowhere in sight.

I had never done anything this consistently in all of my life. Really. Truly. The grass had always been greener. The ideas newer. I had always been onto the next thing. But what remained? At the end of the day what could I count on as being the same? What did I need in order to remain steady? Consistent?

Beat, beat, beat.

I remembered how my dad would say that as a kid I always needed some sort of schedule or rhythm. Without it, I would immediately get sick.

Beat, beat, beat.

So what kind of energy was I squandering every week figuring every detail out anew when there were probably some things that had wanted to stick? What were the things I did or needed to do everyday in order to feel healthy, balanced, consistent? What should I repeat? What was my ritual? What did I pray for? What did I want to let go of? I knew but I didn't know at the same time.

Beat, beat, beat.

Just as the lodge was built, although the drum moved onto someone else, the beat kept going in me. I felt my heart working, wanting to be heard more often.

I joined a group that was making prayer ties by tying bits of tobacco into little sacks along a string.

"These are your prayers," said a girl nearby me. "They will hang above your head in the lodge."

I took another swig of water. It was already four in the afternoon, I was overwhelmed by my revelations, and we hadn't even entered the lodge yet.

"I need three women!" shouted a man's voice from the

lodge. He had just finished covering the dome in blankets.

"Come on," said the girl next to me, "This is a special part that only we can do."

I crawled into the lodge after her.

"We need to line the ground with these," said the girl, coming in with a handful of blankets in her arms. "Make it as smooth as possible, but be sure to leave room around the hole dug in the center. That's where the hot rocks will go."

It felt so small inside. How were twenty-seven people going to fit in here all at once? I focused on my task and made the ground as smooth as possible.

"Next, we need to make sure no light is seeping in," she said as she drew the blanket over the door, revealing a few points of light.

As we patched the holes it got dark. Really dark. The I-couldn't-see-my-hand-in-front-of-my-face kind of dark.

"I think we are all set to begin," she said as she opened the door and people began to line up with their prayer bundles in hand.

As I waited, my fears kicked into high gear, and questioned everything. *Maybe I should have gone to the wedding. Maybe I should have stayed in Vermont. Maybe I should have stayed in that relationship. Maybe I should have, have, have…*

My heart sped up. *Beat, beat, beat…*

I wanted to grab hold of something, anything. Hungry for answers, I started asking questions:

"How long will we be in there?"

"Well, it's hard to say. There are four rounds and each one is its own thing."

"Will it be quiet?"

"Sometimes. But there will also be singing and praying. We never quite know how it will unfold."

"Will we eat right after?"

"No. We'll need to close the ceremony first. You'll see..."

Nothing was sticking. I knew nothing. My "I will be okay if..." mind leapt in to help out:

"I will be okay if I can sit next to the friend I came with."

"Women always enter first. Men and women will sit on separate sides," explained one of the participants.

"Okay... Then I will be okay if I can sit near the other woman that I know and trust. She will help me get through this."

"Oh, I won't be going into the lodge this time," that woman said, "I'm going to stay outside and keep watch."

"Okay... Then I will be okay if, if, if..."

Before I knew it, I nestled into the lodge. I sat three spots away from the open door. My back ran along one of the walls. I squished in to make room for the woman sitting to my right and the woman on my left and brought my knees to my chest as more women started a row in front of me. I backed up as much as I could while encouraging a spider to crawl out under the wall. I looked across the circle to a man who had his hand up in the air. A spider was unraveling its way down to him. "Welcome, little one," I thought I heard him whisper before the door shut and the silence and darkness and heat and the singing and the praying began.

I went through three rounds of sweating it all out. I cried. I gleaned. I held the girl's hand next to me as she kept saying, "I can't do this. I can't do this."

"Yes you can," I whispered to her as I tried to believe it for myself.

I hardly remember the rest of the night, but I do remember this and I'll never forget it: Soaked in my own sweat and tears I made my way to the house between rounds to use the bathroom. Hurrying back, I caught a glimpse of someone in a hallway mirror. Who was that? I stepped back and looked into her eyes. That was a woman. A strong, beautiful woman. I touched my face as she touched hers.

That woman was me.

⌘

Tell the story of the moment when you first recognized yourself as an adult.

What are three things that you need to do on a consistent basis to be at your healthiest?

What is something that you could create a ceremony for right now? How could this new ritual help you to move with more clarity and strength?

EIGHTH MOVEMENT: ANOTHER KIND OF PROVIDENCE

Connect with your Compassionate Creativity by...

94. Graciously welcoming and consciously beginning again.

Providence, Rhode Island. 2013.

I wanted my new graduate students to know about the place that they had just arrived in. The place that they would be living in for the next three years. The place that could easily go overlooked while staying inside making theater all day long. The place that could become a distant memory of just a place where they got a degree and moved on. I wanted to see through one more year with them and here, in this place.

The university is located on a hill on the East Side of

Providence. The theater, where graduate program for actors and directors is housed, is located down that hill on the other side of downtown. In between the two is Kennedy Plaza, the main transit hub for all of Rhode Island. Although all within a mile, the hill and the plaza and the theater are all very different places with very different cultures. And unless taking public transportation, it's easy for the people in each of these places to stay separate.

I remembered when I was in graduate school when we went on silent walks along the river. To see what we heard. And to listen to what we saw. To take in the place and our relationship to it.

For my first class my students that semester, instead of meeting them downtown in the theater classroom, I asked them to meet me in Prospect Park at the top of the hill. There, overlooking the city, I asked everyone raise one foot and inhale.

"See the next three years underneath that foot. All the who-knows-what-might-happen. Who-knows-who-you-might-become. What you might learn. Inhale all those possibilities. The fear, the anticipation, the excitement. And on the count of three, we will take a conscious first step forward into this beginning together and continue silently on down the hill toward school. One, two, three."

We proceeded to take a silent walk through the city as the beginning of our new semester together – to see what we heard and to listen to what we saw. To notice when we wanted to step toward and when we wanted to step away. To notice without wanting or need to change anything. Without judgment, to let everything be as it was as we let ourselves become a part of it.

⌘

What would you like to restart today? Feel free to raise your foot and begin again.

What is a place/time when you felt incredibly welcomed? Why did you feel so welcomed?

What is your favorite way to welcome someone into your home or work space?

95. Talking to strangers.

Durham, North Carolina. 2013-2015.

My hairdresser lives 600 miles away, and her niece just played a birthday concert in my backyard. Only further evidence that everyone is somehow connected.

On my first day off, while working in North Carolina, I wandered out to a Farmer's Market in downtown Durham. I walked from booth to booth between watercolors and peaches, jewelry and carrots, candles and barbecue, seeing how they grew food and art in this particular community.

Through the crowds I saw that poster again: a hand-drawn monkey face with the words "Puppet Show" written along the bottom. Since I had arrived, I had noticed it hanging in grocery store entrances and posted on campus. I made my way to the stand where the poster was hanging, surrounded by various kinds of pottery. A woman's head popped out from behind a set of jars. She proceeded to explain to me how they were made to ferment foods.

As I listened to her describe her process, this woman became an immediate comrade. She was a teacher, an artist, a mom, and a puppeteer, and for many years she had been involved with the huge outdoor spectacle listed on the poster. "People of all ages from around here have been rehearsing together all summer," she explained. "This show is not to be missed."

I bought one of her ceramic trivets and promised to see her there.

I invited a friend of a friend to the show. We had never met before, but he was one of the many recommendations of "people I should meet" when people found out I was working in Durham. I maneuvered through the throngs of people, seeing which one might he him. Recognizing me first, he waved from his seat, and with common joy for our mutual friend, we hugged, and exchanged some stories and snacks before we became surrounded by epic, thirty-foot puppets. The play unfolded into a wondrous tale. The imaginative storytelling filled me with delight. A remembrance of the possibility of what theater without words could communicate to all ages. A realization that a community of thousands throughout this region now had this play, this story, in common.

I hugged and thanked the Puppeteer-Potter for her stunning performance and for encouraging me to come. Full of post-performance excitement, she invited me to her house for dinner later that week so that she could "welcome me to the area and introduce me around" to her family and her artist friends.

"What did you guys think?" I said to a group of people talking outside of their car parked next to mine. Before I knew it, I became a part of their conversation and we were exchanging numbers and they were inviting me to other events.

"I can't believe you just got here," they kept saying. "We

could swear you've lived here for a long time."

"Well, everyone is so kind and inviting," I responded, "It feels natural to fit right in."

"You were the one who talked to us first," the one man pointed out. "You have the magic of momentum."

At the dinner I met the Puppeteer-Potter's sweet, bike-riding, ethical humanist husband and her mom, a striking, eloquent 96-year-old woman who also lived at their home. As we gathered around the table, conversation flowed. When it came up that I had lived in Vermont, the Puppeteer-Potter immediately interrupted me to ask if I knew of a theater there.

"Yes, of course. I've performed there," I explained.

"Then I don't suppose you know this board member?"

"Oh yes! I've worked with him for three years in a row. How do you know him?"

"Because he's my brother and this is his mom," she said, smiling as she pointed across the table to her mom. We all sat in silence for a good moment reveling in such happenstance, while the connected web of relationships took shape in our minds.

"Well then, who's ready for some *Noise*?" the Puppeteer-Potter asked before putting on construction-site-sized headphones to make a coconut-ice-cream-like dessert in her loud blender.

Later that week I added a dress rehearsal for my solo show so that the Puppeteer-Potter and her mom could come on a night they were free of puppet commitments. After my performance, her mom congratulated me and asked if I would like to come over. "I have a special flower," she whispered. "It only blooms once a year and tonight just might be the night."

Although exhausted and ready to go to bed, I accepted. How could I not? This was one of those once-in-a-lifetime invitations.

As I arrived at their house, a Night-Blooming Cereus with two huge flowers welcomed me onto the porch. Layered shades of white stretching out from the center. The inner petals stood tall, while outer petals each the size of an open hand, unfolded gracefully, offering themselves to the world. A hello and a goodbye in one motion. A final corona layer, like a lions mane, encircled the whole.

"Aren't they perfectly beautiful?" smiled the Puppeteer-Potter's mom. "I wait for them every year."

The Carolina nighttime hummed around us as we kept the flowers company and ate another round of Noise. Everything about these people and their home was so special.

Before leaving to return north, I stopped in to say goodbye to the Puppeteer-Potter and her family and to surprise her brother who was visiting from Vermont. As I walked up, worlds collided. The person who he had hired for work Vermont years ago was now standing across from him on his family's porch in North Carolina. "Yes, it's me," I explained. "I've been here doing work and last week, I met your sister at the farmer's market. You have the most remarkable family."

Once he digested the story and connected the dots, he remarked that it made perfect sense that his sister and I had met.

I've returned several times to Durham, greeted by meals made by the Puppeteer-Potter. I eagerly pick up my fork, ready to engulf myself in garden vegetables and fermented things that I never dared to try before while listening to their new stories. The last two times I visited, the Puppeteer-Potter's sister-in-law gave me a haircut in the living room while the Puppeteer-Potter's nephews updated me on their latest glassblowing project, and the Night-Blooming Cereus sat on the porch patiently awaiting new buds.

"Do you know anyone who would want to have a house concert?" the Puppeteer-Potter wrote in between one of my visits. "My daughter is returning from Guatemala and looking for places to play."

Yet another invitation I couldn't refuse! Having a barbecue bash at my house in Providence, replete with ukulele tunes, would be a perfect way to celebrate my birthday North Carolina-style! Sure! Why not?

As the Puppeteer-Potter entered my house months later, she immediately recognized the puppet poster that hung on my fridge. "That's what originally drew me to your mom," I explained to her daughter as I heated up some water for tea. "I also have a teapot made by your mom and I bought this tile from her on the first day we met."

"Hey, I made that!" she said laughing.

And as I placed the tile onto my table, the Puppeteer-Potter's daughter told me the story of how she had carved the two people on it walking hand in hand.

⌘

What ideas did you grow up with about how to treat strangers?

How do you treat strangers now?

How could you connect with someone you don't know yet today?

96. Focusing on healing and sharing your best practices with others.

Baltimore to Providence, Rhode Island. 2013-2014.

"Oh shit," said the orthopedic specialist looking at my MRI. "This is much worse that I thought. Have you ever hurt your knee before?"

"I wore a brace once after I got hurt playing soccer in junior high."

"Well, I think your ACL has been tearing ever since and now it's completely obliterated. Take a look…"

I tore my left ACL: the anterior cruciate ligament, a miraculous band of fibrous tissue that holds the top of your leg to the bottom of your leg, crisscrossing through your knee. The ligament that football players often tear when another huge dude sideswipes them. Me? I did it to myself while pulling a suitcase out of my car before a show I was doing in Maryland… or at least that is what you might read on a trail of medical charts from Baltimore to Providence.

If you had asked how my overall spirits were at the time of the injury, you would have heard the fuller story. It was not a coincidence that days before I tore my ACL I drove eight hours, took two planes, went to a blowout wedding of two people I didn't know, broke up with the guy I had been dating long-distance, and began to create a new play with fifteen high-school students. And that was only the most recent momentum. But when I went to the orthopedic specialists, after the tear, no one asked me about those things; neither did my friends or family. We all focused on the task at hand, my knee, the place that was communicating the loudest that something, many things, were out of balance. Yes, a loud, clear message from the universe to slow down... if only I would listen.

The ongoing, underlying lessons that my injury brought forth day after day focused around learning to let people help me. Friends, family, strangers. *Why can it be so difficult to accept assistance?*

"How important is it to you that you carry all of that into the house yourself," my colleague in Baltimore would joke as I fumbled with my purse and crutches and the ice cream we had just bought.

When I first hurt myself (isn't that an interesting phrase?), he canceled our weekend plans to attend his favorite theater conference, and instead, we went on drives in the country and got oysters in Baltimore. At night we sat and talked about break-ups and breaking bones and making theater and teaching. *Reconnecting is healing.* I was, after all, the eighteen-year-old Buffalo girl who played violin in that same Shakespeare play that he was in so many summers ago. He played guitar and sang James Taylor songs all night – anthems that I continued to use through my recovery. *Music is medicine.*

When frustrated that a surgery would only be the beginning

of a long learning process, with months or years of physical therapy and a new-found relationship to my body, I did everything I could to guide myself forward in gratitude. This was not a terminal illness but rather a fixable thing that I needed to commit to taking care of, and it would require effort and openness on all levels.

Although there were many options for "fixing" my knee, such as using part of my own hamstring or taking from the ligament on the front of my knee, I opted to replace my torn ACL with an allograft. I would undergo a surgery that would take out my ACL and then attach another person's hamstring to my bones.

"The hamstring of a cadaver," I would explain to students and co-workers, just as the doctors had been explaining to me. Their faces would go cold.

"A dead person?"

"Yes. Isn't that amazing?"

The responses would range from gross to weird to a fear of infection, but I continued to see it as nothing short of a heroic miracle. Before dying, a person whom I'd never know made a decision to donate their body to someone like me. Their heart might now be beating in someone else, as their hamstring became the new connector for the top and bottom of my leg. If I asked for the code number on that ligament, I could even anonymously thank the donor's family online.

I thought about returning to Baltimore or Durham for surgery. I considered Florida too. Anywhere would be better than having to relearn to walk on the ice of another

Northeastern winter. And my mom, of course, wanted me to come home to Buffalo to do it. In the end, I decided to do it in Providence. This was my home now. I had spent two and a half years trying to settle there and was finally just beginning to do it. How could I leave now? But I wouldn't be able to recover alone. This choice meant asking my mom to come help me. *Family is medicine.*

She agreed and drove in from Buffalo. By taking me to all of my doctor's appointments and picking up all my prescriptions, she quickly found her way around Providence And she made me laugh the entire way through. *Humor is medicine.*

The night before my surgery, my friend and life coach encouraged me to write down all the things that I dreamed of and put them onto a big sheet of paper. "These are the things you have been moving toward, and that's important to remember." *Something to look forward to is medicine.*

My teacher/mentor from California, now colleague/friend in Providence, accompanied me and my mom to the hospital. When the nurse assumed that he was my dad and said he could stay until I was wheeled away, I didn't correct her. We weren't blood related, but over time we had become family. *Kinship is medicine.*

And on I went to surgery. Even though it was outpatient, it was scary. Any surgery is scary. We don't quite know who we will be on the other side, what will be different or difficult. I came out with a huge brace on my left leg and unable to walk.

The night after my surgery I was feeling great. The drugs

that were supposed to make me sleepy had the reverse effect. After 300 texts telling people all over the world how much I loved and appreciated them, my mom confiscated my phone and forced me to get some rest. *Sharing my love is medicine.*

My mom made soups and smoothies and pasta and changed my ice pack. Learning how to sit on a toilet keeping one leg absolutely straight and letting my mom choose my underwear were both hurdles within themselves. *Redefining dignity.* Other celebrated milestones included the regained ability to drive, take a bath, walk up stairs, hop on one foot, and do laundry. We don't know something quite the same way until it's taken away from us for a while, do we? *Absence makes the heart grow grateful... with many thanks to my ever courageous, patient mom.*

A neighbor called to let me know that there was a homemade quiche on my porch and brought me nightlights when I realized that they would make a difference. Another friend brought prune juice and laid in bed with me for the afternoon. People from the local Quaker Meeting House stopped by to talk and see if I needed anything. Presents and cards and flowers arrived by mail. *Community is medicine.*

People of all ages who did physical therapy next to me gave me the thumbs up. "You look much better today," they would say as they struggled to do their latest exercise.

"You too," I would say as counted another leg-lift. *Compassion is medicine.*

Friends who lived an hour away drove down with their dogs and taught me about herbal remedies. *Animals are medicine. Learning is medicine.*

New friends and old friends came from near and far to help me for a few days at a time. We went duckpin bowling, played games, drew pictures, and shared good food together. *Creativity is medicine.*

I had so much fun and laughed so hard with all of these people, that honestly, when I look back, I remember the fun more than the challenges of recovery. Remembering these moments continued to fuel me as I balanced returning to work with months of physical therapy. *Remembering that I am loved is medicine.*

⌘

How do you pinpoint when you are out of balance?

What is your best medicine?

How did you originally discover these ways?

97. Collaging your life together piece by piece.

Providence, Rhode Island. 2013.

A collage seems to me to be the best way to describe a person. Every being I pass is a perfect, evolving spirit of unique contradictions and correlations. A kaleidoscope. An assemblage of diverse elements, an interweaving of ideas, their own special brew.

When I had knee surgery and my mom came to take care of me, we brought home a lot of waiting-room magazines. Watching them pile up as December wound down, I unveiled the great idea to make collages of what we each wanted to strive toward in the coming year. Vision boards! I didn't know if my mom and I were ready to pinpoint our dreams, let alone explain them, but I thought we could find a way to express ourselves through some good old art making on my living room floor.

Between meals and physical therapy appointments, I excitedly convinced my mom to do it. With scissors and glue sticks at the ready, as if attending an illustrious adult pre-school, we sat quietly for hours scavenging for the exact images, colors, and words that reminded us of what we enjoyed doing most and illuminated our dreams. Slowly these pieces began to layer onto the blank poster boards in front of us, and our unique visions came into view.

Once finished, we sat them side-by-side for late-night museum viewing. We stood taking in one another's choices: looking, seeing, interpreting, comparing, pointing out, justifying, clarifying, and learning. Educated and intrigued, we fell asleep holding one another's dreams for the new year and feeling newly accountable for our own.

Months later, hundreds of miles apart and my knee mostly healed, my mom and I said our goodnights over the phone.

"Remember your collage..." I reminded her.

"Yes, and make sure you are living yours, too, my darling."

⌘

What are 5 things that you would put on your board today?

What part of your collage gets covered up often and why?

How can you enjoy/share in at least one of your collage elements this week?

98. Finding freedom within limitations.

Throughout Rhode Island. 2013-2014.

That Christmas, some older friends invited me to their apartment to share some food and play some music. His mom, Mildred, who lived in an independent living center, and her dad, who had severe dementia, would be joining us. They forewarned me that in this company, one could never quite predict where the conversation might wind up or how the mood might change, and that it could of course repeat or cease depending on several factors unbeknownst to any of us.

We had a ball together. Great food, amazing conversation. I even remember explaining what I did for a living in the most articulate way because: 1) They cared so much. 2) I slowed down and simplified. And 3) Because the entire night was about being present. If I had an agenda to know anything specific or expect any certain answer or response, I had to let it go. But to merely listen and navigate the waters as they came was actually quite liberating. Of course, this was maybe easier for me than it was for their children. Their children had years of specific memories and agendas with each of these people. Heck, they had been living in relation to these people, their parents, for their entire lives, so how could they let go and listen to their parents being confused or weary? How could it not hurt when they saw their parents having such a hard time standing up from the dinner table? These, the people, who taught them to walk.

The night concluded with the singing of Christmas carols around the piano. My friend played as his mom sang from the couch. She loved to sing and had always been in a choir. She knew every verse by heart. My other friend took photos and smiled at the full scene unrolling before her. Her dad, despite having been brought a chair, stood for the full hour plus of holiday tunes, happy to join in on each song and enthusiastically so. If I recognized the melody, I played along on violin, grateful to be part of such an intergenerational group together in the same space realizing each new moment as it came.

Several months later when I went to physical therapy for my knee in the building next to hers, Mildred and I became better friends. I would stop by after my treatment and we would share tea and a chat while looking out at the seasons changing along the Seekonk River. She had a story for every photo and piece of art in her apartment. I came to find out that some of the paintings were done by her late husband, my friend's dad, whom I had never met.

The next spring, Mildred had surgery on her hip. It had been giving her such immense pain, and being in pretty good health up until then, she decided she would do something about it rather than suffer or lose mobility. For Mildred, the most challenging part of this choice was not the surgery itself but rather having to leave her apartment and full calendar in order to do the necessary rehab elsewhere. In this new place, which was more of a nursing home facility, it was difficult for Mildred to see other elders in such debilitating circumstances. Through it all, Mildred grasped for her independence by wanting to do the things that defined her dignity. Tasks like getting dressed or going to the bathroom, which post-surgery she was told not to do without pushing the call button, she just went ahead and attempted on her own. She wanted to show that she was ready to return to her own apartment, her friends, and her life as she knew it. The way she valued it. To her years of accumulated health.

Instead, through a complicated series of infections and additional surgeries and challenges that summer, Mildred made her way around the Greater Providence rehab/eldercare circuit. Meanwhile, her family tried desperately to find a place where she would feel comfortable and have around the clock care, starting to give way to the possibility that Mildred might never be able to go back to the apartment she was longing for.

This story is one that many of us know too well, having traversed it delicately years back, knowing now ways we might have dealt differently. Others of us, bless you, are in the midst of taking on this kind of story right now – accompanied of course by your own jobs and children and finances. The rest of us, if we are lucky enough for our parents to grow to an older age, will negotiate this terrain soon enough. We will learn that there are no easy solutions but rather an ongoing conversation and struggle for dignity while one's body, along with the institutions we've created to take care of it, fail. In this culture, somewhere along the way, we lost a valued reverence for aging. We no longer share a vocabulary for discussing the end of life. Although a horizon for all of us, we avoid talking about, planning around, or looking at death.

One of the places Mildred stayed on her journey was across the bay from Providence. A nice, new place that housed rehab patients, long-term residents, a whole wing focused on memory and more... all expensive attempts to help navigate the many possible crossroads of our ever-aging population. Our friends, our neighbors and our family members. The first time I visited, I saw quiet elders rocking in chairs overlooking the water. They each waved and each smiled in their own way as I entered the building. As I passed through the doors, I realized how proud and fortunate I was to be my age, my face only at the very beginning of having a few wrinkles. Who knows what memories were whirling around in their minds as I passed by? I don' t know whether their thoughts had anything to do with me or not, but I could see their wheels turning about. Gristmills of memories. So many days, years more than I had, floating around in those minds, those hearts. So many times in our world that I would never see or know, but could gain some small insights into if only I would sit down with them, ask, and take the time. The time to listen.

Mildred was excited to see me. She knew that I was performing that week at the new theater festival in town, and she was ready to hear all about it. She had even sought out articles in the newspaper and cut out a mention and ad for the event. After we caught up on how things were going for one another, Mildred begged me to stay and have dinner in her new dining room. She had a new spark about her here. She had begun to find a rhythm and a life with the other temporary residents on this hall. She had found a camaraderie with them, a connection rooted in their common goal to return home.

The dining area was small; maybe five or so circular tables set up only to serve the people staying in Mildred's wing. It felt more like a house in a way, including a regular-looking kitchen that residents or their families could use alongside the cooks and nurses and aides. Mildred approached the tables, purposely choosing where to sit. "Look there," she elbowed me, speaking under her breath as she moved toward the last empty seat. "We can't possibly let those gentlemen sit alone. Come on, pull up another chair."

As I joined in, I was politely introduced to Steve and Mike and Bill. They were all "senior citizens" ranging in age from their mid-sixties to their mid-nineties. All had varying reasons for why they were there – from the loss of a leg to a heart condition to some temporary memory loss. The three men welcomed us with huge grins. Each smile uniquely connected to a map of lines upon each of their beaming faces. The times of their life were drawn in every direction. These guys were a fun crew. They had only known each other for a couple of weeks at most but they already had a template for how they conversed.

Mildred introduced me to the group as a performer who made my own work. She delightedly explained the details of the festival in which I was about to participate. My jaw dropped as I listened to my new press agent going on and on before opening up the floor for questions. Wait, I had approached dinner ready to ask them questions, not to have to answer theirs. "Oh, I know," said Bill, trying his best to understand my line of work, "You're like that woman who wrote the *Vagina Monologues*." The rest of our forks suspended on their way to our mouths. Bill had just casually introduced the word "vagina" into the conversation. This was not a word that was taken lightly while enjoying dinner, let alone being used in front of two women.

"Yes, sort of," I replied, not sure which way to go next. "Do you know that play?"

The others focused solely on their pork chops as Bill began to explain the *Vagina Monologues* to the group. Little by little this brought about an absolutely intriguing conversation about the V word (which wasn't actually mentioned again but was alluded to several times).

"Yes, we didn't really ever talk about those things," Steve offered.

"We didn't even know that word. And if we did, we wouldn't be caught using it," Mildred added.

Could this possibly be happening at any other elder facility across the world? My thirty-three-year-old self was inadvertently, yet openly, talking about private parts and sex with four people over the age of sixty-five. Amazed, I listened with a reverence and innocence I had not yet experienced in my short lifetime. I paid homage to the community theater that had put this play on in Bill's hometown years ago and to Eve Ensler for writing it.

Dinner plates happily cleared, Mildred and I were talked into staying for dessert, and we all enjoyed more thoughts while splitting an amazing chocolate torte. To conclude, one-by-one, our company set down their fork, arose with varying ability, and bid the others goodnight. A ritual that these new neighbors had all become accustomed to. Once all of the men were out of earshot, Mildred looked to me with a glimmer in her eyes: "Well," she grinned, "I'd say we gave them a night to remember!"

A few days later, I kayaked across to the same residence from the Community Boat House. As if on a great ocean liner, Mildred waved me on from her balcony in the distance. "This is my friend. She *rowed* here to see *me*," she proudly boasted to a nearby family visiting with their father – as I sat catching my breath in my lifejacket, utterly amazed by the places in life we happen to end up, and how we arrive there.

In the weeks that followed, Mildred began to decline. Her surgeries had taken a toll and brought out some unknown issues within her heart. She moved into her own room within a special Hospice building dedicated to end-of-life processes. There, Mildred spent her last moments on the planet surrounded by visits from her children, grandchildren, and great grandchildren. They sang. They told stories. They laughed. They cried. And now all of Mildred's relations momentously extend her life by living their own.

Days after her death, her son went to her apartment to begin sorting through her belongings. Many people there, residents and workers alike, came up to him expressing their condolences for his mom's passing. Much to his surprise, they also commented how glad they were that Mildred was able to visit there before she died. Now, admittedly, there is a moment where we all might question whether an elder is actually telling the sound truth or whether they might be speaking through a kind of dementia, but when several elders continue to share the same story in the same hallway, we must all start to believe that it's true. And it was.

Days before going to Hospice, her son remembered that Mildred had asked to borrow twenty dollars. "To be used for a haircut or something," he had thought. Not so. Twenty dollars in hand and fully dressed in her best outfit, Mildred had called a cab and in fact returned to her former apartment complex. Although exceptionally frail, Mildred had somehow mustered the energy, the courage, and the perseverance she needed to spend an entire day walking through her hallways, dining with her friends and going to whatever events were on the calendar. Saying hello and saying goodbye, I suppose.

I can only imagine her at the end of that day, smiling and sitting tall as she was driven back through the streets of Providence. Absolutely exhausted and most definitely victorious. An overwhelming sense of dignity and independence, at last restored.

⌘

How do you define freedom? Dignity?

How do you find freedom within your current "limitations?"

99. Remembering that everyone is just a kid dressed up in older people clothes.

Providence, Rhode Island.

"Today we are going to move from ages zero to one-hundred in one hour."

My new undergraduate clown class proceeded to look at me with their heads tipped like a confused pack of dogs. I was only supposed to have sixteen in this class but fifty showed up. I registered twenty and another six decided to "vagabond" the class for no credit. Clown is a wanted class here. Clown is an essential class.

"Find your own place on the floor and close your eyes, please."

Twenty-six college students run to find their place on the floor. I ask them to floppily raise their knees to their chest and raise their hands above their face. When they open their eyes, this will be the first thing that they see in their baby-state. I let them know that 50% of this exercise can come from their memory and 50% can be completely made up: "Any inspiration is absolutely perfect. Absolutely viable. You choose. Just make sure to take care of yourself..."

They begin by exploring their hands, which led them to discover how to move.

"Everything is an opportunity. Everything is completely new. Curiosity. There is no this-is-this or this-means-this. There is no fear yet."

They throw a ten-second temper tantrum for no reason before seeing something they want and reaching for it and crawling toward it. Falling and laughing and balancing, they learn to walk, they get hungry, they realize when they need people to help them and what they can do on their own.

"Enjoy the privilege of being able to become a baby today," I remind them, "Not everyone has the chance to do this today."

They start to see and play with one another. They imitate each other to figure something out. They start to communicate.

"There is no right or wrong here. This exploration is absolutely for you. What does it mean to be up on your feet?"

They do something that they love.

I ask them to see how they react when they are told they can't or aren't allowed to do that thing.

Some scream and some go sit in a corner.

"Line up for school!" I offer next.

"I don't wanna go to school!" one kid shouts out.

They go to recess and play. They make their way home and are tucked in at the end of the night.

"What is something you are still thinking about? Is this something that you do easily? What is your ritual before going to bed?"

"I want crackers!" someone shouts out.

They all fall to sleep and then wake up into a dream. Parts of the dream are great. Parts are scary. People zip through the room and become super heroes.

"Now do the same thing you are doing now, but fast-forward it to being eight-years-old. How is it different?" People scream and dodge.

"Freeze!" some calls out.

Their dream becomes a reality as I ask them to begin to create or make something. "You love to do this thing. Could be something you do at school, at home, or some place else. If you don't have an idea, keep exploring. Something will come to you."

Some people beat buckets as drums. Others skip through the space.

I ask them whether they want to share what they are making or doing with someone else and how they interact with others.

"Be careful! You are going to hurt the birds!" someone gasps.

Their play then turns into working with a group on some kind of a project in a class. They have one minute to finish in order to graduate. Rushing around, I ask them to translate what they are doing to another activity outside of school. Then I ask them to take ten steps to arrive in this moment in time, to catch up to their present age.

Some smile. Some look taller or gain confidence as they step.

"Now take ten steps into older ages, uncharted territory."

Some celebrate. Some laugh. Some take this very seriously.

As they cruise into their thirties and I remind them that I am thirty-two and that in this exercise, they still have seventy years to go. They play through their forties, choosing whether to have children and noticing what they are doing for work, how they are making money, and how they are having fun.

"Start out with whatever you first associate with that age and let that idea take you down the waterfall to play forward."

They move into their fifties, by making a phone call to someone important.

"I love you so much," says one student.

I ask them to see how that conversation might be different ten years later.

"I'll be right there to help you," one student says.

Into their sixties they possibly have grandkids, and I see them starting to make choices about how their bodies might be changing.

"Oh boy, that hurts!" exclaims one boy.

"You still have forty more years in you," I remind them. "Don't act too old too soon. You'll have nowhere to go!"

At seventy, they remember a game that they played as a kid

and find someone to teach it to and play it with.

"Who are you friends still?" I ask them. "Who is no longer with you?"

They are suddenly surprised by needing to take care of something or someone that needs their help. "What does it mean to really take care of this? Notice how your breath might be different here."

Into their eighties, they take a walk down a street, noticing their sense of family and friends and identify what is the absolute joy in their life.

"It's nice to see you again, Lilly," says one girl.

"As you cruise up to your nineties, what are you loves, hates, hopes, and fears now? What matters now? How are they different from when you were in your twenties?"

They find another person to go on a walk with and share these things in conversation.

"Notice how the way you look out your eyes is different. The way you listen is different."

Their backs are rounded. They are walking slower. Their eyes are squinted.

"Now find a game to play with this person. It is what you always do with this person when you see them. Play it one last time."

The room erupts into loud voices and coughs and laughter.

"There is some reason that this game is a lot more difficult to play."

"Billy! Billy!" yells one student over and over.

"He's such a nice young man," says another.

"Find a place to take a seat together with this person. Every step feels like a month of time. Find a final place to rest with this friend."

They help each other across the room. They move slow. They smile and finally all sit down next to their partners.

"Take a look out into space. Into the distance.

"Oh boy, here we go..."comments one student now being an old man.

"And out there, you have a whole movie playing. It is the memories of your entire life. Over ninety years." I remind them of when they were two, of their dream, of their school project, of class in college, of a job they loved and one they didn't, the people that were important to them, someone who really helped them, of something they are really proud of and could tell a four-hour story about.

The room is silent.

I ask them to slowly look at the hands of the person next to them and then to see their own hands. "These hands have been with you through all of those things. Through your entire life. They were the first thing you saw as a baby. Notice how they feel now that you are ninety-nine. What is the thing you still want to do with those hands? Where do they want to be on your hundredth birthday?"

"Now, take a huge inhale, see whatever you wish for in front of you. On the exhale, you are going to blow out the candles of your one-hundredth birthday."

They all smile, blow, and then their eyes come to a close.

⌘

What part of this journey from 0-100 did you connect with the most? Why?

What fears come up for you?

What age would you like to be today? How will that shift how you see things, what you feel, what you say, and what you do?

100. Leaving room for spontaneous adventures.

Providence, Rhode Island. 2014.

Because I wasn't in a hurry to leave after today's physical therapy appointment, I witnessed the next group coming in. They were mostly older folks. They took smaller steps. Their hands trembled. They seemed down.

"The Parkinson's patients," commented my physical therapist as she saw me watching them. "They are all coming to do their weekly movement class together."

While sitting in the waiting room from time to time, I had seen the flyer advertising this group, *Dance for PD,* and I had been curious about how it worked. Since I wasn't scheduled to be anywhere right away, I asked the teacher if I could watch.

"Sure, but you have to participate."

Walking in, one man immediately looked at me as if I were an alien, "Hey! You don't look like us!"

"I might be a little younger, but would it be okay if I joined you today?"

"I don't see why not."

I took my seat next to him and looked around at the six other people who sat facing the direction of the windows. An aide and a few family members sat along the walls. Although there was an obvious affinity between the group, each individual remained sullen and withdrawn.

When the teacher came in and turned on the music, the mood instantaneously began to shift. Oldies and Big Band melodies immediately took hold of all of us. Without making a conscious choice, our shoulders started moving. Our bodies became marionettes. The familiar tunes became the strings that levitated our joints.

While doing physical therapy at this clinic, I had learned that one of the major neurological issues associated with Parkinson's disease (PD) is that the person being affected thinks they are doing large movements when in actuality, they are hardly moving at all. PD patients are often observed taking very little steps. So this class is focused on doing simple dance sequences. The repetitions and momentum helps the PD patients to gain larger movements. I witnessed each participant's movements growing more pronounced as the hour ticked on.

In the last ten minutes, we all marched down the hallways together. One person's young grandson even decided to join in. Focused on getting the kid to enjoy it, everyone automatically moved more dramatically until arms and legs of all sizes and shapes and ages were flailing with laughter up and down the hallway.

At the end of the class, out of breath, we all sat back in our seats. What an hour! I looked around the room. Those leaving were different people than the ones who walked in.

Everyone now had an extra pep in their step and smile on their face. Even though the music had ended, the melodies still resonated within each of us. An internal concert playing between our muscles, within our joints, and along our nerves. Every cell in our bodies was dancing.

And with some sweat on his brow and a twinkle in his eye, the man who had initially greeted me, patted me on the shoulder. "Well now, that was quite the adventure, wasn't it?"

⌘

What is your relationship with spontaneity?

What's a little spontaneous adventure you could make space for this week?

101. Turning your anger into articulation.

Providence, Rhode Island. 2014.

"Why am I doing this?" I asked as I trod home from teaching through the dark streets of Providence.

"Why wouldn't you go into theater?" I remembered my dad saying long ago, "That's what you've always loved doing."

"Well, I don't love it in the same way anymore," I wanted to yell, shaking my fist to the sky.

I'd been doing theater for fifteen years but now I stood at a new crossroads. I remembered feeling a similar frustration in high school, and my dad getting so excited about it. "Being this furious means that you care so much that you are going to have to do something about it."

Part of me I wished that I didn't care and that I could just move on to another profession, but I couldn't. This conflict was eating me up inside.

My graduate students were dreaming of becoming professional actors. I remembered having this dream once myself, but I was coming to understand that my deeper dream was to foster community. I'm not saying that being a professional actor and fostering community are mutually exclusive things, no, but there is a challenging balance. And as a teacher, I was no longer interested in teaching actors how to be better actors just so that they could wait to be cast in roles that they would then interpret. I was interested in faciliatating a process for people to discover what role they wanted to create for themselves and then help them to make it.

I loved how theater could create a space for this discovery. When theater wasn't an end to itself. When it was a vehicle to learn about everything. To learn about ourselves. When it was a way of continuously falling in love with the world. When it was a way of being with people we knew and people we didn't know. People who had very different perspectives. I loved when theater was about being curious and playing with our unanswerable, eternal questions. When it was a place for everyone to remember what they loved, how to make something, and believe in the power of sharing it. I loved when theater was a place that welcomed people in-person, a rare commodity these days. I loved when theater went beyond sound bytes or headlines that induced fear, assumptions, or judgments. I loved when theater became a safe space to practice empathy together by witnessing stories – full, 360-degree stories. Looking through the prism from every angle. I loved when these stories weren't chosen because they would sell tickets, but rather chosen by relentlessly listening for the stories that had been going unheard. That needed a flashlight. I loved how theater could become a home for these stories. These people. These voices. For me, theater was a valiant reminder that all is not lost when we gather together and share.

I could only teach this. The theater that I loved. The theater I believed in and was so passionate about. I would find a place to do that and do it with all my might, and if I couldn't find that place, then I would somehow create that place myself.

❡

What are five things that make you incredibly angry?

How do these things reveal what you truly care about?

How can you articulate the essence of that care today?

102. Making decisions by gathering three generations around the table.

Burlington, Vermont to Providence, Rhode Island. 2014-2015.

I am the curious young girl chasing butterflies.
I am the beautiful old lady knitting on the porch.
I am the gentle, radiant woman in between.
Learning, listening, and loving.

That spring, I returned to performing by bringing both my solo shows to the Full Circle Festival where 1400 people came together for a stunning weekend to focus on "The Heart and Art of Aging." I immediately fell in love with the intersection of people. Like me, they were extremely passionate about caring for elders, but they were going about it through medicine, business, and government. Part of me started thinking I should jump ship and become a doctor or a nurse so that I could elicit change more directly, but then I started taking suitcases and props out of my car and I was, once again, at home in my art.

My two shows were destined to become one and now, after taking some time away from them, they had become a full-length piece. The loop pedal technology became and IV unit with a call button. The astroterf became the walls of the nursing home, and the wooden ironing board became the door. The old woman character inspired by my grandmother became the mother of the teenage girl who was pregnant. Now there were two acts that moved from an infant home in the 1950s to a nursing home in present day.

Performing both shows in one weekend, still recovering from knee surgery was a challenge, but my mom was there to help, as was a friend from that program in Ithaca thirteen years before.

After my shows the audience was baffled. They didn't understand how I had become all three generations before their eyes. "You were a ninety-one year old woman and then you were a young girl and then you were a middle-aged nurse," one woman responded. "These are such different people. I couldn't wrap my mind around them all existing in one person."

And this was exactly why I had come to love doing solo work. There weren't three actors playing three different characters. The audience witnessed one person transforming before their eyes. I was the nurse helping the old man, but then as I took my hand off the wheelchair I began to age. Within moments I became the old woman getting and MRI. I was the mother holding her pregnant belly but as she moved across the stage that pregnant belly, a sweatshirt, passed through becoming a baby in her arms to being put on by that baby thirty years later.

My hope was that after seeing these transformations happen in the theater, the audience would more readily be available to see the possibility of transformation in their families, in their friends, in their co-workers, in strangers, and ultimately in themselves.

"How does a young woman like you step into the body of a ninety-one year old woman?" asked one audience member.

I had done it for so long that it was second nature to me. But these were doctors and nurses and government officials.

When I put my body in the shape of an elderly person and take a deep breath, I start to feel like them. On the next breath, I find how they gesture. On the next one, I add a sound to match that gesture, and then I let that sound evolve into a word. This word teaches me something about what that character wants. Then, they start looking for that thing and they see it. And seeing it changes them. If it is, in fact, the thing they were searching for, then they are overjoyed. If it turns out it's not that thing, then they are disappointed. For me, this is the embodiment of a character. Through this process, I begin to look out through their eyes, and I see an entirely different world.

"At first when you entered as the nurse, I got so mad at her for how she was talking to the elderly woman," said another audience member, "But then when the nurse explained how after her twelve hour shift, she had to go and take care of her own mother, I suddenly saw her in a completely different way."

When I first started doing these shows, the characters were more surface level. The grandmother was mean and the young girl was innocent and the nurse didn't care about her job. But as I spent time being these people, I started to have more empathy for them, and I realized how much more complex their relationships were. The Nurse, The Old Woman, The Granddaughter. They weren't just one thing. Nothing was cut and dry or easy to figure out. All these people had secrets. They had joyful moments and angry ones. They all wanted to love and be loved. They had reasons they did what they did and needed what they need.

"At the end of the show, I didn't understand how the granddaughter could possibly make up with the grandmother, but somehow she did."

"I didn't understand how she could either," I responded, "And neither did she…"

By the time I decided to go and visit her,
I was ready to scream at her for days
For how she treated my mother
For how she never cared for me
But then I saw her.
Just laying there
So helpless.
"Hello," I said.
"The snow is coming down so hard right now."
She looked exactly like my mother…

That day in rehearsal, I remember debating over how to end the show. I started playing with the objects in the show and jokingly, like a puppet, I made the slide projector tray become the head of the old woman in the wheelchair. A friend of mine came in as I was doing this and said, "That's it! That's it! Keep going!"

The old woman started looking around and I spoke as the granddaughter taking her out of the nursing home:

She pointed and I drove
Until finally we pulled up to a blue house.

The lights were still on.
"It's real nice in there," she said.
"There's a little family in there
And they are just at the very beginning..."

"Being here with all of you makes me hopeful for the elders of the world." I said to the audience of festival participants at the conclusion of the talkback. "That they, that we, will all be taken care of."

"I feel the same hope by being with you," said one of the participants as she went on her way to the next event.

⌘

What is a current decision that could be helped by more generations being around the table?

How does your Compassionate Creativity help you find an access point for empathizing with people of different ages or professions?

103. Recognizing how much your current story affects your every move.

Providence, Rhode Island. August 2014.

I just ran a whole mile without stopping! The sweat still drips off my wrists and finagles its way around the edges of my eyes. Typing is a beautiful challenge. I can't find each key quickly enough for these thoughts, the result of my efforts still running through my mind.

Now I know that, to some of you, this achievement might not seem like a big deal at all, and to others, it might seem like a huge deal: a mile. Running is another one of those very relative things. Me? I've never been a runner per se, but I have always related to and understood the world around me by moving through and with it.

Since my injury ten months ago, I haven't been able to move like I'm used to and this has been endlessly frustrating. Healing was quick and noticeable at first but then it came in tiny doses. I went to physical therapy but I didn't feel like anything was changing. I began to doubt that I was ever going to get better. This lowered my spirits, which made my knee hurt more, which made me feel worse, and then I had absolutely no motivation to get better. Rather than starting with what I could do, I focused solely on what I couldn't do.

"My bad knee..." was the beginning phrase to every story I told to myself and to everyone around me.

One week ago, my physical therapist said that my next task would be to run a mile. This was something that I could hardly do even before the injury. (I still remembered that fifth grade race and the mean, doubtful voice persisted: *Running had never been my strong suit. This was going to be impossible.*)

But tonight after standing in the outfield attempting to play softball with a group of new neighbors, I stopped at the track on the way back home and started running. *Why not?* Smiling and without hesitation, I easefully went around the track.

One lap! Little did he know his power, but a man standing at the side of the track smiled my way as I passed him. "Keep going. You got this," he waved.

Two laps! I started telling myself the same thing: *Keep going. I got this.* I remembered the time in Brazil when I surprised myself by doing a back-hand-spring because the teacher assumed I could and wouldn't take no for an answer.

Three laps! I reveled in the accomplishment of each step, instilling faith in my two legs, my body, my balance. I remembered how much I loved to move freely whenever and however I wanted.

And four laps! One mile! Just like that, I reached the seemingly impossible goal, and I am now telling you the story that I never thought I would be able to.

Although I needed the expertise of those who have studied

the body in and out, along with the gifts from all of the people who supported me, ultimately I had to embody their gentle kindness and gift it to myself. I am the expert of my own best healing, and the story I tell myself is my most potent medicine.

⌘

How might your current story be limiting you?

How can reframing your story help you to break through?

104. Remembering that you are never alone. There are too many people in the world.

Providence, Rhode Island. September 2014.

I used to say how much I wished that all of the people I loved could somehow live in the same neighborhood. Eventually I realized that neighborhood was the world. But even amidst a life traveling as a performer and teacher I often found myself slipping into feeling isolated and becoming "busy" doing my own thing.

When a student expressed an interest in helping me to share my writing with more people, the *Compassionate Creativity Project* was born.

This project quickly became a community that included 111 people from around the world: my teachers from high school, my best friend's mom, people I met in college, my new boyfriend, colleagues from Italy, neighbors, people I met on airplanes, former boyfriends, classmates from graduate school, people from Quaker Meeting, students, one of my company members and his aunt, friends of friends, people who I had yet to meet, and my mom.

Every day I sent one of these 111 values to them. The email would be automatically sent out at 3am so, no matter what part of the world they lived in, everyone would receive it on the same day. When I woke up, I ran to the computer to see who had written and what they had said. My mom was connecting with my company member's aunt in Switzerland. My orchestra teacher was connecting with an engineering professor I knew in college. My colleague from Italy was connecting to my classmates from graduate school. My young students were connecting with my older friends. These connections energized me more than I could ever describe.

Driving to Pennsylvania to do my solo show, I felt like all these people were in the car with me. When I was on the stage doing the talkback, I couldn't wait to tell them about what I had heard, what I learned, and how I was defining and redefining the potential of Compassionate Creativity.

After the first few weeks of sharing, I took pieces of all the community responses and collaged them into this poem called *Great Observers of Life's Many Facets*:

On the cusp
I'm at a crossroad
Morning coffee by water's edge
I needed a day off
With a new attempt to heal
A tree fell in the woods near where I grew up
Silent
Retreated into my imagination
A dark hole somebody will eventually coax me out of
Holding a candle
Passed down from generation to generation
To see the view outside my window.

I am not enough.

Longing for longing
I wait
Seeing now clearly
All of the untraveled passages
That will never be
The water too dark
Too dense
Too deep to swim
My heart then too heavy
I would not float
I caress the clarity
That lives between these stones.

Ella Fitzgerald, Count Basie, Tony Bennett, Steve and Eydie
On a dairy farm
A weekly knitting group and 2 book clubs
A 1940s vacuum cleaner
The M train as it passes through Williamsburg
My first bike
A task of integration
Synchronicity
A meteor falling fast
Where love is the most important thing in the world
A symbol for everything I have compromised and accepted
Cousins with self-forgiveness and discipline
Colored squares and rectangles
A dog sniffing along for the next step.

It all begins with rummaging through my mind
Before anything gets out of my mouth

And I need to experiment now and just see what feels right
But at times the guilt overwhelms.

I have met my quota of road time
But I'd still span the length of the isle of Manhattan
and I'd bring it to where you are
But that's just me
We are all working toward a kind of resolution.

Dear mirror, thank you
Your birthday is tomorrow
What a collaboration
No matter what.

Remember this beautiful site on a Saturday morning
They want to love you
Relax and let them
Just watch the happiness on their faces
Joy at so many junctures
Ask them to share their stories with you
You just have to wait
All in its own time.

Gratitude for all in this moment.

Bless you.
Stay there.
Listen.
You are.

On day thirty-two of the project, one of the members wrote a message to the community that felt different. Her note wasn't directly related to the value of the day, but rather, a request for support. She described how she was getting ready to go to a critical job interview that day. Feeling that she needed support, but for various reasons wasn't able to share this news with her family or friends, she decided to share it with all of us. As I finished reading her words, I understood that this interview was minutes away. I hurried to write to her, but as I scrolled down, I saw that over twenty other people had already responded to her. People whom she didn't know, people from all over the world, let her know that she was supported. People wished her luck by sending her energy, silly dances, and words of inspiration, along with interview advice of all kinds. This vital connection is the heart of Compassionate Creativity.

⌘

When you feel lonely, how and where can you reach out?

What challenges you to connect with new people? What inspires you to take a step closer?

NINTH MOVEMENT: ALWAYS IN PROCESS

Connect with your Compassionate Creativity by...

105. Letting your beliefs continue to evolve as you do.

Buffalo, New York. 2012-2014.

"I hope they're all up there together. Eating and laughing and playing cards and being happy."

"I don't know if they are really people anymore doing people things."

"Oh, come on. It's so nice to think about them like that, isn't it? Happy?"

"But they already were happy, weren't they? They did all that already."

When my mom mentions heaven, I don't know how to respond. I'm trying to convince myself that these people aren't here anymore. That they don't exist and that they aren't coming back. But when my cousin's five-year-old son asks me if my dad is in heaven, I respond by saying, "Yes," not quite sure what I might be getting myself into...

"Where is heaven?" he asks swinging on a swing between two trees in front my cottage.

"Where do you think it is?"

"High up in the clouds," he says pumping his feet back and forth.

We both look up for a long minute.

"Are you ever going to see him again?" he asks.

"Sure, I see my dad all the time. In the sparkle on the water today and in the sun coming through those leaves right now."

"Where? I can't see him."

"It's more like I see his spirit in all of those things," I say.

"What's a spirit?"

As I play with the grass between my fingers, considering how to respond to him, he jumps off the swing and flows right into the next thing, "Kāli, can we go to the playground now?"

And as we walk to the park, hand-in-hand, I remember how I concluded that conversation with my mom and how she too, sees my dad's spirit in the beauty of the world every day:

"I think heaven is here. On Earth. And that it's good that we have endings. That nothing is forever. That way we enjoy it for what it is while we are all here."

⌘

What do you believe happens when people die?

How have your beliefs shifted over time?

How do you compassionately listen to people who have different beliefs than you?

106. Believing that you can love anew.

Bloomsburg, Pennsylvania. September 2014.

"Yes!"
Whispered the woman
So that the whole world could hear.

Elbow back and fist clenched
Eyebrows raised
The moment before embarking
On a wild shoulder bouncing celebration
Round and round
Arms raised in abounding gratitude
A reminder of so many things.

And what had sparked this fervor?

A beautiful soul, of course.

Meeting her halfway
Between three year blocks
And fingers on a keyboard of play.

A ceremonial, sweet, graceful, loving presence
With laughing lips and flippant hair

And a glowing beard that lifted her palm.

And how could he hold her from hundreds of miles away
All throughout the night?

So gently
Perfectly
Easefully ready.

A rock
A tree
An ongoing gift of life.

⌘

Describe a time that you fell in love.

How did this moment shift your worldview?

107. Letting the readiness find you.

Providence, Rhode Island. December 2014.

I pulled the car over to talk on the phone with a friend whose fiancée had just called off the marriage. Unsure of how to help and knowing that we both loved dogs, I promised him I would go find a great dog to pet and from there I would send love to his breaking heart. I had an extra half-hour before my next orthopedic appointment, and I had heard that there was a shelter in that area. I curved round the new roads thinking of my friend and how excited he had been to become engaged. How ready he was to get married. Maybe she wasn't?

When I pulled up to the address of the shelter, there sat a tiny cement building surrounded by dumpsters and a barbed wire, chain-link fence. The truck pulling out stopped me at the gate: "Sorry, ma'am, we're closed for the day."

I checked the time. I could swear their website said they were open until 3:00pm. I still have twenty minutes.

"Yeah, but we're closing up and… we don't have any dogs here anyway."

"You don't have any dogs?" I looked at her. "Really? None? I just wanted to pet a dog."

"Well, there is one, but... well... Oh, I don't know. Go inside and see if Mary will let you in. She might already be locking up."

I nearly turned around, afraid to infringe on Mary's schedule, but then I turned back. I was right here. I was so close. Why not at least go in and say hello?

As the metal door creaked open, Mary happily welcomed me in. "How can I help you today?" she smiled while sweeping up around her desk.

"The woman out there said there was one dog and I was wondering if I could pet him."

"Sure," she grabbed the keys off her belt, "I guess we have a few minutes yet."

As she unlocked the door, I readied myself for the beast behind it. It could have been anything: A little pug or Chihuahua, a scared Pit bull. See, I love all dogs, but the little ones or shorthaired ones don't quite do it for me like the big shaggy ones do. If you and I were walking down the street and we came upon a large furry dog, I'd excuse myself as I uncontrollably ran toward the dog as if he were my long lost companion. Bypassing the person attached to its leash, I'd be down on the ground ready to get slobbered and start petting the soft, bushy ears of that dog as if it was my own.

As Mary opened the door, she introduced me to Maxwell. And there he was. The fluffy, tail-wagging, smiling dog I had always dreamed of. It was love at first sight for both of us. I steadied myself, attempting to hide my outlandish excitement as I made my way to his cage. After all, I was only here for my friend.

"He can be a little timid and you might…"

But before she could finish we were nose-to-nose and looking into one another's eyes in absolute bliss.

"Wow. He sure likes you. You can have him if you want. No one's claimed him for three weeks. He needs a new home."

I could have him? Wait, I had just come here to pet a dog.

I wasn't ready to have a dog, but I was ready for Max, the mascot, who now sits nestled at my feet as I write. He comes to every class I teach, and I'm fully enrolled in his on-going, daily course on unconditional love.

⌘

How do you know when you are ready?

108. Asking questions that don't have answers.

Providence, Rhode Island. 2015.

I knew I wouldn't be able to answer my students' questions about why a student on campus had committed suicide. Hell, I hadn't begun to process the loss myself. But not having answers wasn't reason enough to avoid engaging in a conversation with them. Although many of us might not have known this student, he was one of our community. Yesterday he was here and now he wasn't. He could have been any of us.

As the students entered the room, I could feel their heaviness. It was as if it took every ounce of their being just to show up.

"I don't think I'm going to be able to play today," one student said as she passed me.

These young, grief-stricken people sat before me. Not knowing what to do, I asked them to gather round. No one wanted to move, but they did pull themselves up and find their place in the circle. I felt their fear of what they were going to have to do next. I felt the preciousness of this moment.

Was I about to deny what had happened and simply press on? No. I had been teaching them about inclusion – good and bad, happy and sad, life and death. About the power of connection. Of play. I needed to trust in my teaching and call on all that we had been learning together to help us now.

The room hovered.

Word by word, I acknowledged the loss and that I did not know what to do, how to start, or whether to have class at all. I asked for a moment of silence to notice whatever we were thinking, to feel whatever we were each feeling, each wanting to do. We had started every class this way, but today was different.

Next, I delicately opened up the floor. Responses trickled in little by little. People who knew the student chimed in. Others noted how this event reminded them of other people they had known who committed suicide. I tried to listen without commenting. Without needing to make it all better.

No one made eye contact. Everyone wanted to be anywhere but here. Should I let them go? No. I felt that it was best to stay together, but people didn't want to connect. Not yet.

"Let's all find our own place to lay on the floor and close our eyes," I offered.

They all gratefully melted into the ground.

I encouraged each person to take a further moment for themselves. To not having to say anything or do anything for anyone. To acknowledge for themselves what they were needing. Who they were thinking of. That wherever they were was perfect.

I laid down too, still not knowing what I was going to do next. The room held a kind of stillness that I had never before experienced. It seemed like everyone wanted to just stay lying there forever.

After a few more minutes passed, I felt people starting to breathe. To release. To catch up to themselves. I felt this in my body too.

Little by little I started to sing a simple, made-up melody. It was the only thinking I could do that I knew would unify us without talking. Sound and movement. My sounds helped me to stand up. I moved to one of the students. I looked down at her and sang the song to her as she opened her eyes. She smiled, looking up at me. I reached my hand to her, helping her to get up as she joined in the song. We tiptoed around the room to choose the next person. Then together we continued our song for them as they opened their eyes to see us. We helped them up before we all moved on to include the next person and the next.

One by one we gathered and walked as a group throughout the room singing. The song grew in volume and continued to evolve with each newly added voice. Eventually, all twenty-one of us stood in a circle humming and making music together. This, our sound of grief. Of not knowing.

Sounds that reminded us that our creative process is not therapy but it can be therapeutic. Healing. Connected now, we opened our arms into movement. We flowed into play. Living within the unanswerable questions together, we created a safe space for expressing our relationship with all that we will never know, and somehow, amidst our loss, we each found our own way to bask once again in the beauty of one another and our time here together.

⌘

How do questions and answers play into your process of figuring something out?

What is a question that you can ask today without needing the answer?

How can simply asking it open up new ways of being for you?

109. Inviting your ancestors to dinner.

Providence, Rhode Island. 2015.

Halloween is my dad's birthday, and I never know what to do on that day because, as you know, my dad is no longer alive. I could say that a million more times and even though it has been over sixteen years since I've seen him, I'm not able to fully believe it: My dad is not alive anymore. He is dead. He has passed away. He is deceased. Any way I put it, he is not here. I lost him some years ago, and I have looked for him in airports as I wait to board the next plane. I've often had that millisecond thought to call him, especially when something great happens. My dad has made an appearance in my dreams every once and a while. He usually wears fancy suspenders, something that I don't remember him ever doing in the waking life.

I miss my dad more than I could ever imagine anyone could miss anyone or anything. That's the best way to describe my experience of it, I guess. There really are no other words. Years later, while traveling in Brazil, I learned that they have a Portuguese word that doesn't exist in English: "Saudade." It means to miss someone or something with such a longing that it's beautiful. Because there is so much love and remembrance in the missing. That word might get a little bit closer to what lives in my heart.

Grief isn't the thing that makes me want to stay in bed all day and not get out, afraid of the world and overwhelmed by all its possibilities. No. Not grieving or ignoring my grief is the reason I might feel that way. When I let it linger in the corners of my heart without giving it the opportunity to move throughout my body, it nudges me and sometimes aches desperately to get out. To flow. To literally be expressed. This movement of grief is not easy. I could never write anyone a script on how to do it, nor could they for me. No. But I have come to learn that grief has a voice of its own that wants to be heard. It is the most empathetic, loving character we'll ever meet.

Halloween is my dad's birthday, and I never know what to do on this day. This year he would be turning sixty-four. This year I am going to celebrate. I'm going to let him turn sixty-four. I am going to plan for his visit. I'm going to clean even though that probably won't matter much to him. He's never been to Providence, so I am going to show him around and introduce him to my boyfriend and our dog and cats and neighbors. They will all be talking so much that we'll skip the Farmer's Market and head south toward the water. We'll go to an indigenous museum that none of us have ever been to before, walking through a bird sanctuary I know he would find cool. Next, we'll eat dinner at an oyster farm restaurant that might end up being his favorite restaurant in the area or maybe ever. We'll philosophize about theater and dinosaurs, and he'll definitely request that there be no phones at the dinner table after he takes an important birthday call from my mom and responds to a text from my brother. We will either watch the sunset there as we have our chocolate dessert or we'll go sit in the marsh somewhere nearby. We'll take a couple of pictures but not too many because we'll most likely be too busy remembering things we haven't remembered in a long time. We'll be picking up rocks, comparing the sunset to that of Lake Erie – a place which we are both very familiar and very fond – and we'll dream of when and how to take a vacation together to the Southwest once it starts snowing this year. Then we'll come home for a bonfire. I'm sure we'll tell some new stories about the formation of the stars while intermittently singing ridiculous cowboy songs... and who knows, my dad might even accompany the night on the guitar, which he could easily have learned to play by now.

Throughout the day my dad might be talkative or quiet. He might have trouble walking up some of the stairs or he might feel young and vibrant as ever. He might drink or he might not. We might agree on some things and disagree on others. If he still smokes, he'll have to go out to the sidewalk, because that is our new rule for guests. Whatever the day brings, I will surely talk about him in the present tense and I will play him a special surprise version of *Happy Birthday* I have prepared on my violin, followed by some *Scheherazade*, if he's lucky. Before we say goodnight, I will share this book I am writing with him and ask him what he thinks of the title and if it's okay if I quote him once or twice.

My dad will be here. My dad is here. My dad is out on a pyre. My dad is on Lake Erie. My dad is in the outback. My dad is happy. My dad is sad. My dad is ready. My dad is tired. My dad is proud. My dad is... my dad. My dad *is* Thom Quinn.

⌘

Who is an ancestor could connect with today? What do you want to share with them?

110. Practicing what you teach and teaching what you practice.

Manchester, New Hampshire. 2015.

I sit in a introductory birth-education workshop as one of thirty women. Wanting to learn more about the details of giving birth, both for the themes of my performance work and for my own curiousity, I signed up for this weekend. Here, at this half-way point I was already full and in awe. I'd been around friends and family that had given birth, but I had never heard about these parts.

We just finished observing a class for pregnant couples and the instructor has opened the floor for questions. We all are fixated on one particular part of the class when, without any warning, as if interrupted by it herself, the instructor began to act out what it was like to give birth. She didn't talk about it. She just did it. Her extreme contractions lasted for several minutes beyond my comfort level, but I couldn't look away. I had never witnessed anything so violent, sensual, sexual, loud, scary, and primal. I now understand in the birth-education world, this approach is referred to as "labor theater," and it is rarely played out as realistically as she had demonstrated.

The woman behind me raises her hand and asks what most of us seemed to be wondering: "Do you always do this in your classes? Aren't you afraid that someone might get up and leave?"

Without emotion or attitude, the instructor calmly and comfortably held her ground. "If someone wants to leave, then they can leave. This might not be the class for them. I wholeheartedly believe that showing this truth will shift the birthing culture in our country."

And with that, and some extra encouragement – whether we had ever given birth or not, whether we were health care professionals or not – we all proceeded to scream and laugh as we endured a five-minute contraction of our own.

⌘

What is your expertise?

How are you an artist?

How are you a teacher?

How are you an activist?

111. Prioritizing your own well-being.

Providence, Rhode Island and Buffalo, New York. 2015.

In my college students, I began to see myself. They were quickly becoming burnt out and strung out. Running from one thing to another, they didn't seem to be eating very well or sleeping very much, either. Bent on doing things to satisfy other people or standards, they were harder and harder on themselves but they couldn't seem to pinpoint what really mattered. They took very good care of everything else, but they were leaving themselves out of the equation.

"You are the show," I started to say to my students thinking that might be a good place to start. "And the show can't go on if you don't go on."

But how could I expect them to take care of themselves when I wasn't doing the same? Who was teaching them how to do this? Anyone?

That spring when I was told that someone else was given the longer-term job that I was hoping for, I finished the semester and for the first time ever, I didn't have a plan of where to be next. My first response was to start to figuring out how to patch up this gap of time with ten million new projects, but then I decided to practice what I had been teaching. Embracing not knowing, listening, and piecing it all together little by little while having faith that it would somehow accumulate into something that I couldn't quite see yet, I began living every moment as it came, listening to what wanted to happen next.

Drive west, said my gut.

Go home, said my heart.

California or Vermont or New York or, or, or... asked my head.

I started driving and stopped in Buffalo first. Without my usual agenda, everything looked different. Memories and moments that I usually cut off or holed up started to morph and move. Forgotten sparks started to reignite. And much to my surprise and the wide eyes of my family who was used to me blowing in to quickly say hello and goodbye over the course of the last sixteen years, I decided to stay.

Interesting, isn't it, how when one member of a family or a community makes a shift, it has a ripple effect on everyone? Every little thing can't help but start to shift in some way too. In no particular order, but rather like a bed sheet moving in the wind, each of us the corners connected by thousands of threads, my brother got engaged, my mom planned a vacation to Switzerland, and I decided to stay and do nothing. For us, none of these choices were everyday, ordinary events. Something unusual was in the air. Out of sync. Or maybe more in sync than it had been in a while.

So there I sat at my family's cottage on Lake Erie for three weeks. The first few days included having smiling lunch with my brother and spending quality time with my mom before she left for Europe. While making meals and freezing the leftovers for my stay, my mom gave me the rundown on how to take care of the place. Once she flew away, I returned to the lake by myself. At first I tried to be on a schedule: running, biking, eating, swimming, writing. But then I realized that the only one enforcing the schedule was me. The me that was still feeling the need to produce. To make. To share. To move along. Sitting still and being silent and spending time by myself had never been my forte, but I was ready to try something new.

So I stopped. And I sat. And I slowed down: Remembering. Thinking. Reflecting. Crying. Reading. Listening. Eating. Sleeping. Looking at rocks and walking two dogs along the beach each morning and as the sun set each night.

I watered the flowers one by one with the same watering can my mom had used for years.

I accepted meals from neighbors who had known me since I was six.

I sat writing in the same recliner that my dad sat writing in years ago.

Sometimes I felt guilty for being able to take this time. I wanted to give it to someone else who deserved it more. Other times, I felt that I was wasting time or I was just too uncomfortable to be in my own company. But then the wind would waft in off the lake or a bird would call to its mate, and I couldn't imagine anything better than this. This place. This precious time. For me. To come home to myself.

And by September, breathing deeper into my own rhythms, I returned to Providence and was finally able to proudly say this: "I am committed to not teaching, performing, or seeing any theater until next year."

Great... and this was scary as hell. How was I going to make ends meet? How and from whom would I have to ask for support? How could I just stop doing without people thinking that something was wrong? I was the one who said yes. I drove the extra mile and enjoyed being that person. I showed up to every conference. It was one thing when I had knee surgery last year and I told colleagues that I couldn't work or explain to friends that I couldn't make it out for coffee that day. But what about if I said no because I just needed to take time for me and I couldn't articulate all the reasons why? How would I explain this?

This would be new: "I will be a better colleague and collaborator and friend when I return, but for now I am choosing to be on a low-input, low-output diet. If my dream has become to open a Center for Compassionate Creativity, well then, I'd better be a student there first. I'd like to live the gift that I want to give to other people."

Perhaps there are good reasons why I didn't calibrate my momentum before this. I accomplished a lot and I don't regret a peck of it. But now, as I've slowed down, and I mean really slowed down – enough that I hardly recognized myself – I've started to see all that was going unheard, unattended to. By not moving so much on the outside, by simply sitting and listening, so much started to move on the inside.

This is the place I have been writing you from.

Taking my time instead of letting time take me. Seeing the clouds as they pass, remembering what I love, and making something.

Welcome to the Center for Compassionate Creativity…

⌘

How have your priorities shifted as the years have gone by?

What kind of decisions are you thinking about at the age you are now?

How could a younger or older person's point of view help to give you perspective with a particular decision?

A CODA: OPEN DOORS

Starting here and now...

Rise and shine!

A new work begins
Sits waiting for you at the dawn of task-filled days
 What is your practice?

I remind myself as I remind you
These times are not meant to be easy
Change and resistance always want to be friends
Distractions perpetuate other momentum
And nothing might feel like enough

I encourage us not to make do but to let be.
Not inhaling pent up and staying at home there
But rather exhaling and stepping outdoors
Standing at the ocean
 Arms open
 Significant AND insignificant

This is who I am.
This is all I have for you.

Grief becomes Love
    Digging into the earth
    Held down by the sky
    Wilting, heavy
    Lose hope
    Eat fear
    Drown into the core of devastation, loss, sorrow
    Befriend all ends
    Remnants
    Covered in dirt

The moon begs us to emerge, resilient
    Relinquish your craft.
    Your life's work is you.
    You have everything you need.
    This is your practice.

Go!
    With the gut of a dog
    Intuition of an elder
    Innocence of a child

Gather community as diverse as the stars
Welcome them
Tell them what you've seen
Where you've been
What you need
    Head
    Heart
    Gut

Humbly perform your eternal questions
Without any need for answers
Metaphor a guide
A gift

Include their stories and infinitely repeat
    Gratitude as the sixth sense
    Humor as the seventh

Look and see each other:
    Ritual
    Lineage
    Privilege
    All

Create a culture that values playing together like this...

    Celebrating the beauty and mystery of it all
    Remembering the dreams of the world
    Written upon our bones

Perform your own contagious Acts of Compassionate
Creativity everywhere you go...

Remember that you are never alone if you don't want to be.
There are too many people in the world.

    Everyone is an artist. *
    Everyone is an actor/activist.
    Everyone is a teacher.
    Everyone an expert.

Start here.
Start now…

[Singing.]

* See other art often and want to love it.

⌘

What are your core values?

Write them down and walk with them every day.

ACKNOWLEDGMENTS

Thank everyone profusely.

From preschool, when I talked out lesson plans as I rode to school with the teacher who also happened to be a neighbor, to my first grade teacher who today is still one of my best friends, to those who encouraged music and imagination in my life, to those I never met but who founded schools in places I would spend so much time learning so much. To a lineage, a tradition of people researching movement, creativity, human connection, compassion, theater, love.

I have always been blessed to have the most incredible teachers and mentors, companions and neighbors.

The tollbooth worker with the extra smile on mile 541. The mailman who had no idea what letter he was finally delivering to me. My students who all showed up on time and hungry to learn when I thought I was too tired to teach. Especially those the eight from Solo, Clown, Movement, and Creativity at Brown, Trinity, Rochester, Bucknell, MUW, Putney, Vermont Academy, and Duke. To Action Plans. To Miche and Rachel. To Candy and Barb and Tina and Mr. Ross.

If we could know one word in every language, one word that would get us by in every country or culture, it would be "thank you."

The airline stewardess who let me know in a look that we would be safe. The busy guy who made my sandwich without mustard. My mom for redoing the basement when I came for a visit. To the leaders of the world and to knowing that we are all leaders. To Emily.

To Mimi for asking me what my dreams were and encouraging me to go for the biggest one. To Jeff for believing in my work and helping me to share it. To Jake for coming along on the ride.

To GUTWorks and Dan and to Jon and their families.

To Jerry and Rupa. And Stephen and Peter.

To Deena and Ruby and Danny.

Thanks to the animals that talked to me. The seal. The bat. The whales.

To Sam and Pepper and Vita.

And to my Goose and her Goslings and Paul.

Great thanks.

To physical therapists and baths and highways. To wrist surgeons and knee specialists. Tom, Jenn, Hulstyn, and Dr. Meghan. To Steve and Gerritt. To Emily. To Jerry. To Lauren and Laura. To Marcus. To Kevin and McDonogh. To Clara and Rebecca. To Cynthia and Chris. To Tommy and Karen. To Rollie.

I find that once I start thanking people or even thinking about the things and people that I am thankful for, the feeling goes exponential. A web. A waterfall of gratitude.

To my co-worker in Little Rock for making sure I had health insurance. To my brother for leaving me that unexpected voicemail mid-day with a funny Russian accent. To the mystery person who gave me a part in that Shakespeare play when I needed it most. To the lady at the corner store who always asks for my ID. To that guy on the track. To Eric. To Nick. To Heather and Jim. To Charles. To Jules. To my grandmother who has long since passed away but still reminds me to eat well. To Sudha and Griff. To Maryellen. To Danielle. And all Aunts and Uncles and twenty-four cousins. To Jakob.

Infinite thanks.

To Rochester and Ithaca and Vermont and California. To the Adirondacks and all the highways in between. To Nigel and Mervyn. To Sally and Chris. To Tucker. To Aadika. To JB and Eddie. To Anthony and Monica and Amanda and Jimmy. To Caren. To Michael. To the Bellows Falls Opera House. To The Pearl. To the Bloomsburg Theatre Ensemble.

To being a Dell'Artian and part of La Famiglia. To Michelle and Jen. To Adrian and Eleni. To Bea and her family. To Eric. To Dan and Eli. To Chris. To Ben and Kristin and Izzy. To Bill. To Audrey and Malin. To Wyckham and Brody. To Joel. To Joan and Michael and Carlo and Donald and Jackie and Phillip and Evamarii and Cal and Ronlin. To caves and drums and wooden floors. To Dorsja and Anthony. To Alicia. To the Pacific ways and waves. To Jeff who auditioned me and only continues to inspire.

To Tuscany and Accademia dell'Arte. To Brazil and Grupo Galpão and Cine Horto. To Eduardo and Flor. Rodgrido and Fernando and Marcinho. To Ana Amelia. To NYC and Kristin and HERE.

Obrigada.

To Alisha and Mark and the whole Network of Ensemble Theaters.

Only more and more...

To Buffalo and its suburbs and Frontier and Lake Erie. To the neighbors who gave me quiche and chicken and sea glass and music. To the one who saved me from the bat. And from the fire. To backgammon and hot tubs at coffee shops. To Annie and Amy and A Beauty Way. To Rune Hill. To 4ᵗʰ Street. To Pat. To Wendy and Shannon and Zoe and the 111 pioneers around the globe.

To the Quakers. To the Brian who helped me do so much more while getting the VW on the road.

To the Herons: Barry and Carole. Daniel and Sally. Paul and Susie. To Mildred.

To Gil who endlessly edited this book while making me only more coffee and salmon and hot chocolate.

To Samadi who taught me how to learn from my resistance.

To Daniel who was at every intersection teaching and believing with such expanding love and curiousity.

To Alex and Mary and Carm and Chris.

Thankfulness abounding.

To Lake Erie and Snyder Beach.

To Max and Skiba for their rhythms and abilities to love unconditionally. To Heath and Dempsey. And Beckett.

To my beloved Shaw who has always been with me and always believed in and encouraged me toward every dream and center. Who is teaching me how to dance. To his family close by.

To my mom and dad and the infinite love they share. To those who made them and raised them. To Evan and Vonessa.

Resounding.

To Theater.

To Providence.

And to the comrades who spent lifetimes dedicated to infinitely discovering until their very last moment, I extend my work and practice with your strides in my walk, your passions in my heart, and your eternal questions in mind.

The river goes on and on and on.

To Love.

To Compassion and Creativity and the combination within me.

⌘

And to you and your collage.

Thank you.

For reading.

For listening.

For being.

You are a blessing.

Onward ho...

TO INSPIRE FURTHER CONNECTIONS

BOOKS

Spider Speculations by Jo Carson

Narrative Medicine by Lewis Mehl Medrona, MD, PhD

Kitchen Table Wisdom by Rachel Naomi Remen, MD

Creating the Work You Love by Rick Jarow

Bowling Alone by Robert D. Putnam

Small Wonder by Barbara Kingsolver

When Things Fall Apart by Pema Chödrön

The Smell of Rain on Dust by Martin Pretchtel

Extremely and Incredibly Close by Jonathan Safron Foer

When Elephants Weep by Jeffrey Moussaieff Masson

Joy and Sorrow by Kahlil Gibran

Anatomy of an Illness by Norman Cousins

Being Mortal by Atul Gawade

Creatively Independent by Jess Pillmore

Birthing from Within by Pam England

PRACTICES, PRACTITIONERS, & PLACES

Life Coaching: Samadi Demme

Proponent of Play: Jeff Smithson in CT

Alexander Technique

Rubenfeld Synergy Technique: Rupa Cousins in VT

Tai Chi: Philip Gerstner in CA

Authentic Movement

Feldenkrais Method

Pilates

Postural Restoration Institute

Network of Ensemble Theaters

Todd International Theater Program, U of Rochester

Dell'Arte International in Blue Lake, CA

Accademia Dell'Arte in Arezzo, Italy

KO Festival in Amherst, MA

HERE Arts Center in NYC

Los Angeles Women's Solo Festival, CA

New England Youth Theater, VT

Bloomsburg Theatre Ensemble in PA

Putney School Summer Programs in VT

Green Heart Healing Center & Farm in Springfield, VT

Clown Without Borders

Odyssey of the Mind

Patch Adams & The Gesundheit Institute

A Beauty Way

Dance for Parkinson's & LSVT BIG Therapy

Music and Memory

Camp Good Day and Special Times in Keuka Lake, NY

Extraordinary Rendition Band in Providence, RI

Grace Note Bedside Singers in Providence, RI

Providence Friends Meeting in Providence, RI

Hallowell Bedside Singers in Brattleboro, VT

Full Circle Festival in Burlington, VT

Shakespeare in Delaware Park in Buffalo, NY

Grupo Galpão in Minas Gerais, Brazil

⌘

ABOUT THE AUTHOR

Kāli Quinn is a facilitator of Compassionate Creativity through innovative storytelling and physical play. She is from Buffalo, NY and now lives in Providence, RI where she has taught clown, mask, movement, devising, and creative leadership at Brown University and worked as Stateside Faculty for Accademia dell'Arte (Arezzo, Italy). Kāli has facilitated Compassionate Creativity at: Creative Medicine Series at Brown University, McDonogh School, United Natural Foods, Pearl Theatre Company, Celebration Barn, New England Center for Circus Arts, MIT, Duke University, Putney School Summer Programs, Vermont Academy, Connecticut College, Boston University, Emory College, Bucknell, Clowns Without Borders in Guatemala & Grupo Galpão in Brazil. Kāli served on the Board for the Network of Ensemble Theaters from 2009-2014 and received training at the University of Rochester, with an MFA from Dell'Arte International in Northern California.

For more information & to connect with Kāli, visit:
compassionatecreativity.com

COMPASSIONATE
CREATIVITY
www.compassionatecreativity.com

Made in the USA
Middletown, DE
15 August 2019